Studies in Rhetorics and Feminisms

Series Editors, Cheryl Glenn and Shirley Wilson Logan

WOMEN'S IRONY

REWRITING FEMINIST RHETORICAL HISTORIES

Tarez Samra Graban

Southern Illinois University Press
Carbondale

18 17 16 15   4 3 2 1

Library of Congress Cataloging-in-Publication Data
Graban, Tarez Samra.
Women's irony : rewriting feminist rhetorical
histories / Tarez Samra Graban.
    pages cm. — (Studies in rhetorics and feminisms)
Includes bibliographical references and index.
    ISBN 978-0-8093-3418-6 (paperback)
    ISBN 0-8093-3418-6 (paperback)
    ISBN 978-0-8093-3419-3 (ebook)
1. Feminism and literature. 2. Irony in literature.
3. Feminist theory. 4. Feminist literature—History.
5. Women and literature. 6. Feminism—Philosophy.
I. Title.
PN56.F46G73 2015
809'.89287—dc23   2014045163

CONTENTS

5. TOWARD AN IRONY PARADIGM 165

ACKNOWLEDGMENTS

Not all projects have a clear point of origin. This project, however, did originate in a particular kind of intellectual space that only certain teachers could construct. I give thanks first and foremost to Patricia Sullivan, Victor Raskin, and Janice Lauer, whose courses and methodologies inspired this project. Their commitments to history, theory, and ontology have had a profound impact on all that I do. Along the way, Shirley K Rose has exercised patience and persistence in helping me develop a theory and practice of archives, for which I am grateful. I acknowledge the generosity of Paul Schueler and Kathy Atwell at the Tippecanoe County Historical Association (TCHA) in Lafayette, Indiana, for mentoring me in and providing access to the archives while I worked on the Helen M. Gougar Collection. I also acknowledge the largely invisible but significant work of former TCHA archivist Sarah M. Cooke, whose notes on the first iteration of the Gougar Papers reflect treasures of their own.

Women's Irony has had a long journey to completion, and it warrants an expression of gratitude for the many informal conversations and formal dialogues that brought it to fruition. While I may not remember all of the former, I can certainly acknowledge the latter, and I am grateful to Ira Allen, Dana Anderson, Penelope Anderson, Christine Farris, Kristie Fleckenstein, Shannon Gayk, Rae Greiner, Laura B. Johnson, Rebecca Jones, Michael Keene, Rhea Estelle Lathan, Joan Pong Linton, Nicole Converse Livengood, Lisa Mastrangelo, Kathleen J. Ryan, John Schilb, Amy Ferdinandt Stolley, Kathleen B. Yancey, Xiaoye You, and Harvey Yunis, who read and sometimes commented on various parts of various versions of the book, and without whose genuine responses, reactions, and suggested resources or reenvisionings I would not have been able to make it cohere. Special thanks go to my colleagues at Florida State University for generously engaging with this project and embracing it with all my others, as well as making time for me to write. I sincerely thank the graduate students in my seminars at Indiana University and Florida State University, whose curiosity and powers of reflection caused me to rethink almost every claim throughout the book. And to my cohort at Purdue, thank you. Without your quiet brilliance, stamina, generosity, and love, I would be neither the scholar nor the person I am today.

Thanks are due in solid measure to my family, for their consistent love and unwavering support, and for modeling by example that life's greatest pleasure is to make the most difference for the most people. Eric Graban especially challenged me to prove how distant rhetorical projects could be made salient for nonrhetoricians in the contemporary world.

Two anonymous reviewers for Southern Illinois University Press provided formative feedback, which helped shape my revisions of this book, and Margaret Morris's and Joyce Bond's expert eyes caught numerous transgressions in the final draft. Cheryl Glenn and Shirley Logan have supported the development of this project from its very beginning, while the entire staff of SIU Press have expertly guided me through every phase of its completion.

An early version of portions of chapter 1 appeared in print in the December 2007 issue of *Rhetorica*, while I was still making an argument for linguistic noncooperation in Anne Askew's discourse. An early version of portions of chapter 3 appeared online in the October 2011 issue of *Gender and Language*, while I was still intent on demonstrating irony's intentional *use* in Helen Gougar's suffrage discourse. In the years since I started this work, my rhetorical and methodological stances on irony have drastically changed. It is my hope that readers will find the changes offered here to be useful and rich, and broadly applicable to questions they might take up.

WOMEN'S IRONY

INTRODUCTION: Why an Irony Paradigm for Feminist Historiography, and Why Now?

> Irony not only trades on incompatibilities, but its study embodies them.
> —Kathryn M. Olson and Clark D. Olson, "Beyond Strategy"

The July 1969 US edition of *Vogue* magazine featured Israeli film star Daliah Lavi in leather "manna," copies of painted scrolls, and a cultural profile of Israel's status in the post–1967 war period, alongside excerpts from an interview with then prime minister of Israel Golda Meir, which became politicized in the following line: "We [Israel] don't thrive on military acts. We do them because we have to, and thank God we are efficient." Against a backdrop created by head scarves and fall fashion, the ironic repercussions of this statement resonated then and still reverberate now, almost seventy years after the United Nations General Assembly proposed Resolution 181,[1] some ninety years after the British Mandate of Palestine, and more than two thousand years after Aspasia's earliest political influencing. In its *actual and politicized* contexts, Meir's statement is problematic on its own. When read as a statement of Israel's national identification, it supports the notion that nationalism is only as conscious and embedded as a set of qualifications that can be "checked," "verified," or "suspended" at a security border (Khalidi 1). When read as a statement of Palestine's defensive ideology, it refutes the notion that a cultural identification can be more enduring than its surrounding political events. Taken completely out of context, it instantiates what had become a decades-long tradition of ambiguously named and "administered" territories as a result of a failed plan of partition and separation (Benvenisti 229–31), or it coolly and tactlessly overlooks what would become an international refugee crisis. In its *historicized* contexts, however, it obfuscates any clear vision of the sources of difficulty in navigating between not two, but multiple sets of interests—Palestinian, Israeli, and the Western "other" broadly defined.

1

Ambiguation is what I work against in articulating the linguistic and philosophical impediments to realizing women's rhetorical identifications in the histories that we choose to write, and this international conflict is just one example of a contemporary diplomatic challenge that is rife with complication, because of its various communicative ideologies, and ripe for examination through a feminist lens,[2] because of the many ways that studying it limits us. The simple recognition of irony in Meir's work, whether or not she intended to use irony in the way that we interpret it, is valuable on its own. Yet too few theories in rhetorical studies complicate women's ironic discourse beyond intentionality, something that Linda Hutcheon attributes to an overattention to the point of view of the ironist (116) and an inattention to the "slipperiness" of intentionality (118). We note irony's use for diplomatic self-positioning and audience construction, yet our critical language—what Richard Rorty might call our metavocabulary (*Contingency* xvi) and what Leo Strauss might have called our politicized phenomenon of "reading between the lines" (30)—brings our descriptions of it back to the same few aims: reflective self-deprecation, conservation of inferiority stereotypes, and maintenance of a strong but properly feminine persona (Bilger, "Laughing" 51).[3]

Often these critical descriptions rely on such binaries as those derived from Sally Miller Gearhart's "Womanization of Rhetoric," in which she sought to broaden rhetoric's ends from "conquest and conversion" to communication and relationship.[4] Or they are measured against a "collaborative and noncoercive" dichotomy, such as the kind that Annette Kolodny noted in second-wave feminist readings of Margaret Fuller's *Woman of the Nineteenth Century* (138). Or they become historicized in diminutive and uncritical descriptions of gendered speech (Zwagerman 25; Barreca 6). In contrast, this book argues for irony as a critical paradigm for feminist historiography, specifically for the ways it challenges critical historical methods in rhetoric. In fact, this book argues for irony as a phenomenon that serves both discursive activism and critical disruption, by looking to the political past.

Meir's statement simultaneously represents the greatest challenge in national identification and poses the greatest opportunity for disruption of ironic targets, subjects, victims, and frames as they are delivered—and when they are enacted—by women. To call it *ironic* means to embrace its richer context and to acknowledge that its employment in popular media spurred various theories about its role in place, time, and memory. Indeed, to call it *ironic* means to acknowledge how irony *persists*, as Robert Coles has written, "in the various faiths we uphold, in the political and social and psychological ideas we have had handed down to us, [and] in the lives we live" (9). Furthermore, to acknowledge the immediate and epistemic function of this irony means to accept that the statement itself hinges on contingent myths of selfhood, beliefs about statehood, and the preservation of culture through a feminist lens. More importantly, to acknowledge irony's critical significance requires considering the potentialities of irony for writing women rhetors into political history at all, no matter how clear or distorted the written record. The fact remains that in political performances involving some negotiation between contingent circumstances or subject positions, or some ironic distancing between subjects and their agents, a woman's options for rhetorical positioning veer slightly to one extreme or another: humorous or humorless. Even the contexts in which they appear cannot soften this dichotomy.

In its many rhetorical contexts from antiquity to the present, *irony* has been alternatively associated with the nature of the speaker, audience, and situation, first as a condition of how little or much the speaker's reputation was enveloped in the truthful content of the speech (Aristotle, *On Rhetoric* bk. 3, ch. 19), then as a classification or subclassification of facetious behavior intended to secure an audience's goodwill (Cicero, *De Oratore* bk. 2, sec. 67; Volpe 322–23), and eventually as a logical diversion or projection of linguistic deceit (Swearingen x, 202). Irony has also been theorized as both a figure and a trope (Quintilian, *Institutio Oratoria* 9: 2), an instrument of deferral (Gans 66), a device that highlights the incongruity between what is expected and what is presented (Gibbs and Izzett 145), and "not a discrete linguistic phenomenon, but rather a family of attitudes" (Brown 111). However we wish to define it, *irony* lingers historically in women's political discourse, perhaps because it is simultaneously symptomatic of Eve's antediluvian predicament (Coles 20, 26) and emblematic of a kind of literary self-criticism (Coles 108). As a result, rhetorical analysis often describes what irony *does* according to whom it excludes or what it explicitly targets, and determines its success according to whether it elicits laughter or whether it upholds or violates some principle of cooperative communication in a fixed historical moment.

Yet while our notions of feminist discourse in rhetorical studies have been liberated from the kinds of essentializing paradigms that cause us to evaluate women's texts according to a single subject position, our application of irony to feminist discourse has not. In treating women's irony as "feminist," our options—even in the twenty-first century—seem limited to justifying it in terms of a *feminine* construct: a construct of acting male or of not acting female. These constructs do not allow us to see how each writer appropriates discursive power in her various (historical) contexts or how her ironic discourse provides opportunities for ideological disruption (or harm), nor are we permitted to imagine alternative ways in which her irony positions her as a political and rhetorical agent or to understand how we are positioned as historical agents in return.

IRONY AS AGENCY

While we do have alternative lenses or frames for assessing women's work beyond "masculine" (patriarchal, agonistic, power-wresting) or "feminine" (antipatriarchal, nonagonistic, power-yielding) styles (Buchanan, *Regendering*; Ronald and Ritchie, *Available*; Mayhead and Marshall; Miller and Bridwell-Bowles, to name only a few), when we approach women's ironic texts as *works*, we are not completely free from the bifurcations of real and ideal or logic and emotion that guide our methods of analysis. Thus an underrepresentation or misrepresentation occurs. What Sean Zwagerman says about studies of gender and humor I can say about studies of irony: when these studies fail to—or simply cannot—accommodate the "transideological" potential of the discourse being examined (as per Linda Hutcheon), they will serve only to reinforce binaries that impede more critical and metaphysical work (5).[5] As a result, our rhetorical analyses obfuscate, rather than clarify, the gaps among linguistic, rhetorical, and philosophical approaches to the construction of irony. This in turn binds women's ironic performances more pervasively to humor, lying, or evasion, since those three registers are perceived as the easiest to observe.[6] Perhaps because humor and irony share the same basic mechanisms, one of the most common outcomes of being ironical is to be perceived as funny (Giora, "On Irony" 256). Yet this delimits irony's interpretive possibilities to questions of static representation and rhetorical intention—for example, *Who did what to whom, for what reason, and at what cost?*—and undervalues irony's epistemic potential beyond its first occurrence.[7]

I suggest that we begin at another place: with the presumption that feminist ironic discourse is of greatest value to rhetorical studies not for these reasons—how women's texts reveal the elision of gendered conflicts, the overturning of hegemonic discourses, or the refusal to participate in certain discourses—but for others. Feminist ironic discourse is of value to rhetorical studies based on how it (re)defines the ways in which women ironists participated in various traditions, the possibilities for their participation, and what it means for them to participate at all. I suggest broadening our understanding and examination of ironic discourse situations across time and space, including ourselves as implied readers among its multiple targets and participatory agents. In sum, I suggest developing a panhistorical approach to irony based on its consciousness-raising potential—*on its ability to draw readers and writers of history into a simultaneous reexamination of their methods, theories, and practices* and on its ability to demonstrate how responses to rhetorical exigencies can evolve (Sowards and Renegar 537). While rhetorical agency can be straightforwardly defined as "refe[rring] to the capacity to act, that is, to have the competence to speak or write in a way that will be recognized or heeded by others in one's community" (Campbell, "Agency" 3), this definition does not preclude the important question of how many critical and historical agents it takes *to realize an ironic event*. For that reason, I find it historically plausible to read irony into an event where it has not been explicitly noted before.

This book does not offer a single response to the questions of why and how women rhetors have used irony in their political discourse. Instead, it presents irony as a useful form of ideological disruption then and now, argues for the complex and contradictory uses to which it has been put, and demonstrates its potential for redefining agency, language, and history. Anne Askew's, Anne Hutchinson's, and Helen Gougar's political ironies push the limits on existing analytic paradigms for explaining their success and justifying their historical significance. Rather than suggest what I think these women writers *intended* by their irony, I consider the value in examining their irony as shared, apart from an intention or the negotiation of truth claims (Hutcheon 117). Rather than define more comprehensively *what irony is* when women enact it, I dislodge expectations about how and why it occurs at all. In other words, what I refer to as "women's irony" throughout this book does not simply disrupt the historical events in which women participated; it dislodges the whole event in which their discourse is disseminated and perceived. The parameters of their discourse encompass implied, intended, and unintended audiences across historical time and critical space. In this way, ironic discourse opens up conditions for activism by inviting readers and their subjects to behave like agents, where "agency" is a reciprocal construct, relating authors, texts, contexts, and metatexts.

Thus another goal for this book is to equip rhetorical critics to study women together—meaningfully and purposefully—who might not have been studied together before and to see in the analysis of irony rich, complex spaces for doing so. I demonstrate how their irony affords us and them agency by answering such overarching questions as the following:

- What can be known about irony's potentialities—about how it is used, read, interpreted, and historicized—as a feminist rhetorical practice?
- How can and do recovery scholars study women's ironic discourse more critically and with more possibilities for consciousness raising among themselves and their readers?
- What bearing does this consciousness raising have on "more productive investigations into the . . . conditions of agency" (Geisler 9)? On the (re)construction of historical paradigms in rhetoric and writing studies?

I do not argue for feminist irony as agency in terms of skill or embodiment; rather, I discuss it as a phenomenon in which both rhetor and audience consciousness are "shaped by arrangements external to that consciousness" (Geisler 13).

IRONY AS HISTORICITY

What can be the feminist rhetorical historian's role in brokering deconstruction and displacement of certain phenomena and in tackling questions of nationhood and belonging, yet without discounting other systems, histories, methods, and traditions? The vitality in such a study is in proactively questioning how irony has been and can be historicized in women's political texts, where *historicization* involves the act of being historical or being perceived as historically actual. Janet Atwill once alluded to historical methodologists as puzzle changers, providing temporary solutions for the historical problems that scholars know they currently face (Octalog, "Octalog II" 24). This book, then, presents "recovery" as the qualitative disruption of a critical paradigm, rather than the quantitative building of a corpus. Because they entangle the political present in the political past, the analyses that I perform throughout this book offer temporary solutions to two particular problems: Given a text, history, or archive, how can irony provide *a way in* to feminist theorizing? And given irony's disruption of intentionality and of the singular female subject, how do historians analyze what amounts to a knotworking of contingencies and instabilities where irony occurs? Like Candace Lang,

I am less interested in codifying irony as a rhetorical *trope* and more interested in discovering "the kind of ironic universe implied by the critical practice of explaining everything—texts, behavior, life, the world" (15).

However, Lang's definition of paradigmatic irony as "disguised intentions" still differs from my own, because I discuss irony apart from intentionality as much as possible.[8] Ultimately, I present irony as a critical paradigm for feminist historical work by making case studies from the ironic discourse of three women who, at various junctures, have been remembered as "stumping" (Glenn, *Rhetoric* 117), "reducing to confusion" (Hall 311), or "out-speaking" ("Gougar on Murphy") their examiners or political opponents. Martyred under Henry VIII, Anne Askew (1521–46) represents one of rhetoric's early and influential female participants in a principally male tradition. Publisher Johan Bale and martyrologist John Foxe remarked that the king's bishop and councilors at Newgate Prison eventually lost patience with Askew's tactical silence, refusal, and syllogistic challenges to their interrogation. Born and baptized within fifty years of Askew's execution, and descending from some of England's "good literary stock,"[9] Anne Hutchinson (1591–1643) endured a two-day church trial in the young Boston commonwealth that resulted in a verdict some historians say was due more to her examiners' fatigue and frustration than to evidence of her wrongdoing. In 1904, the *New York Times* editorialized Hutchinson as the Colonial woman "ahead of her time," whose sole misfortune was in trying to bring a public argument to resolution ("Tragedy"). Though neither a martyr nor a defendant, Helen M. Gougar (1843–1907) died while her movement was young, suffering heart failure ten years before the state of Indiana adopted universal suffrage and thirteen years before the Nineteenth Amendment granted all US women the right to vote. Gougar did significant work toward securing municipal suffrage in four western states, yet she was memorialized by the editors of the *Lafayette (Indiana) Morning Journal* as one who "was graduated into the political arena at a time when it was considered profitable to abuse one's opponents" (qtd. in Kriebel, *Where the Saints* 215).

Little more than a transparent line connects Askew's, Hutchinson's, and Gougar's performances throughout history, although various reliances on women's use of irony between the English Reformation and American Suffrage may show traces of an indirect path in the vernacular training of women rhetors.[10] All three of these women have been remembered—to varying degrees—as political and rhetorical agitators. All three ironists are bound together by a cultural logic of interruption, their work unfinished as performers, as politicians, and as rhetoricians—and, more than likely, historically underserved. All three ironists suffered scrutiny often, or exclusively, for performing public debate, and not one of them succeeded in escaping the continual reification of the "weak but empowered," "gendered female," or "iron/tart" stereotypes that preceded them. Consequently, one or more conditions of their historicization as either *rhetorical* or *political* figures require a disambiguation that only irony can provide by bringing into deeper relief the various motives, positions, and attitudes *against which* and *in which* they worked. Askew has been textually interpreted through the subjectivities of others, Hutchinson has been historicized as part of a Colonial schism, and Gougar has been miscast as a political pariah in ways that are disproportionate to her archival neglect (Stowitzky; "Helen Gougar"). While Askew's two-part narrative, *The First and Lattre Examinacyons*, has been rhetorically reconstructed as an important feminist text whose author could perform while also subverting expectations of the genre (Beilin, *Redeeming*; Glenn, *Rhetoric*), its greater ironic potential is in confounding the genre expectations of Askew's immediate and distant audiences, then and now. While Hutchinson's trial discourse has been well historicized for its seeming confusion and contradictions, its ironic potential is in eliding the public-private dichotomy that caused Hutchinson's examiners to interpret them as licentious "lyes" or "erroneous claims" in the first place (Hall 345). And while Gougar remains understudied as a rhetorical influence on women's suffrage in America, a taxonomical look at the contexts in which she is perceived to have been speaking or writing reveals that her ironic discourse was more invitational than agitational.

These analytic attitudes—confounding expectations of genre, eliding *dissoi logoi*, and recognizing invitation—challenge the construction and evolution of feminist research methodologies and bear significantly on the question of how and why we do recovery at all. Furthermore, these analytic attitudes help me define a broader class of events, responses, and interpretive actions for historical work than are typically applied to women's performances. I consider how irony "serves to define what should be studied, what questions should be asked, and what rules should be followed in interpreting the answers obtained" (Ritzer 7). I also approach irony as a "collection of questions, viewpoints and models that define how [those] who subscribe to that paradigm, view and approach the science" (Salter and Wolfe 22). This approach enables the fusion of rhetoric's discursive and self-referential dimensions, allowing rhetorical theory to be viewed as synchronic and diachronic (Oravec and Salvador 174, 180) and allowing critics to read women's texts as *moving assemblages of loyalties and interests,* rather than as representative entities of particular stances or positions.

Read together through this lens, Askew's, Hutchinson's, and Gougar's texts reveal how irony can create the conditions for what Elizabeth Maddock Dillon calls "category disorder": patterns in their discourse where "forms of agency and power float across different relationships, rather than reside only in the hands of [prescribed] authorities" ("New England"). This concept of *floating across different relationships* is reflected in what I call "interstitial witnessing" in chapter 1, "panhistorical agency" in chapter 2, and "a typology of discursive attitudes" in chapter 3. In other words, if there is any relationship to be maintained among Askew, Hutchinson, and Gougar, it reflects the ties that *they do have with other writers,* the ties *they could have with one another,* and the ties *we can have with them.* In their discourse, irony occurs in the myriad places where critics note contradictions, occurring for different audiences within the same utterance. While all three women do not necessarily perform the same way, their discourse alternately reveals and obscures the terms of its own politicizing. As a result, this book argues for irony as a critical paradigm because it is an optimal site for actively questioning and making knowledge about feminist rhetorical and historical practices.

IRONY AS ACTIVISM

In spite of—perhaps because of—its title, this is not a book about irony or one that celebrates irony as a woman's trope, construct, or subject. Rather, it is a book that understands irony as a critical resource for *making knowledge about* feminist rhetorical and historical practices and for rethinking those practices that we have claimed as disciplinarily sacrosanct. In that sense, "women's irony" is meant not as a declarative statement, but a generative one, and my fascination with the term is not surprising. I was raised in a third-culture context—fairly caught between home and host cultures—and my earliest memories are of limited and limiting modes of cultural and linguistic accommodation. Owing to my father's immigrant status as a displaced Palestinian, my siblings and I already understood ourselves to be neither fully American nor fully Arabic but were very aware of the times and spaces in which these identifications converged. Additionally, my family lived for twenty years as Americans on the politically censored Arabian peninsula, which meant that we often shuttled between not only the eastern and western aspects of our parentage, but also the mores of two eastern cultures (Saudi and Palestinian) that were often diametrically opposed—one with a strong national identification and the other marked by an existential belonging. Growing up in these contexts, I had few viable models for public expression. As a result, I was not fully cognizant of the pragmatic functions or rhetorical uses of my own "first" language, English, until coming of age in a profession devoted to it. Naturally, I would be drawn to complex forms of expression, particularly when taken up by strong women in oppositional contexts—women who disproved their own historically limited capacities for communication, overcame the awkwardness of public misidentification, and articulated subject positions that seemed too perplexing to identify, let alone to linguistically convey.

At first irony fascinated me because of what it allegedly allowed women *to do.* Irony allowed them to *speak up and speak through various circumstances* when their right to speak had been revoked, to reclaim agency where it was categorically denied them, to say something other than what they meant and have it be understood by a hidden party to the exchange, to insult, to condescend, to preserve selfhood, to subvert, to stump, to demonstrate wit, even to penetrate the boundaries of time and space by making incongruous references that would take on a new significance with some implied reader in some other context. Later, I realized that these attributes still do not account for what I see as irony's greater historical and theoretical significance. These attributes do not fully explain the complexities that irony brings to feminist discourse, touch on irony's potential to penetrate structures that keep other discourses hidden from view, or describe how irony matters to the past, present, and future histories of our discipline.

Women's Irony explains what I now recognize as irony's activist potential for feminist discourse and for rhetorical theory, by demonstrating how it can function as a historical method, an investigative lens, and a typology all at once. I do not argue against the notion that women have *used* irony as a humorous tool or as a rhetorical and political strategy. The evidence is plentiful and clear. Askew, Hutchinson, and Gougar all responded ironically, in some sense, whether or not it was their discursive norm. Yet their perception as politicians, social and religious reformers, or public intellectuals has been more often tied to their production of a deviant discourse. Instead, I propose their invention of a discourse that is neither masculine nor feminine, neither dominates nor capitulates, but demonstrates a useful contradiction of public and private powers. I propose that irony's historical significance is in its tendency to portray *agency* as the way a writer (or speaker) embodies things, whether those *things* are material or immaterial, actual or imagined, *kairotic* or temporal. The principal function of the case studies constituting this book, then, is to demonstrate the critical, interpretive, and meta-discursive capacities that irony *allows*.

In light of recent calls for reader-centered interpretations of irony in historical work (Galewski; Olson and Olson), for feminist theories of "incarnate argument" or "rhetorical enactment" (Campbell, *Man*; Campbell and Jamieson), and for renewed discussions of what should count as feminist goals and objectives (Foss and Foss), feminist scholarship in rhetorical studies is ripe for an irony paradigm that accounts for the simultaneously disruptive and representative nature of language and that allows for the reciprocal nature of historical work (Royster and Kirsch 68). A number of theories of irony with rhetorical implications are often oriented toward intentionality *or* toward language, toward understanding irony as either a strategy *or* an aesthetic, but not toward both at once. Nor are they oriented toward irony as contingent on shifting subjects and contexts.[11] In grappling with its linguistic and extralinguistic nature, I have learned that irony's dual role as function and metafunction creates the conditions for what contemporary philosophers call *counter-finality* and for what feminist rhetoricians call *moving between resource and restraint*. Drawing on Jean Paul Sartre's term, I use *counter-finality* to denote the "negative exigency" in an event (196) or the unintended outcome of a process that is meant to preserve a group's identification but instead reveals some tension between historical forces and individual agency in the construction of that identification.

This book argues for an ironic paradigm whose semantic dimensions do not operate at the expense of its metaphysical dimensions, and it argues for expanding our research methodologies so as to achieve a nuanced interpretation of irony (Hutcheon 6; Olson and Olson) that does not reify a singular intention or assume a solitary female subject. For me, the clearest indication that such a paradigm is overdue occurred several years ago at an international rhetoric conference where I gave a presentation on irony and shifting contexts in Protestant women's discourse. Afterward, two members of the audience delivered skeptical praise. The first admired the methodology but admonished me to "be free of the analytical box" in assigning semantic value to what I read in these women's texts. To this audience member, any textual marking was too prescriptive. The other admired the depth of analysis in marking a single utterance for dual contexts and multiple audiences but said that my analysis was insufficient for demonstrating how irony deconstructs the text. To this audience member, textual marking was inconclusive. In fact, both responses stemmed from the assumption that in my paper, I was offering a stable definition of irony with which to syntactically identify the speaker's intention or to make a structuralist interpretation of Protestant women's discourse. Instead, I was demonstrating how irony's multiple functions—its behavior as *form and phenomenon*, as *language and lens*, as *discourse and metadiscourse*— could be compatible in critical, historical, and feminist contexts.

The kind of textual examination I was proposing does not require that readers necessarily "trust" in their stable properties or extract from them inherent truths. For irony to occur, two or more agents must share some presuppositions; that is, when the speaker makes an initial utterance, some hearer must assume that the speaker meant something else or that the utterance was inappropriate given the context. Yet not all analytical assumptions about how irony *works* (or seems to work) are necessarily and exclusively bound by linguistic function, by rhetorical intention, or by the broader and more complex notion of "intentionality" for which Linda Hutcheon argues (118). Not all theories of irony require an overattention to false distinctions between intentional and nonintentional or an inattention to the multiple roles that are involved in interpreting an ironic event. These difficulties in categorization likely emerge from overlapping theoretical approaches; however, as Candace Lang, Hutcheon, and Zwagerman note, the success of one theoretical approach need not preclude all others.

Indeed, what binds Askew, Hutchinson, and Gougar (together and with other female rhetors) is temporal and atemporal, discursive and metadiscursive at the same time. Where their ironic discourse acts as a predictable form, it also raises consciousness of how that form elicits (un) desired effects. Where their ironic discourse reveals the tensions between semantic and pragmatic interpretations of the same passage, it invites us to locate linguistic sites where gender and power struggles can be more closely examined. Where their ironic discourse defies a stable intention or unified cause, it reflects the limits of historians' own understanding and how those limits may be "moved and removed" (Ratcliffe 30). Ultimately, what draws together Askew's *Examinations*, Hutchinson's trial, and Gougar's suffrage discourse is the understanding that their language is both transparent and material enough to demonstrate—for immediate and distant audiences—its failures in implicating them on set charges. All three cases provide a theoretical space for considering where language and history intersect or collide in feminist rhetorical criticism. All three cases equip discourse analysts, rhetorical theorists, and historians to *reexamine, reread,* and *reuse* feminist texts, histories, and archives, bringing into greater relief the activism in their discourse.

SHAPING THE PARADIGM: HISTORIES *FROM* VERSUS HISTORIES *OF*

In sum, *Women's Irony* argues for irony as a critical feminist paradigm because it *provides insight into nascent moments and ways of being, disrupts rather than reinforces understandings, and promotes a triad of perspectives—among those who register historical evidence, those who write history, and those who read history—as equally vital.* In more ways than one, this book responds to a question put forward by Jacqueline Jones Royster, Cheryl Glenn, Andrea Lunsford, and Patricia Bizzell in a featured session at the 2010 meeting of the Conference on College Composition and Communication: What comes next in historical studies of women rhetors? Gesa E. Kirsch and Royster have further observed that feminist rhetorical inquiry has expanded so vastly over the last three decades as to disrupt prevalent knowledge paradigms in the history of rhetoric and writing, evident in our focus on women as principal rhetorical subjects, on geographically decentered rhetorical activity, and on redirected attention to nonelite groups who are writing and speaking in counter-public arenas (641). Both of these occasions call for a revised understanding of feminist histories in rhetoric and writing and for a rethinking of the role of archival inquiry in feminist rhetorical studies, beyond the "three Rs—*rescue, recovery,* and *(re)inscription*" (647). What defines new inquiry, they say, is the nature of its impact on operational patterns in rhetorical scholarship (647)—that is, how it helps scholars in histories of rhetoric redefine their terms of scholarly engagement at all.

To that end, a paradigmatic relationship shapes this book. Each chapter builds on the previous in terms of illustrating how feminist discourse reveals irony's knowledge-making potential. The analysis of Askew's, Hutchinson's, and Gougar's performances enacts an epistemic shift from reexamining the narratives that have circulated around Renaissance texts (chapter 1), to rereading Colonial histories of rhetorical participation (chapter 2), to using suffrage archives for more than historical recovery (chapters 3 and 4), in the same way that Jean Carr, Stephen Carr, and Lucille Schultz offer "watersheds" from their tripartite investigation into nineteenth-century textbooks as archives (202). The theorizing that occurs around this analysis further exemplifies that epistemic shift by first describing how their ironic discourse complicates theoretical relationships between women and agency (chapter 1), language and history (chapter 2), and archival location and memory (chapters 3 and 4), and then suggesting new ways to question women's political histories and consider how today's feminist discourses may be historicized. The final chapter (chapter 5) looks at how all the chapters together demonstrate that a serious examination of irony in feminist rhetorical criticism encourages historiographers to expand our cultural memory, rethink the ways we form cultural norms, and rethink how we produce historical knowledge.

Rather than conduct a transhistorical analysis of Askew's, Hutchinson's, and Gougar's ironic texts, I work *panhistorically*, offering a set of principles guiding how we can reasonably expect their irony to demonstrate reciprocal agency across traditional historical parameters and a set of methodological questions to apply to more contemporary ironic events. Although I demonstrate ironic agency primarily through textual examples, the kind of historical study I do throughout this book aims neither to limit the material locations of ironic texts nor to privilege their generic conditions. Thus my marking of women's discourse is not intended to mark properties inchoate in particular texts or in limited notions of the rhetorical situation, nor to locate irony in tacit features, but rather to note their historical *residue*—the possibilities for relating and interacting all of the elements that converge on the irony event—and consider how that leads to a metadiscovery of historical processes.

While I do understand irony to be reception based throughout this project, I also understand reception to be encompassed by the broader concept of rhetorical motive. To be clear, what I call *irony* in women's texts—and the reasons why we might label their irony as impactful or effective—is not so called because of some property of these texts, but because of the expectations feminist critics can bring to our readings of these texts and for its potential in helping them become more empathetic interlocutors. The processes and practices through which feminist ironic discourse is historically recovered should reflect both its potentialities and its actualities, but especially the *existence* of potential, like the Aristotelian *dynamis* (*Metaphysics* bk. 5, sec. 1017a). My descriptions of "ironic" discourse are more concerned with its role in place, time, and memory, with how it represents an inclination to act, similar to Kenneth Burke's reclaiming of *dynamis* as a kind of *attitude* (*Language* 206)—a leaning or movement toward. My goal is to open up possibilities for what feminist irony does achieve, has achieved, or *can* achieve. Irony's *agentive* potential is best seen in how it enables the writer and the writer's feminist audiences and historiographers, as we begin to rethink not only the histories they help us write but also our attitudes toward writing histories in general.[12]

If I propose to (re)locate women's irony in the rhetorical traditions, it is because I wish to consider how irony allows us to rethink our rhetorical histories in terms of "theories" and "systems" at all (Graff and Leff 11) and to be mindful of how my assumptions and motives about their irony cause me to (re)locate them the way I do (Graff and Leff 21). As such, *Women's Irony* is not a purely historical project. Like Linda Ferreira-Buckley, I value the productive tension between *doing history* and *doing theory*, relying on the secure place of theory in historical work and thriving on the disagreements among historians about which theories to obtain (Octalog, "Octalog II" 26). Like Barbara L'Eplattenier and Royster, I study the histories of rhetoric and writing studies because of my interests in building theory, bringing about social change, and understanding how knowledge is made in the discipline. For L'Eplattenier, simply leaving her "calling card" as a historian is insufficient to describe her approach in, her attitudes toward, or her ultimate desires for archival work (133). For Royster, simply offering new spatial metaphors for women's rhetorical participation was never enough to relandscape the discipline ("Disciplinary," 149). For Nan Johnson, historical research and history writing must work toward both "archaeological *and* rhetorical" ends (10). And it is the same for me. In its most useful state, this book constructs a paradigm in which to theorize about communities of discourse more broadly, even as it disrupts certain notions of when, where, and how women are permitted to speak.

1. ON WOMEN AND AGENCY: Ironizing Together

Agency . . . emerges in performances that repeat with a difference, altering meaning.   —Karlyn Kohrs Campbell, "Agency"

The answerer's task is, in a way, to make the questioner's work
more difficult. He is to do this . . . by holding the questioner's
argument to the highest standards, so that when the answerer's
thesis is defeated it will be because of its weakness, not the
answerer's.
  —James Allen, "Aristotle on the Disciplines of Argument"

Who counts as "us" in [our] own rhetoric? Which identities are
available to ground such a potent political myth called "us," and
what could motivate enlistment in this collectivity?
  —Donna Haraway, "A Manifesto for Cyborgs"

In their presentation of feminist rhetorical studies as a robust framework, Jacqueline Jones Royster and Gesa E. Kirsch reflect on the ways
in which field scholarship has pushed conceptual frameworks of agency
"well beyond . . . basic issues of identity and representation," striving
toward multidimensional analytic methods that show feminist subjectivities as interrelated and complex (48). In fact, since Cheryl Geisler's
synthesis of the 2003 ARS position statements on rhetorical agency, several theoretical shifts have invited new considerations of what it means *to
have critical agency*: a move toward "more productive investigations into
the consciousness and conditions of agency" (9); an interplay between
"what rhetorical agency, in *fact*, is and what it, in *value*, ought to be"
(Geisler 9, original emphasis); a stretching of agency's varieties and available means well beyond the postmodern critique of autonomous agent
or humanist individual (Geisler 10); and an interplay between two questions that *Women's Irony* serves to bridge: "What agency does the rhetor
have?" and "What agency do we have as historiographers of rhetorical

activity?" (Geisler 15). My bridging these questions acknowledges that they can and often do function together in historical projects. At such a critical juncture as this—one in which we aim to have more conscious control over our historiographic practices—it makes sense to reconsider attitudes such as Barbara Biesecker's and Karlyn Kohrs Campbell's notion of consciousness-raising because it has proven to be an unsettled term. Although this idea emerged two decades ago, and primarily as a second-wave feminist concept, I still find it useful for illuminating historicized events (or sets of events) in the twenty-first century by broadening our understanding of their ironic constraints.

Arguing against the ideology of individualism in constructing feminist histories ("Coming" 156), Biesecker appropriates Lloyd Bitzer's "consciousness-raising" as "bringing to the surface something that is hidden, the task of making manifest something that is concealed or covered over" ("Coming" 158), while Campbell defines it as "a form of discursive practice . . . that links the recovery of texts [and] their recuperation through criticism" ("Consciousness-Raising" 45). Neither Biesecker nor Campbell advocates for simply accommodating new textual discoveries or for more altruistically representing the texts that were produced by women during specific historical periods. Rather, each of them draws on rhetorical agency to foster a reciprocal examination of textual evidence. Indeed, Campbell's definition reflects what I ultimately see as irony's greatest potential for feminist discourse: it accounts for a process that is both discursive and metadiscursive.

Women's Irony demonstrates irony's critical offerings by making this reflection agential for more than the ironic subject and its temporal context. It examines how various writers reach beyond their own acquaintances (Strauss) and unsettles the manner in which master narratives are sought, challenged, or overturned in the first place (Biesecker, "Coming" 141; Octalog, "Octalog II" 29). The book's epistemic shift from *unsettling narratives* to *unsettling the ways in which the narratives are remembered* begins in this chapter, with a reexamination of the narratives that have circulated around women's Renaissance texts and a description of how feminist ironic discourse can complicate theoretical relationships between women and agency.

Anne Askew is not an unknown figure to feminist historians, yet a reappropriation of her ironic discourse as multilayered and dualistic may offer historians new ways to valuate her stumping, her refusals, and her silence. The same can be said for Anne Hutchinson in chapter 2, although what is at stake in rereading her trial discourse is a reappropriation of "wit" that does not preclude a Colonial woman's ability to participate in the public arena.[1] In chapter 3, I argue that Helen Gougar has been neglected as an archival figure—although she delivered as many lectures as Elizabeth Cady Stanton and was cited in periodicals from Hawaii to the eastern coast of the United States—and reinscribed through a series of tropes, and it is both the critical archival turn in rhetorical studies and the ensuing push to reconstruct suffrage histories from obscure figures, institutions, and texts that have made her neglect and reinscription take on real consequence.[2] For all three women, in calling their discourse "ironic," I note the interplay between the conditions that are present in their performances and how those performances enact or contain a theory of agency when they are read, disseminated, and analyzed across historical and critical contexts. Moreover, I locate the reciprocal conditions under which they are able to act ironically *and we are able to historicize them as such.*

Askew makes a good first figure for demonstrating this reciprocity because her self-identification has historically been situated in the tension among her roles as author, actor, and agent. As ironic identification involves not only revealing the cultural logics that drive a particular discourse community but also using discourse to recover the critical distance between ironic agents, an examination of Askew's irony sheds light on three things: how her responses could have challenged established rhetorical traditions when read across historical lenses; how her performances can make new possibilities for gendered communication in Renaissance and early modern texts; and how our historical readings of her text can make new possibilities for examining Englishwomen's political discourse as agential rather than transactional.

Unfortunately, there is still this need. Paul Zahl mentions Askew as one of five influential women in the English Reformation, all of whom were "extremely well educated by the standards of their time" (1) and involved in a religious movement that transcended gender on the basis of their being theologians, yet having principles shared "point for point with many men who worked alongside them" (5). Of the women Zahl mentions—including Anne Boleyn, Katherine [*sic*] Parr, Jane Grey, and Catherine Willoughby—he describes Askew as especially accomplished and influential but "a harder character to love, as she was tart, ironic, and also iron" (40). Zahl's positioning as a systematic theologian may complicate this characterization somewhat, although his historicization

is as influential as any other in portraying Askew as "totemic" among
other women in an "enduring search for [Reformation] role models" (8),
and yet "totemic" is not necessarily *agential* where irony is concerned.
It takes a strong historical reimagining to suggest reciprocal agency for
the present and future.

In this chapter, I suggest an alternative positioning for Askew and
alternative ways for historiographers to valuate her work. I urge us to
consider her ironic *positioning* as something that occurs over time, long
after one set of meanings has been activated. Rather than mark Askew's
text for *intentionality* or even propose a more correct *intention* in reading her work, I point to a residue of historical interactions that the irony
makes possible, becoming conscious of the multiple occasions and needs
for regendering her practice beyond the topoi she has traditionally been
assigned. Instead of the "tartness" that results from our assumptions
about how she performed in an unprecedented discursive space, we might
achieve transhistorical readings of her performance and other performances like it. And instead of the "silence" that results from our assumptions about her ambiguation of truth or refusal, we might achieve more
critical noise. In arguing for a critical paradigm for irony that functions
separately from humor or intention, I face the same challenge as Candace
Lang: arguing for more concrete differences between humor and irony
without resorting to prescriptive characteristics of what should be a fairly
contingent and flexible phenomenon. A reexamination is necessary to
reveal more opportunistic moments for critical disruption in Askew's
textual dynamics, then and now.

REEXAMINING RENAISSANCE TEXTS

The trial of Anne Askew was remarkable in that she was the first gentlewoman to be illegally rack-tortured and sentenced to death on grounds
of heresy, ultimately condemned without firm charges (Beilin, *Examinations* xxvi).[3] One of four female martyrs who burned at Smithfield during
Henry VIII's tenure, Askew is the only woman who left behind a written
record. *The First and Lattre Examinacyons* (hereafter referred to by its
modern spelling, the *Examinations*) is a two-part, self-recorded narrative
of her arrests and imprisonment, which she wrote prior to her death in
July 1546, "in order to set out publicly the significance of her sufferings"
(McQuade 2).

The *Examinations* gained such popularity as a religious text that it
was reprinted in more than six editions before 1550, both in England

and abroad. In their written commentary on her work, Johan Bale and John Foxe remarked that the king's bishops and councilors eventually lost patience with Askew's tactical refusal and syllogistic challenges to their questions and said that she owed her greatest success to the employment of silence and divine intervention. Without overlooking the numerous references Askew makes to divine intervention and fortitude as she exhorts believers to hold fast and "praye, praye, praye" (*Lattre Examinacyon*, Bale edition, line 392), it seems necessary to consider that Askew may have been modeling an alternative civic role for the religious woman—assertive and loquacious, rather than "weak but empowered" (Beilin, *Redeeming* 31–32). While Askew performed ironically for the bishop's council, ultimately stumping the interrogation (a fact we can discern based on their failure to indict Askew on a definite charge), she later recalled this performance in another passage directed to fellow reformers: "I do perceyve (dere frynde in the lorde) that thou art not yet persuaded throughlye in the truthe concernynge the lordes supper" (*Lattre Examinacyon*, Bale edition, lines 38–39).

Elaine Beilin notes that by the nineteenth century, Askew's story appeared in several collections of women's biographies, while her writings appeared in anthologies commonly consulted by historians, biographers, religious writers, and novelists (*Examinations* xl). Beilin and Elizabeth Mazzola have also recognized the *Examinations* as an important feminist work for Askew's various resistance strategies, and Cheryl Glenn has described Askew's syllogisms and "self-portrait" as regendered and expert forms of *disputatio* (*Rhetoric*, 154). All of them have noted Askew's systematic refusal or silence when it came to offering information about her domestic affairs and revealing the identities of fellow Protestant sympathizers. While a number of Protestant reformers and historians, including her first publisher, Bale, have looked on Askew's strategies as evidence of divine intervention, Beilin and Mazzola further argue for Askew's self-assured authorship, intellectual fortitude, and rhetorical prowess prior to the interrogations—enough to warrant that the *Examinations* was meant to defend herself before her readers and demonstrate a calculatedly strong and ironical witness as she performed the text (Mazzola 159).

This rhetorical notoriety is neither surprising nor unjustifiable. Like other Renaissance Englishwoman writers, Askew had the unique challenge of "discover[ing] an appropriate persona, subject, and form" for lack of sufficient prior examples (Beilin, *Redeeming* 269). However, unlike other Renaissance Englishwoman writers, Askew wore her "learned and virtuous" character as an empowerment rather than a limitation (Tebeaux and Lay 55), constantly reminding the Protestant reformers that "courage, constancy, and fortitude, since they could not be a woman's, must have come from God" (Beilin, *Redeeming* 30). Beyond merely increasing her virtue (chastity, obedience, and humility) and womanliness, Askew's tenacity "ironically subvert[ed] the restrictions on women's roles" and diverged from the intended silent role (Beilin, *Redeeming* xxiii). Indeed, Askew's first *Examination* opens with explicit audience construction:

> To satisfie your expectation, good people (sayth she) this was my first examynacyon in the yeare of oure Lorde M. D. xlv and in the moneth of Marche, first Christofer dare examined me at Sadlers hall, beynge one of the quest, and asked yf I did not beleve that the sacrament hangynge over the aultre was the verye bodye of Christ reallye. Then I demaunded thys questyon of hym, wherfore S. Steven was stoned to deathe? And he sayd, he coulde not tell. Then I answered, that no more wolde I assoyle hys vayne questyon. (*First Examinacyon*, Bale edition, lines 21–29)

On the surface, this represents a kind of rhetorical refusal. As the narrating subject, Askew portrays authorial and ironic control by not entertaining Christopher Dare's "vayne" question, presumably because it would lead to the kind of heretical sand trap (the "ynsavory symyltude") in which Dare and the bishop's council had hoped to catch Askew. Her narration disrupts certain acts of identification and interpretation, eliciting several responses from an audience that was likely expected to give only a single response in accordance with the genre (Schilb, *Rhetorical* 142). In his chapter on "Tudor Writings," Walter Ong notes that this kind of rhetorical control became prevalent in the polemical outlook one century later, mixing with "witty raillery" as a way to deliver criticism on science, logic, and stylistics of the day (*Rhetoric* 66, 101).

Beyond a surface reading, however, Askew's question about Stephen is not the rhetorical refusal. In the combination of her text, her extratextual commentary, and Bale's elucidation of the text, readers are not given an overarching or logical explanation for precisely why she counters with this question. Askew may be testing Dare's hagiographic memory of martyr tales or simply asking him to predicate his accusation on the actions of Stephen's successors even when they could not find fault in his arguments or testimony. If Dare's first question really had been intended to gauge

Askew's publicly spoken and privately held views on transubstantiation, then her use of deferral as a constant rhetorical strategy would certainly allow her to demonstrate that the question was a reciprocal one. She would be implying, first, that both she and Dare have insufficient knowledge to explain it and, second, that some interrogative questions are more productive and worthwhile than others, strongly hinting that the premise underlying Dare's question was as heretical as Askew's alleged teachings. The ironic nature of this whole exchange accommodates (and is accommodated by) any of these possibilities.

However, if Dare's first question had been motivated by some other desire, such as to confirm Askew's guilt on some extant charge, then several additional possibilities for Askew's deferral should be considered:

- Askew could be refusing the occasion to turn what is a fairly straightforward statement into an epistemic debate;
- Askew could be responding in such a way as to let her examiners fulfill the role they construct for themselves; or
- Askew could be reminding her examiners of the fundamental points on which they *do* agree, in this case a point echoed in the New Testament book of Acts chapters 3, 7, and 17 that "God dwelleth not in temples made with handes" (*First Examinacyon*, Bale edition, line 38).

The precise nature of this disruption raises critical questions about the role of audience competency in determining Askew's success and in naming her techniques beyond "silence," "resistance," or refusal (Glenn, *Rhetoric*; Beilin, "Askew's Dialogue")—in fact, in understanding her irony as agential—as something that *is or acts as* an agent. Beilin notes that Askew casts herself as an "uncooperative reader" of the texts her interrogators grill her about and succeeds in carrying out "both the Reformer's essential task of discrediting doctrine and the woman writer's search for an authoritative voice" ("Askew's Dialogue" 314).

Another option is not to read such statements as rhetorical refusals at all and to read them as illicit participation in something like civic debate. At three instances in the narrative, Askew describes herself as responding to her examiners with silence or gesture, rather than with an answer. In the second of these instances, Askew justifies her response by denying the validity of the charge, eliding the narrow subject position in which her examiners want to cast her:

Besydes thys my lorde mayre layed one thynge unto my charge, which
was never spoken of me, but of them. And that was, whether a mouse
eatynge the hoste, receyved God or no? Thys questyon ded I never
aske, but in dede they asked it of me, whereunto I made them no
answere, but smyled. (*First Examinacyon*, Bale edition, lines 224–28)

Yet while she claims to have "made them no answere," where witnessed
or observed, Askew's writings and speeches betray an informed understanding of theoretical—even metaphysical—argumentation. Accounts
of her birthright and marriage indicate that she was given an exceptional
education by her father, Sir William Askew (Glenn, *Rhetoric* 125). As a
humanist, Sir Askew would have supported a liberal education for gentlewomen, even if it did not equip them for public service or to speak with
the same authority and in the same venues as gentlemen (Clarke 38;
Donawerth, *Rhetorical* xxi; Glenn, *Rhetoric* 150). This tradition emphasized literacy as the key to Christian knowledge and was largely centered
on a renaissance of classical texts, including Cicero's *De Oratore* and
Quintilian's *Institutio Oratoria*.

Thus it seems reasonable to assume that Askew was schooled in both
logical and decorative forms of argument and was aware of Leonard Cox's
The Art or Crafte of Rhetoryke. She may even have been influenced by
Agricola's *De Inventione Dialectica*, which stressed invention and judgment as two parts of logic.[4] If this were the case, then Askew would have
appreciated the various associations of irony to proof, truth, character,
empathy, and eloquence that occurred in its theoretical developments between Aristotle's *eironeia* and Augustine's "didactic indirection" (Swearingen 202); she might even have mastered argumentation beyond them.
In any case, if we insist on defining this event as a rhetorical refusal, it
becomes clear that Askew is refusing not the role of participatory subject,
but rather the limitations put on critical and historical participation at all.

I am not the first to establish that the ironist is not the only agent in
an ironic event (Kaufer, "Irony, Interpretive" 452; Hutcheon 122) nor to
problematize the role of ironist as an intentional actor (Hutcheon 122).
Linda Hutcheon's metaphor seems more complete for describing Askew's
irony: it is "the superimposition or rubbing together of [the said and the
plural unsaids]" (19), and this makes it necessary to reexamine. I agree
with Beilin and Mazzola that Askew sought to portray a different persona
than one who believed she was weak but simply became strong in the act
of speaking. However, Askew's use of irony effectually reinvents religious

discourse for her own civic purposes, because she knew the nature of the record she would leave behind, and for this reason her texts deserve a reexamination beyond their motives and outcomes. Thus while silence and refusal are useful concepts for rhetorical reexamination, they are not sufficiently agential for panhistorical study if they obscure interstitial awareness—the awareness of *how looking at the gaps* raises the historian's self-consciousness of *how s/he looks at all*. I propose reenvisioning them as movable relationships that reflect what Debra Hawhee and Christa J. Olson call a "pan-historiographic" attitude toward histories, archives, and texts (91): an attitude that endures the growth of a discipline's questions, combining "conceptual, theoretical, and practical reasons" for doing history (95). If we can achieve this, I anticipate four worthwhile and immediate repercussions: rethinking "silence" as a function of/in Renaissance women's discourse; relinquishing truth claims as a function of scholasticism; viewing rhetoric, logic, and dialectic as jointly constructed endeavors in feminist inventions of reformation arguments and texts; and as a result, inventing something like a "civic" discourse for Renaissance writers like Askew.

Rethinking Silence

With such direct and subtle mediation provided by the *Examinations'* publishers, it is not surprising that Askew's posthumous reputation has been steered toward silence, resistance, or refusal. Both *First* and *Lattre* were combined and published as a single volume, first in 1546–47 by Protestant reformer and bishop Johan Bale, while he was exiled in Germany, and later by martyrologist John Foxe in Latin (1559) and in English (1563) as part of his *Actes and Monuments of These Latter and Perillous Dayes* (Beilin, *Examinations* 35).[5] What distinguished the two editions were Bale's "elucydacyons" and prefatory and concluding commentary. Primarily interested in using Askew's text to undermine the threat of papal rule in England, Bale interspersed his own commentary with Askew's narration throughout the *First Examinacyon*, often highlighting a charge that came against her, providing a brief scriptural exegesis, or directing the reader's attention to Askew's various political "resistances" (Beilin, *Examinations* xxix). Ultimately, he included an alphabetized table of chronicled events and ended with the 54th Psalm of David. Bale's *Lattre Examinacyon* also included his elucidations, prefatory and concluding commentary, a table of chronicled events, and a "Ballade" written by Askew while awaiting execution at Newgate Prison.

Foxe adopted Bale's version for his own *Actes and Monuments* but omitted Bale's commentary, perhaps as a way of letting Askew "speak for herself" (Mazzola 160). Thus his version contains no breaks except those that Askew created by the insertion of occasional descriptive headers. However, he did include a brief eyewitness account of Askew's burning with three other prisoners, in which he described Askew as someone who "divulges no name, and by her silence . . . proves stronger than the machine" (Beilin, *Examinations* 194). As a result, "[her examiners] stand dumbstruck, and are driven mad by the delay: yet they achieve nothing" (Beilin, *Examinations* 194). And in his 1559 Latin edition, Foxe published an epitaph as a way of recognizing Askew's contribution of silence—or, more specifically, of not revealing the names of the queen's "inner circle" members. In both of these editions, Askew's *perceived use* of irony is both persuasive and divergent from the traditional forms of persuasion that typically determine the scholastic debate. By undermining the purpose of a public examination (which is to establish evidence by bringing names, places, and events to the surface), Askew's ironic responses could elide expected outcomes. That Askew chose to respond ironically, or not to respond at all, could exemplify her participation in such feminine rhetorical strategies as taking an oath of silence (Barratt 9), invoking formal styles of argument, employing dissociation (Perelman and Olbrechts-Tyteca 191), and using humor as a form of evasion. Like other Renaissance women writers, Askew helped challenge and call into question not only the discursive stability of the genres in which she wrote but also the ideological stability of *genre* itself.

Although it is historically valuable to understand silence in its various modes as a rhetorical art (Glenn and Ratcliffe 3), a silent subject position nonetheless remains limited in historical valuations of irony, because it assumes that the ironist either ambiguates truth or elides charges of falsehood.[6] In *Rhetoric Retold*, Glenn argues that even the most outstanding, erudite, and clever women writers in the Renaissance were marginalized, according to their limited tendency to break with convention (142).[7] She places Askew within this rhetorical tradition of silence for demonstrating when it was advantageous to speak or not to speak, for knowing how much or how little to provide, and for providing answers that were extraneous to the question at hand (153–54). Each of these strategies describes vital rhetorical operations within a shared linguistic context. To extend any or all of these strategies to Askew's *ironic* discourse requires two things: that they be understood as something more than a rhetorical foil for Askew's pragmatic cooperation or noncooperation; and that this understanding in turn be liberated from the limitations that come with analyzing her irony as a single speech act or discursive event. For this reason, I willingly depart from the analytic constraints of looking at the *Examinations* as a speech act—even a broadly understood speech act that is determined according to social understandings of wit (Zwagerman 212)—in reexamining Askew's exchange.

Rather than evaluate Askew's *Examinations* according to one of these things—how completely irony seems to ambiguate the topic, how successfully it evokes or defies cooperation, and whether it restores truth to Askew's statements—we might understand that her irony constructs, and is recognized in, a productive tension between ironist, victim, and observer(s). And instead of watching for irony to subvert the hegemonic expectations of various discourse communities, we might imagine how Renaissance audiences *could* employ irony to reinvent the epistemic functioning of their own and others' discourse.

This small paradigmatic shift provokes a reassessment of the kinds of textual personae that Renaissance and women writers could portray and the logocentric nature of the genres through which they portrayed them. In some respects, I am—like Hutcheon—interested in how the ironists and the interpreters can "ironize" together.[8] In other respects, I am less interested in how this reciprocity gives readers more explanatory power and more interested in how it enables a kind of *interstitial witnessing*—what Sean Zwagerman refers to as "turning a Burkean lens" onto their joined interests (Zwagerman 162; Burke, *Rhetoric* 20).

Relinquishing Truth Claims

Zwagerman asks an important question of women's humor more broadly: How can we traverse the Derridean constraints on speech acts that cause us to view them as performative failures (129)? However, where Zwagerman and I both strive to reach a "transcendence of ambiguity and disconnection" in the discursive relationships we study (9)—where we both strive to *not* be limited by poststructuralist assumptions about language—Zwagerman retains a connection between words and deeds that I wish to disrupt. Rather than ground my query in the deconstruction or reconstruction of speech acts, I ground it in the metacritical space that occurs when questioning whether it is even possible to read irony as a signature event *rather than as a complex interplay of motives, attitudes, and contingencies*. This results in a discourse practice that acknowledges irony's dialogism—its qualities of *asignification*—where language does not just reveal or overturn objects of understanding but inspires what H. Lewis Ulman calls a "philosophical transformation" (181).

I see inventive potential in ironic discourse in spite of—*because* of—an unclear intention at its center. Like Lang, I note the problems of determining irony only in terms of how much it diverges from a predictable or expected truth—an other, an ideal, a *real*—for the ways it metaphysically and ethically limits irony and, I would add, for the ways it delimits the kinds of relationships that can be constructed between irony's users and its subjects. To more fully take into account nonhumorous or nondeceptive motives in rhetorical and discursive theories of irony, and to apply relevant-appropriateness conditions to the ways that critical readers valuate ironic utterances (and not only to the ways in which ironists use them), the parameters of the ironic event would need to be redrawn so as to account for meanings that are discursively contextualized (Hutcheon 97), that either "access directly or make available a strong prior context" (Giora, *On Our Mind* 69), and that support an immediate and subsequent phase of comprehension without overlooking the role of multiple critical readers in order to determine whether and how these phases occur. In still simpler terms, for the irony to be successful, its processing and interpretation theories no longer (or need not ever) rely on one audience recovering and restoring all meanings in one context before activating any or all meanings in another context.

Intentional rereadings of her irony may move Askew's performance beyond caviling and undermining, but they do not necessarily open up her performances to critical possibilities beyond linguistic determinism. Such questions ground her performances—temporally and critically—in historians' desire that *discourse* be reconstructed as compositional and transcendent (Yarbrough 108), that attention to discourse can make historical narratives more or less accurate, more or less powerful, and provide more or less insight into the totality to which Askew and her readers belong (Yarbrough 109). Yet rather than point to linguistic activism—which is a worthy goal for historiographic investigations of performances and situations where we suspect agency has been removed—I want to consider Askew's and her historians' activism more agentially through its logical gaps, without assuming that their language necessarily reveals power, motive, and common or dissonant ground (Yarbrough 50), and through the lens of what Hutcheon calls irony's "multiple operations" (Hutcheon 46), linguistic or not.

When searching for the silencing mechanisms around *irony*, feminist critics should not only broaden the parameters of the event but also extend the conditions in which it is rendered salient. In Askew's ironic self-positioning, feminist critics may see a more agentive participation within and against dominant discursive traditions by drawing on definitions of verbal irony that do not merely reinforce felicity or appropriateness conditions in their analysis and interpretation, but challenge them (Attardo, "Irony" 822; Giora, *On Our Mind*). As a result, they may find a self-positioning that is interpretive, provides insight into moments and ways of being, and disrupts extant understandings of when and where Renaissance women can be perceived to speak. Thus the first step in making the paradigm shift I outline in this book—from *reexamining texts* to *rereading histories* to *(re)using archives*—comes in dissociating irony from the truth-conditional expectations that underlie humor and deception, indeed from the pragmatic expectation that all ironic speech acts must either support or overturn truth conditions (i.e., must reflect either humor or lying).

Linguistically, this dissociational move already occurs in theories of irony that rely first on an utterance being contextually inappropriate and second on the utterance being situationally relevant. Recent analytic methods such as those posed by Salvatore Attardo, Rachel Giora and Ofer Fein, John Morreall, and Amadeu Viana do help rhetoricians argue that the ability to detect "funniness" in a text relies on more than Paul Grice's "cooperative principle."[9] In Gricean pragmatics, a bona-fide cooperative principle is being either observed or opposed ("Logic" 58), making hegemonic disruption in gendered discourse more markedly visible but also more markedly limited.[10] In response, Attardo's relevant-inappropriateness definition makes it clear that, though it is often interpreted as humor, irony does not need humor support ("Humor" 166), which is to say that irony *need not* indicate the opposite of a statement's "literal" meaning ("Humor" 148) *or* support Gricean distinctions between bona-fide (humorous) and non-bona-fide (deceptive) communication.

Instead, irony results from the incompatibility or inappropriateness between the context and mechanisms of an utterance (Attardo, *Humorous* 103). Not all audiences need to arrive at a particular meaning first (Attardo, "On the Pragmatic" 52). In addition, Giora's "irony salience" requires only that an ironic utterance be contextually minimal to be relevant to a context in which it is perceived (*On Our Mind* 26). Thus while humor and irony share some basic mechanisms, they are distinct. Attardo notes that what semanticists perceive as irony is often dependent on what they perceive to be a text's narrower *first sense* or literal meaning, yet irony comprehension does not in fact require that this meaning be arrived at first at all. This loosens the interpretive constraints from purely Gricean terms, which require that both speaker and hearer be committed to the literal truth of what is said according to initial presuppositions that they both share (Attardo, *Humorous* 117). Even for linguistic examinations of ironic discourse, the processing of irony need not rely on the identification of a single literal meaning or on "literal" meaning as truth-conditional.[11]

For example, the following passage from Askew's *First Examinacyon* begins with Dare's "quest," the formal inquiry by an appointed jury of twelve men, and concludes after several interrogations showed insufficient evidence to detain her. In this part of the text, Askew is asked to respond to a total of eight charges of heresy and misconduct, followed by a charge she claimed "was never spoken of me, but of them"—that she had denied the Catholic doctrine of transubstantiation in asking the question "whether a mouse eatynge the hoste, receyved God or no?" (Bale edition, lines 222–25). When asked whether she had publicly stated some things antithetical to the doctrine, she replied by quoting the New Testament book of 1 Corinthians. Afterward, she was sent to the lord mayor of London and to the bishop's chancellor for repeated questioning:

> (A) Then the Byshopes chaunceller rebuked me, and sayd, that I was moche to blame for utterynge the scriptures. For S. Paule (he sayd) forbode women to speake or to talke of the worde of God. I answered hym, that I knewe Paules meanynge so well as he, whych is, i. Corinthiorum xiiii, that a woman ought not to speake in the congregacyon by the waye of teachynge. And then I asked hym, how manye women he had seane, go into the pulpett and preache. He sayde, he never sawe non. Then I sayd, he ought to fynde no faulte in poore women, except they had offended the lawe. (Bale edition, lines 277–84)

Passage (A) already represents a fairly complex elision in several ways.[12] It is important to note that the audience for this transcript could have included the king's Privy Council, not just Askew's fellow Protestant reformers, since she remarks in the *Lattre Examinacyon* that her illegal rack torture was reported to them while still in jail. And while Mazzola argues that Askew's written autobiography acts the same as the spoken testimony—"as if she's still defending herself before her readers" (159)—it can also be argued that the noncooperative aspect of Askew's irony is more apparent in the written autobiography than in the interrogations themselves, because the readers necessarily share a context with Askew that Askew did not share with her interrogators.

Mazzola argues for this strategy as a kind of mockery of the law, but it seems necessary to acknowledge that irony occurs over multiple or shifting contexts. In its most basic definition, irony (as a *trope*, a *device*, or an *event*) involves speaker S uttering u in context C, while meaning presupposition p for audience H, as depicted in figure 1.1. The u is somehow inappropriate in C, but H may or may not detect this inappropriateness. While the first irony (or set of ironies) is fulfilled when H both detects and interprets the inappropriateness, the second irony (or set of ironies) is fulfilled at any time, as long as there is a witness. Thus Askew's presupposition is ironical because H expects a blatant disagreement—an affirmation or denial of a truth claim. Askew's denial of 1 Corinthians 14 both contradicts the truth of what her examiners expect (i.e., that she had at some point preached in public) and predicts the kinds of public (re)circulation her testimony would eventually have.

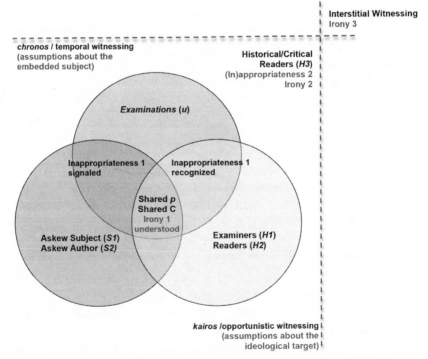

Figure 1.1. Interstitial witnessing model, depicting how various audiences and readers access irony in Anne Askew's First and Lattre Examinacyons.

The perceived presupposition of the bishop's council is that they are rebuking Askew for having disagreed with this scripture by preaching in public at some point in time, even though Askew circumvents the rebuke by citing and discussing 1 Corinthians 14 in the presence of her interrogators with no other audience present. If there is mockery here, it relies on a context made possible by Askew's presupposition that she is narrating her first performance for a second audience. H may or may not recognize this "second crime," because it relies on a different context made possible by Askew's presuppositions. However, given how many of these ironic exchanges appear to have resulted in a "stumping" or redirected course of questioning, it seems more likely that irony recognition and irony processing do not always occur at the same time and by the same audiences within a single shared context C. And in fact, it is important to realize that C shifts in any of these theories, serving more as a variable than a historical constant.

First Corinthians 14 acts simultaneously as a declaration of Askew's knowledge of scripture and as a reference to the elision of gender roles that an ironic reader would understand. That is, her utterance u would be interpreted as relevant-inappropriate for her examiners, who were expecting a declaration or a confession, and relevant-inappropriate again for her immediate and distant readers, who were expecting an elision of that first speech act. Also, Askew's reference to Paul would be understood not just as a covert demonstration of why she cannot answer the examiners' question, but as a metahistorical explanation for why she cannot answer it sufficiently by merely demonstrating the scholastic limitations on her gender.

Finally, the irony created by the incongruity of her response (because it does not meet with either the examiners' or her readers' expectations of possible responses) would not only equip Askew and her immediate readers to assume different rhetorical roles than the ones prescribed but also enable Askew's examiners and her critical or historical readers to have a measure of agency in the discourse. More agents than just her adjudicators would need to feel simultaneously accommodated and impeded, more agents than her immediate readers would need to understand that paradox of impeding, and more agents than her critical readers would need to benefit from such a paradox. In turn, more interpretive possibilities become available for reading the passage inventively because it allows for an interstitial witnessing of multiple shared and unshared contexts and, consequently, for the construction of several relationships between irony's users and its subjects, not only those relationships that are bound by literal performance and truth claims.[13] In that context, uttering Paul's maxim about women in general allows Askew to achieve the following: to avoid incriminating herself; to commit as normative that which they accuse her of and which she had not done before this moment; and to undermine the validity of the interrogation.

Askew's most notable strategy here is deflecting the question back to her examiner by demonstrating an uncommon knowledge of scripture. Glenn already notes that Askew responds to the query in a four-part move: citing the New Testament (1 Corinthians 14); posing her own question; exacting an answer; and drawing a conclusion to discomfit the questioner (*Rhetoric* 154–55). She also responds to the chancellor's request for personal information (*Did you preach before a congregation?*) with a maxim about women in general (*Paul says no women are preaching to a congregation*; *You ought not to charge women unless they break the law*). The meaning is finite, the interrogative request is settled in a denial—or an elision—of the first pragmatic expectation, and the speech act is evaluated according to whether Askew's performance is cooperative or noncooperative. And these same discursive patterns are employed continuously throughout the interrogation of the eight separate charges:

> Fiftly he asked me, what I sayd concernynge confession? I answered hym my meanynge, whych was as Saynt James sayth, that everye man ought to acknowledge hys fautes to other, and the one to praye for the other [James 5:16]. Sixtly he asked me, what I sayd to the kynges boke?[14] And I answered hym, that I coulde saye nothynge to it, bycause I never sawe it. (*First Examinacyon*, Bale edition, lines 128–29)

However, questions of whether Askew tells "the truth" have stunted more vital discussions of precisely what can be achieved for Renaissance rhetoric by reexamining her responses apart from their adherence to truth claims. There are richer definitions of performativity and cooperation that can accommodate rhetorical motives and felicitous goals whether or not they recount "real" events or subscribe to truth claims (Zwagerman 22), so I propose an even broader understanding of *discourse* that raises metalinguistic consciousness of the kinds of framing and delimiting that historians do (Hutcheon 194).

Probability, rather than truth, is a more reliable measure of effectiveness in Askew's arguments for readers then and now, because "effectiveness" need not rely on whether the audiences fail to uncover all of the discourse goals while thinking that they do. While the interrogation appears only to proceed from—and to affirm—previously established certainties, Askew positions herself as both a product of and a reformer of a tradition of scholasticism in the way that her responses leave room for questioning, then and now. Although it may be true that Askew's interrogators become increasingly frustrated by her ironic statements in the *Lattre Examinacyon,* we know concretely only a few things about their response: they follow her lead when she redirects the line of questioning; they persist in their questions; they fail to find grounds for arrest; and they ultimately resort to illegal rack torture and burning. When, after repeated interrogations, the bishop himself tests Askew on her beliefs about transfiguration, she replies by asking him "how longe he wolde halte on both sydes?" a reference to the Old Testament book of Kings to indicate a wavering between two opinions. When the bishop asserts that she should be burned, Askew responds that she can find no textual basis for Christ or the apostles putting anyone to death, provoking the bishop to command her to stand aside (lines 280–85). Not long afterward, and after refusing to sign a written confession, Askew is sent to Newgate to await execution.

Historically and ideologically, the dissociation between irony and truth-conditional expectations has yet to occur. Seeing and believing in formalist properties of language do not necessarily guarantee that language performs only formalist functions when it is studied historically, although it does guarantee to overturn the assumption that "all evidence is interpretive" (Flynn 154), most likely because language and history tend to be studied as separate disciplines, in spite of significant theoretical work toward destabilizing language. In terms of how irony has functioned in Western rhetorical paradigms as a set of linguistic signs, it has typically been understood as a failed discourse (Swearingen 195). Ultimately, these methods categorize a text's interpretive or extralinguistic content in ways that are temporally bound—that is, they depend on irony resulting from the incompatibility or inappropriateness between the context and mechanisms of a single utterance in a specified moment (Attardo, *Humorous* 103), rather than by accounting for multiple, embedded, or evolving contexts. As well, verbal theories of irony cannot claim to fully distinguish humor from lying. In strictly Gricean (or pragmatic) terms, irony is a non-bona-fide mode of communication because it relies on implicature, violating one or more of Grice's maxims, although it can become bona-fide once the violation is resolved. As a result, it is not hard to imagine why irony's tropological functions for rhetoric have tended to lean more toward coherence than disruption, more often "used to reinforce rather than to question established attitudes" (Hutcheon 10).

Often, irony studies are framed by a typically Western rhetorical understanding of irony as an elicited effect and intended outcome, they are identified through Wayne Booth's depiction of irony through its stable or unstable properties, or they are evaluated within Kenneth Burke's establishment of the comic frame. Yet historical methodologies that rely on purely pragmatic assumptions leave few options for valuating women's discourse beyond cooperative or noncooperative aims, and this is my greatest contention with them. By the time of her interrogations, Askew likely would have acquired an appreciation of irony's communicative potential beyond the forms that were considered mundane, especially if the principal treatises on irony—Aristotle's and Augustine's—imply a prohibition on mundane ironic forms that influenced Askew's historicization, then and now.

In the *Nicomachean Ethics*, Aristotle addresses truth telling as moral and *eironeia* (irony) as "the pretense of understatement, or mock modesty" (Swearingen 127), while in *Enchiridion* and *De Doctrina Christiana*, Augustine indicates that rhetors who use ambiguous language necessarily mislead their audiences on matters of religious authority (Swearingen 202). Aristotle's *eironeia* contains linguistic contingency and semantic autonomy at once (Swearingen 76), because it depends on shared contexts between the rhetor and his various audiences, but at the same time it acts as a complete discourse somewhat independent of its originator and audience. Augustine's emphasis on using rhetorical persuasion to teach and disseminate religious texts—in fact, his belief that rhetoric should serve the communication of scriptural truth (Lauer 30)—makes clear distinctions between cooperative and deceitful persuasion, prohibiting any humorous forms from being considered authentic communicative strategies during this period. For Aristotle, irony served as an "understatement and verbal dissembling—a guarded version of what one means" (*On Rhetoric* bk. 3, ch. 18; Swearingen 127). For Augustine, irony was a known referential error—strategically expedient or plausible—thus "the quintessential rhetorical lie" (Swearingen 213). This is perhaps too simple a dichotomy, given irony's long and complicated evolution between their treatises,[15] yet something like this dichotomy still dominates the rhetorical study of feminist texts.

In Askew's case, and in feminist rhetorical criticism more generally, the precise nature of failed meaning that dictates most intention-based interpretations of irony may actually open up possibilities for interpretive discourse, where *discourse* both reflects and shapes individuals' interactions with society, politics, and culture, yet does not necessarily "achieve such an accurate representation of itself or anything else" (Rickert 53). I too have had difficulty making my subjects' performances fit extant templates for the analysis of feminine irony, perhaps because the dominant templates require some linguistic and discursive separation of irony or because they link irony to the bifurcation of Hegelian or "romantic" irony that promises "a primary and originary Intention" behind written words (C. Lang 2) and Socratic or humorous irony that shuns the "simple splitting or duplication" of meaning (C. Lang 115).

There are alternative methodologies to those that rely purely on marking ironic utterances for semantic protocol, and I argue that those methodologies would better serve feminist rhetorical recovery by opening up critical and historical space for considering feminist ironies as multilayered and even multidimensional, beyond merely cooperative or not. Kathryn Olson and Clark Olson propose to raise metalinguistic consciousness of rhetorical irony by classifying various responses as "optimistic," "cynical," or "skeptical" according to readers' expectations of what can be achieved through persuasion (25). On the one hand, such a reader-centered theory of irony opens interpretive space that "the rhetor cannot shut down" in spite of his or her choices and explains the theoretical unevenness or unpredictability of irony—it does not fail to meet one set of communicative objectives simply because it meets another. On the other hand, a reader-centered theory of irony reinforces a Burkean distinction between ordinary and pure persuasion, even as it tries to demonstrate that verbal irony contains both (27).

In my reexamination of Askew's text, a reader-centered theory of irony would lead me to respond in one of several ways. As a *cynic*, I might be attracted to the "powerful narcotic" (Olson and Olson 31) of the linguistic devices that carry Askew's embedding subjects and shifting ideological targets, such as her use of evidentials and examples. As an *optimist*, I might be compelled to take some immediate action, such as passing judgment, though not necessarily an action that is consistent with Askew's goals. As a *skeptic*, I might withdraw from one or more of the messages being communicated to me before becoming "energized and nourished by [both] the text's pure and ordinary persuasion" (Olson and Olson 31), depending on my relative interest in the possibilities that

Askew's irony afforded her and affords my historical reading now. While
these are all worthy goals for examining irony, in order to arrive at a new
logic of identification for the ironists I study, I want to be able to mark
what Burke calls irony's "strategic moment of reversal" and its "unresolved
symbolic tension" *without* reinscribing the primacy of language (Burke,
Grammar 517; Olson and Olson 27).

Philosophically, such a move has already been suggested by Candace
Lang's efforts to distinguish irony from humor as a critical paradigm
for postmodern (re)constructions of literary texts that do not rely on
romantic notions of author, audience, and intention (42), specifically to
argue for *humor* as "any non-truth-oriented mode of discourse" and *irony*
as that discursive mode that can account for other pluralities of meaning
(42), and ultimately to posit rhetorical irony as more than a mere stylistic
device (49). In fact, Lang's discontentment with Wayne Booth's discussion
of stable ironies is one that I share. For as much as it moved rhetorical
theories of irony beyond the acknowledgment of purely ideal or aesthetic
forms, Booth's definition ultimately relies on eliminating the contradiction between an original utterance and the context in which it is uttered
(Booth 43).[16] Booth's "rhetorical ironies" are classified by degree of openness or disguise, degree of stability in the reconstruction, and scope of
the "truth revealed" (234). By justifying irony's domains based on "one's
critical purposes and principles" (233), Booth constructed a semantic
map for guiding rhetorical inquiries into irony by the "variations in how
authors and readers relate" (234), ultimately arguing that "no reader can
hope to be fully successful [in getting all of the possible meanings] with
any but the simplest ironies" (242).[17]

However, a reader-centric theory is not where I want to end up, either;
there would still be limitations to overcome. Those methodologies that
account only for audience response may place too much intellectual currency in visceral outcomes that are informed by historians' perceptions
of what might have or should have been an appropriate response. My
goal with Askew's ironic discourse is to demonstrate how it promotes a
metalinguistic consciousness without merely reorienting its linguistic
features toward the reader by basically leaving room for questioning or
by raising questions rather than simply affirming or denying extant facts.
Critical discourse studies can and do emerge from a theoretical linguistic
space, even in a postmodern world where the relationship among "things,
thoughts, words, and actions" transcends the realistic principles of any
given period (Ulman 2).

Marrying Logic, Rhetoric, and Dialectic

In fact, reading Askew's ironic discourse apart from the support or elision of truth claims may accommodate a rejoining of logic, rhetoric, and dialectic more advantageously than Renaissance histories have been able to do thus far. Three aspects of irony are important to negotiate the complex and shifting positions of Renaissance women writers: the fact that irony need not implicate the opposite or converse of literal meaning; that it need not be read as a semantic "failure"; and that it need not be located exclusively (or principally) in audience. Wilbur Samuel Howell's *Eighteenth Century British Logic and Rhetoric* cites an evolution of Renaissance systems of logic and rhetoric according to how new political structures or public desires more closely aligned systems of communication with systems of learning. While the *Examinations* is not necessarily borne of an emerging political structure, a strong case can be made for its alignment with both logical and rhetorical invention. Askew's ironic discourse functions logically in accordance with sixteenth-century scholasticism (Howell 66) in that it reveals not only Askew's talents in explicit disputation but also her potential for raising contradictions. At the same time, its semantic reversals help collapse stark distinctions between what Howell has historically termed "artistic" and "inartistic" forms of Renaissance invention, depending on whether they were concerned with creating arguments through the process of questioning (i.e., finding available means) or witnessing already available proofs (Howell 68). Thus in some ways, Askew's historicization as logically cunning demonstrates a more varied rhetorical craft with the examination genre than was commonplace.

As Natalie Zemon Davis has argued about sixteenth-century pardon tales, Renaissance women's performances—whether they are authored or mediated—do not just disrupt the plots and genres that were permissible (111). They also challenge the critical and historical lenses that were often used to examine their logical structure, even to the point of employing fictional or implied readers. Such "fictional" aspects of historical narratives are not fictive, but rather represent the "shaping choices of language, detail, and order [that] are needed to present an account that seems to both writer and reader true, real, meaningful, and/or explanatory" in their recovery of Renaissance texts (3). Thus a successful study of sixteenth-century pardon tales should rely as much on what that discourse community values in storytelling as on the events depicted in each tale, since those qualities of forming, shaping, and molding are as vital to the outcome of judicial speech (or confessional discourse) as are other rhetorical forms.

To a certain extent, I agree. As both a confessional and a trial defense, the *Examinations* provides narrative possibilities that readers later see reflected in the contrived audiences of Sor Juana Inés de la Cruz, as she wrote letters justifying seventeenth-century women's scholastic education, and in John Fowles's postmodern depiction of events leading to the birth of Ann Lee, as he blurred stark boundaries between historical novels and historical accounts of the eighteenth-century Shaker trials (299). Without comparing fiction to nonfiction, I note the similarities between Fowles's narration and the various narrative tropes that have been applied to historicized accounts of women's trials and confessionals from the Renaissance through the eighteenth century. When women are being historicized in rhetorical spaces where ecclesiastic and civic duties collide, certain topoi emerge to present them as alternatively speaking from or through certain traditions, while the acts of speaking are themselves used to undermine the topoi they reflect.[18] The most important effect that these "fictions" have is not on commonplace assumptions about their genre, but on the dialogic construction that occurs between the genre's various subjects. Askew enacts the expected topoi of confession and polemic, including an appropriation of the vernacular in what Elizabeth Tebeaux and Mary Lay call addressing skepticism (53) and including what Alexandra Barratt calls appropriating and assimilating masculine authority via the role of translator, mouthpiece, and historian (10). What results is a co-constructed dialectical form.

An ironic and co-constructed reading of the *Examinations* disrupts critical expectations of what can be and could have been debated in a particular genre and forum. Logic and rhetoric become one another's domains in Askew's ironic discourse, wherein the rhetorical is not bifurcated from the dialectical, the devotional is not bifurcated from the speculative (Ong, *Ramus* 232), the experiential is not separated from the doctrinal, and the lay is not distinguished from the expert (Ong, *Ramus* 225). This is significant because these are binaries that Walter Ong notes would not be rejoined until the rising popularity of sixteenth- and seventeenth-century method books (*Ramus* 232), and yet our historicization of Askew's performances can no longer overlook them within a panhistorical context nor assume that they were not at work for some of Askew's audiences. Wilbur Samuel Howell already notes that English Reformation rhetoric—largely in response to Peter Ramus—challenged the idea that a logical speaker need only link a given proposal to a bound system of agreements (11). Whether or not this is an expectation of which Askew was aware, her ironic discourse achieves historically more than (dis)agreement.[19] For its emphasis on accuracy, Askew's whole response to the interrogation reflects how she negotiates theological preparedness—the most visible demonstration of personal aptitude she could offer her interrogators at that time and her historians later on.

An ironic and co-constructed reading also shows Askew's statements to be reflective, rather than declarative. Rather than conforming to or diverging from finite identifications for the Renaissance woman teaching doctrine, they are sites for developing new or unexpected content by reflecting on what critical readers project onto the breaks in conversation. They are spaces through which Askew enables multiple audiences to gain empathy for the dialectical possibilities of doctrine, then and now. Askew's text may well demonstrate what Ong argues for as a recasting of Medieval *method* in rhetoric to reveal a "broader paralogical notion of an intelligent approach . . . to a complex problem" (*Ramus* 227). In other words, Askew's text demonstrates both a method of identification and an inventive identity politic, ultimately demonstrating how irony can blur stark distinctions between modeling and responding and how doctrine can blur the divisions between existing persuasive moves and the suggestion of new rhetorical practices.

More often, Askew's ironic performance transcends precise expectations of what the logical structure of confessions should be and of how the logical and rhetorical dimensions of Renaissance discourse should interact according to the lenses it provoked. Her performance reveals an assembling and dissembling of words such that Askew (or Bale or other agents of her text) may safely harbor disagreement or promote discord. If Howell's view of Renaissance logic has any bearing on the historicization of Askew's ironic discourse, especially that it concerned itself "chiefly with statements made by men in their efforts to achieve a valid verbalization of reality" (3), then Askew achieves a logical persuasion that challenges—indeed, that *operates apart from*—the constraints of such validity markers as the categorical syllogism and arguments of definition or classification (Glenn, *Rhetoric* 153).

Inventing a Renaissance "Civic" Discourse

Perhaps Askew's historicized performance achieves a kind of proto-feminist genre that enables critics to interrogate the linguistic basis for

"negative and disempowering definitions of women" and to note patriarchal limitations on women's historically available roles (Merrill, *Social* 158). They could conform to dominant discourse, select less valued
"feminine/private" discourses in which to perform, or create new genres
for discourse, yet this limitedness is as much a factor in contemporary
critical readings of women's texts as it was in the women's actual performances, primarily because the genres in which women performed were
not extant, but rather embodied rhetorical contexts made possible as
they performed. Such a collision of language and history echoes the key
question in Jacques Derrida's "Law of Genre": What happens to genre
when or as the text is being produced? Rather than propose an analytical
apparatus to mark *for* genre or a way of justifying the discourse *as* genre,
I consider how the critical interstices of Askew's ironic discourse reveal
an epistemic space. *Genre* is more than simply the tacit recognition of a
set of features or behaviors that do or do not belong; rather, *genre* reflects
a set of cognitive and social commitments (Journet 103) that describe the
"dialectical relation between written texts and the contexts and actions
that constitute them" (Journet 103–04).

The interrogative genre jointly performed by Askew, Christopher
Paul Prior reminds us that we have multiple lenses through which
to study—and with which to apply—*genre*, where not even particular
media, sites, or modes can stand in the way of finding new ways to classify and taxonomize discursive activity or to understand its functions
and outcomes (17–18).[20] In fact, *genre* may well reflect a "sense of loss"
that historians experience on recognizing "the gaps that exist . . . when
our words fail to capture the inner webs of meaning and feeling that we
had meant them to convey" (27). This *sense of loss* guides my interest in
determining what we still can do with irony in the valuation of women's
texts and what irony can do for us.

The interrogative genre jointly performed by Askew, Christopher
Dare, and the members of Dare's first "quest" illuminates one way that
a *civic* positioning can emerge from a theological one, and this may be
the principal reason why, a century later, Bathsua Makin credited Askew
as one of the women who motivated the movement toward reclaiming
classical and practical educations for gentleladies and realizing a woman's
capacity to work with languages and texts.[21] Paula McQuade calls the
Examinations one of the earliest examples of "specifically English female
textual production" for the way it challenges contemporary notions of
the relationship between gender and jurisprudence in early modern England (12). Even in Bale's published edition, wherein he elucidates Askew's

"attacks" on the Catholic Church, McQuade notes that Askew's principal strategy in the dialogues with the Privy Council was not to attack doctrine, but rather to "bid for legal recognition as a female English subject whose common law rights have been violated" (2).

By foregrounding in her text the occasions when her common-law (or juridical) rights were being violated or suspended by ecclesiastical law, Askew could redirect attention from her own case toward the ongoing jurisdictional conflict between the two court systems (McQuade 2). For example, Askew wrote, "We thought that, I shuld have bene put to bayle immedyatlye, accordynge to the order of the lawe. Howbeit, he wolde not so suffre it, but commytted me from thens to preson agayne, untyll the next morowe" (*First Examinacyon*, Bale edition, lines 1102–05). Furthermore, by positioning herself as suspended between her civic and religious identities, Askew could maintain her own beliefs without incriminating herself under the Act of the Six Articles (McQuade 7).[22] Finally, by reciting scripture in response to her interrogators' remarks and by making frequent textual references to the manner, frequency, and attitude of her repeated indictments, Askew could demonstrate her practical knowledge of the Religion Act of 1543, a reform passed by Henry VIII that explicitly required a "quest," a trial by jury of one's peers, before any indictment could be made (McQuade 6). For example, she wrote, "The counsell is not a lyttle dyspleased, that it shulde be reported abroade that I was racked in the towre" (*Lattre Examinacyon*, Bale edition, lines 1170–71; in a letter to fellow martyr John Lassels). By her second *Examination*, then, we can style Askew "as a Protestant, female subject with legal rights equal to men in the only forum available to her—the ecclesiastical courts" (McQuade 11).

In this way, McQuade argues, Askew did not perform as a saint, as Bale portrayed her, but as a forerunner in gendered argumentation, or at least an early participant in the gradual development of English women's civil liberties (11), revealing or constructing certain privileges of authority. Knowing that ecclesiastical law recognized women as autonomous (religious) subjects when common law did not, Askew and her historians may have looked on these ironic performances in the ecclesiastical court as providing some civic advantage. Thus Askew's ironic performance seems best described as a complex self-positioning of multiple and shifting agents, rather than a deflection of her interrogators' charges, and an analytic method is required that is robust enough to trace this shifting activity between temporal and historical contexts.

LOOKING INTERSTITIALLY

The task of analyzing discourse in time—or analyzing particular instances and uses of irony over time—need not preclude a more metaphysical understanding of discourse as a phenomenon that reveals how audiences and readers access it opportunistically across texts. Understanding irony's powers of language need not preclude a more critical understanding of *ironic discourse* as a series of agentive, multistable utterances. It is the simultaneously metaphysical and multistable properties of discourse that I am interested in here when I examine Askew's discourse interstitially. *Looking interstitially* means looking between positivist approaches to language and the apositivist historical narratives that language supports—finding gaps in historical processes that lead to new procedures, new claims, and even new attitudes toward those procedures and claims.

Both *Examinations* invite us to notice two or more simultaneous performances: a conversation with Askew's interrogators, and a witnessing of that conversation for anticipated audiences. Whereas the *First Examinacyon* is mainly a dramatized version of chronologically ordered but separate events in Askew's interrogation, the *Lattre Examinacyon* acts explicitly as a dual performance—a spoken testimony before the king's council and a written testimony for fellow reformers, women martyrs, and other members of the Parliament. The *Lattre Examinacyon* chronicles Askew's second arrest and interrogation, her torture, and the events leading to her execution, and it demonstrates most of her direct audience construction through metadiscourse and commentary.

On one analytic level, Askew often achieves a role reversal and subject shift made possible by what Cheryl Glenn has termed an embedded syllogism (*Rhetoric* 155), in which Askew is perceived as redirecting the questioner with a question path of her own. The move from "what have you (Askew) done?" to "what have you (interrogators) seen?" shifts the interrogative subject from herself to her interrogators and embeds more than one implication in a single statement, making other assumptions (valid or otherwise) possible for all audiences to the exchange, what Beilin calls "destroy[ing] the very bases of the interchange" ("Askew's Dialogue" 318). This acts in many ways like a reversing or narrowing of the field for Askew's examiners and a broadening of the field for other audiences, and it occurs frequently throughout both *Examinations*, most notably in examples such as the following: "Then he asked me, whye I had so fewe wordes? And I answered. God hath geven me the gyfte of knowledge, but not of utterance. And Salomon sayth, that a woman of fewe wordes, is a gyfte of God, Prover. 19" (*First Examinacyon*, Bale edition, lines 802–04). It also results in a shifting of ideological targets or, more accurately, a blurring of the roles of subject and target (or victim) in the ironic exchange. Acknowledging flexible or unshared contexts at this level allows for the possibility that Askew's irony manipulates the interrogation in such a way that it is unclear whether the cooperation principle gets restored to functionality. More pointedly, Askew achieves ironic communication in spite—or perhaps because—of unclear evidence that the utterances are relevant and that violated maxims have been restored.

To explain this further, I borrow from David Ritchie's extension of Coulson's "frame-shifting" from semantic properties of humor in general to irony in particular. Responding to semantic theories of humor that would posit irony as "exceptional and peripheral to 'bona-fide' referential and propositional language use"—thus reinforcing its ties to truth claims—Ritchie suggests *framing* and *frame-shifting* to describe how the irony works (276). Frame-shifting is not just activated in a salient interaction among ironist, observer, and victim within a specific temporal context. Instead, that interaction becomes a site for illuminating how salience can be determined atemporally, allowing us to see in irony "a complex array of contextual effects and relational objectives" (283). "Frame" becomes a metaphor "for a particular set of neurological connections," and "frame-shifting" becomes a metaphor "for the activation of a new set of connections and suppression of a previously activated set" (290). Ritchie's frame-shifting occurs where readers in all the different contexts realize they are contributing vital questions to textual studies as a whole.

What this means for the *Examinations* is that to interpret any irony as a denial, an insult, or a refusal is to overlook the ways it makes meaning apart from a single, historicized subject position and context. It is the difference between reading Askew's statement "By commonynge with the wyse, I maye lerne wysdome" as proactive, unapologetic, and generative versus reading it as responsive, defensive, and declarative (*First Examinacyon*, Bale edition, lines 357–58). Read together, Askew's responses in both the interrogation and her narrative account of the interrogation do more than just break frame with the rhetorical expectations of her immediate examiners or challenge the frame (and its underlying premise) that her examiners bring to the rhetorical situation (Schilb, *Rhetorical* 9). Rather, they make generic possibilities for historicizing the *Examinations* as more than just an interrogation of a speech act or a singly authored narrative. It becomes possible to witness a dialogue that is recursively constructed among Askew, her examiners, and her various readers across time and space in ways similar to Hutcheon's "transideological" irony: irony that "can and does function tactically in the service of a wide range of political positions" (Hutcheon 10).

Once viewed in this light, it is easier to note patterns to the interrogative discourse that do not necessarily reinforce topoi characteristic of the confession or interrogation genres but that create possibilities for interstitial witnessing at various intersections of *chronos* and *kairos* experiences, in turn revealing atemporal relationships between all of the text's ironic agents. By "interstitial witnessing" I mean the dialogic construction within and between the subject positions of the *Examinations'* various users, then and now—what Campbell might call "points of articulation" that give texts and their histories a special force ("Agency" 14). A notable tension among ironist, victim, and observer is best reflected in several additional conditions on Askew's whole discursive event, such as the conscious questioning that becomes possible by noting how a single ironic interaction represents a continuously (re)negotiated contextual inappropriateness. While the first irony (or set of ironies) is fulfilled when the examiners not only detect but also interpret Askew's inappropriateness, the second irony (or set of ironies) can be fulfilled at any time, as long as there is a witness. This implies that contexts shift in ironic discourse when they are accessible to some audiences but not others, that more than one presupposition is always at work in the irony, and that multiple audiences are always implicated in the irony.

I demonstrate this kind of interstitial witnessing in figure 1.1, modeling how irony enables its interlocutors to shift modes and subjects without betraying a shifting linguistic context or assuming that the irony is intrinsic to the text. The model describes how audiences draw conceptual connections within and between ironic contexts, and it reveals how the discourse can raise doubts about the topics being discussed (Ritchie 287). For example, in passage (A) from Christopher Dare's first "quest," Askew's performance as both subject and narrator shifts the terms of the examination in order to call into question the nature of interrogation at all, disrupting actual or historical expectations on her gender's ability to reason. For the audience we identify as H1 (Askew's primary or immediate hearer or reader), the argumentative premises shift from the charge of "utterynge" the scriptures to "going into the pulpett and preache." For the audience we identify as H2 (Askew's secondary or more distant hearer or reader), Askew assumes the questioner's role and reassigns the role of respondent, having the last word in each segment. Given the differing presuppositions between H1 and H2, this exchange supports a range of subjects, including Paul (and 1 Corinthians 14), Catholic doctrine, and limitations on a woman's role in the church. Catholic doctrine becomes paired with Askew's own alleged behavior in a single response, making interrogation the new literal subject of the exchange in more than one context.

In addition to raising doubts about the topics being discussed, looking interstitially at ironic discourse helps destabilize the historical motives and outcomes of other agents in the exchange. During her twelve days in jail on the first arraignment, and following her interrogation by Christopher Dare, the bishop's chancellor, and the lord mayor, Askew was visited by a priest who questioned her on five points: why she was put in prison; whether she denied the sacrament of the altar; if she had been formerly absolved by a priest; what she thought about transubstantiation; and whether she intended to receive the sacrament on Easter. Passages (B) and (C) reflect the fourth point, the transubstantiation question on which Askew was principally charged, and interstitial witnessing reveals a shift or movement between embedded subjects and ideological targets (or between temporal and opportunistic expectations) across contexts in (B):

(B) Fortly he asked me, if the host [bread] shuld fall, and a beast [mouse] ded eate it, whether the beast ded receyve God or no? I answered, Seynge ye have taken the paynes to aske thys questyon, I desyre yow also to take so moche payne more, as to assoyle [resolve] it your selfe. For I wyll not do it, bycause I perceyve ye come to tempte me.

(C) And he sayd, it was agaynst the ordre of scoles, that he whych asked the questyon, shuld answere it. I tolde hym, I was but a woman, and knewe not the course of scoles.[23] (*First Examinacyon*, Bale edition, lines 379–85)

As in passage (A), this exchange relies on flexible and unstable contexts—some shared, others unshared. The shared context between Askew and H1 is that she is being asked to state her beliefs about transubstantiation, but other unshared contexts are made possible by considering the different presuppositions of Askew, her examiners, and other historical witnesses or readers. One presupposition of Askew's response is that because she is a woman, she does not know the rules of debate concerning Catholic scholarship ("I . . . knewe not the course of scoles"). The perceived presupposition of the priest is that he intends for Askew to reveal her disagreements with official standard doctrine. Askew's second presupposition is to elide the interrogation and exempt herself from stating her beliefs about transubstantiation, but this would be noted best in a second context by readers bringing that expectation to the text. Again, according to figure 1.1, the latter presupposition creates two simultaneous possibilities for the exchange: Askew complies with official standard beliefs about women's low intellectual status; or Askew points to the problematic and paradoxical nature of the text in question, as it prevents women from being knowledgeable enough to know when to respond or not to respond on matters of church doctrine, both realizable in the second context.

As a result, Askew does not remain the subject of the exchange. Rather, the path of questioning becomes complicated as it allows Askew's discourse to make gender roles the embedding subject—women are not legally permitted to know the rules of scholastic debate. This shifting or blurring of subjects may work as follows:

situation → question of compliance (B)
compliance → question of motive (B)
motive → official standard doctrine → statement of classification (C)
classification → problem of gender (C)

As well, those agents who reinforce gendered roles—either in actuality or in memory—become ideological targets. The priest becomes a target when Askew invites him to "resolve" or "explain" the question himself, as a kind of mockery of his deductive rigor. The monarch Henry and the official standard doctrine become targets for providing Askew with a way to exempt herself from the interrogation. The consequent shifting of targets looks as follows:

sacrament → Askew's competence (B)
Askew's competence → priest's compliance (B)
priest's compliance → priest's motivations → priest's competence (C)
priest's competence → nature of interrogation → pursuant power-
    holders (C)

A similar shift can be witnessed during a summative portion near the beginning of the *Lattre Examinacyon* in passage (D), which is significant to note because it represents a segment of Askew's narration that both employs and anticipates dual audiences and contexts in her assertion that she has left the question of her divorce unfulfilled:

(D) . . . I beynge before the counsell, was asked of mastre kyme. I answered, that my lorde chancellour knewe all redye my mynde in that matter, They with that answere were not contented, but sayd, it was the kynges pleasure, that I shuld open the matter to them. I answered them playnelye, that I wolde not so do. But if it were the kynges pleasure to heare me, I wolde shewe hym the truthe.

(E) Then they sayd, it was not mete for the kynge with me to be troubled. I answered, that Salomon was reckened the wisest kynge that ever lyved, yet myslyked not he to heare. ii. poore common women, moch more hys grace a simple woman and hys faythfull subject. So in conclusion, I made them non other answere in that matter. (*Lattre Examinacyon*, Bale edition, lines 127–37)

In justifying what she perceives to be giving the bishop's council "no other answer," Askew's discourse again demonstrates the interpretive possibilities of historically shared and unshared contexts:

interrogation → marital status (D)
marital status → council's authority → royal audience (D)
royal audience → king's priority → Solomon's grace (E)
Solomon's grace → king's grace → female subjects (E)

With gender again as the embedding subject, the consequent shifting of targets across contexts looks as follows:

Askew's competence → council's motivations (D)
council's motivations → king's authority (E)
king's authority → council's authority → nature of interrogation (E)

This movement between familiar and unfamiliar contexts provides an enduring lens for reexamining Renaissance women's discourse, showing what continues to be achieved in both literal and nonliteral meanings long after one set of meanings has been activated (Attardo, "Irony" 801; Giora, *On Our Mind* 70). Both *chronos* (temporal) and *kairos* (opportunistic) dimensions of history must be at work in processing and interpreting these passages. In fact, both time and space are factors in interstitial witnessing, given that this kind of reexamination involves a linguistic "tacking in" and "tacking out," to borrow strategically from Jacqueline Jones Royster and Gesa E. Kirsch (76). Where Royster and Kirsch adopt these metaphors to describe a shift in commitment between engaging closely and dialectically with primary sources (tacking in) and standing back "in a conscious awareness of what we have come to know" (tacking out), I borrow them to argue for interstitial witnessing as an appropriately panhistorical analytic methodology—robust enough to "use tension, conflicts, balances, and counterbalances more overtly" for critical inquiry and reflexive enough to use them imaginatively and hopefully (Royster and Kirsch 72, 73). Just as Schilb notes the enduring value of a rhetorical refusal even when *chronos* has changed the context in which it is so recognized (*Rhetorical* 114, 139), I note the qualities of a third irony that encourages vital questioning or a context in which meaning is constructed as a result of expectations that have formed *over historical time and within critical space.* The presence of other agents becomes much clearer—and the recovery of intentionality much less crucial—in this third irony, in the various interstices of historiography. In short, Askew's ironic discourse affords historians an important merging of the temporal and the spatial that allows for a disruption of what readers might label—linguistically or discursively—as a single isolated event and that raises the interpretive probability of any event.

The strongest justification for this is in how Askew's ironic discourse interweaves language, authority, private character, and public self (Baumlin 230). Early in the *First Examinacyon*, the interweaving becomes clear, first in Askew's statement of not knowing the underlying purpose of her internment, and second in her denial of having ever provided a spoken confession:

> (F) In the meane whyle he commaunded hys Archedeacon to commen with me, who sayd unto me. Mastres wherfor are ye accused? I answered. Axe my accusers, for I knowe not as yet. Then toke he my boke out of my hande, and sayd. Soche bokes as thys is, hath brought yow to the trouble ye are in. Be ware (sayth he) be ware, for he that made it, was brent in Smythfelde. Then I asked hym, if he were sure that it was true that he had spoken. And he sayd, he knewe wele, the boke was of Johan frithes makynge. Then I asked hym, if he were not ashamed for to judge of the boke before he sawe it within, or yet knewe the truthe therof. I sayd also that soche unadvysed and hastye judgement, is a token apparent of a verye slendre wytt. Then I opened the boke and shewed it hym. He sayd, he thought it had bene an other, for he coulde fynde no faulte therein. Then I desyred hym, nomore to be so swyft in judgement, tyll he throughlye knewe the truthe. And so he departed. (*First Examinacyon*, Bale edition, lines 586–99)

This same interweaving is clear again in a proverbial maxim that Askew recites, presumably and markedly for more audiences, occasions, and contexts than simply her adjudicators':

(G) Then brought he fourth thys unsaverye symylytude, That if a man had a wounde, no wyse surgeon wolde mynystre helpe unto it, before he had seane it uncovered. In lyke case (sayth he) can I geve yow no good counsel, unlesse I knowe wher with your conscyence is burdened. I answered, that my conscience was clere in all thynges. And for to laye a playstre unto the whole skynne, it might apere moche folye. (*First Examinacyon*, Bale edition, lines 661–66)

Neither passage depends on a positioning of Askew that can only be proven or disproven, nor on an identification of her examiner as having a singular motive. Instead, both passages together offer insight into how certain figures position others and are themselves historically positioned. In short, both passages together help raise the questions of who *owns* the text and its ironic functions and how Askew's persecution can invite a retrospective self-interpretation of that ownership (Strauss 26).

What this means in practical terms is that pragmatic events can bear witness to multiple unstable, evolving relationships among subjects, implied targets, and audiences. They need not be temporally bound or temporally determined in order to have historic possibility—in order for them to reveal or conceal ruptures in context. Askew's ironic discourse need not be seen as a *refusal* in order for it to call into question the historical relevance of such an exchange, including the way that it challenges assumptions about women's scholastic ability and obfuscates the tasks that have been assumed to be carried out. Looking beyond only those shared contexts in which irony is assumed to occur can help readers note what is paradoxical about Askew's response: that it demonstrates doctrine as a site for *making new meaning* from discourse in Renaissance women's texts and not merely a site for *declaring expected meaning* or *eliding intended meaning.*

In each of these examples, few if any stark distinctions can actually be made between local and contextual information without promoting linguistic determinism, but that is not my goal in looking interstitially. Each of these constructs—subjects, targets, audiences, and motives—is not semantically true of only one context in the irony, but rather all of the constructs potentially surface across all contexts. Irony becomes most useful in the critical reader's ability to understand it as nuanced and to doubt. However, articulating these interstitial shifts as *visible* constructs reveals the potentially disruptive nature of the *Examinations'* discourse and enables the following questions:

- What can these ironies reveal about women's performances (then and now), and how should we define the parameters of each performance?
- How do the various ironies demonstrate how readers and writers relinquish or maintain control over self- and other-representation in these performances? Furthermore, how should we understand "control" in Renaissance texts?
- How can these notions of "control" contribute alternative methods of locating, classifying, and evaluating Renaissance women's discourse?
- Finally, what does it mean for discourse to enable its own critical (re)reading?

INHABITING DISCOURSE

This project hinges on a definition of feminist agency that recognizes *how rhetors and their audiences jointly embody situations* that are material or immaterial, actual or imagined, *kairotic* or chronological. What makes ironic discourses agential is not that they are autonomous entities waiting to be realized in time, but that they are defined by the functions, uses, purposes, and practices in which they occur and from which they result. In this way, ironic discourse is *inhabited.* What makes ironic discourse useful for reexamining Renaissance women's performances is that it necessitates a closer examination of texts whose authorship and mediation have historically been questioned or left undetermined. Indeed, most discussions of Renaissance women's rhetorical arts stem from a neoclassical turn to Cicero and Quintilian, yet most Renaissance instruction stemmed from contemporary Machiavellian notions of goodness, religiosity, candor, and craft (Baumlin 236).

Read interstitially, the *Examinations* complicates any notions we may have that irony must be temporally defined in order to give agency to women's texts, signaling an enabled capacity to reason beyond simply establishing a pattern of responses that were "good ynough for the qyestyon" (*First Examinacyon*, Bale edition, line 824). The most enduring aspect of Askew's ironic discourse is that it reveals the places where critical and historical readers are most likely to perceive an absence or presence of power and oppression and where they are most likely to note or overlook powerlessness when reading a historical event. It provides one way to theorize agency beyond a set of attributes contained *in* the text or held *by* the writer, thus highlighting the duality between what drama theorist

Alice Rayner might call a "capacity" and a "willingness" in defining agency (Ratcliffe 26; Rayner 7) or, more simply, highlighting the duality between the writer as both harbinger and enactor of the text.

If we define feminist agency as "communal, social, cooperative, and participatory . . . constituted and constrained by the material and symbolic elements of context and culture" (Campbell, "Agency" 3), then we understand that agency is learned (6), is negotiated by authors who are best understood as "points of articulation" rather than "originators" (5), and can be divisive or destructive (7).[24] My desires for feminist historiographic agency, in particular, concern the capacity of multiple rhetors and audiences to act, empathize, and understand, noting—like Karlyn Kohrs Campbell—the chaotic and flexible nature of women's social movements and embracing the idea "that women's liberation never was . . . a cohesive, organized effort to produce certain well-defined social changes" ("'Rhetoric'" 139). Much as feminist reading is not merely a practice of overturning hegemonic narratives, neither is feminist historiography merely a practice of piecing together coherent metanarratives. It is an opportunity to destabilize maxims about women's performance and feminist interpretation when they are applied to the irony event and to articulate how *reading historiographically* can become a process of inhabiting. I have found two such maxims in reexamining Askew's performances and hence two ways to argue for this reading as agential.

Disrupting genre and promoting generic contemplation. The fact that the *Examinations* represents both a spontaneous performance and a meditated verbal transcription may explain why Beilin considers it polemically useful and why she positions Askew "as the worthy opponent of numerous officials of church, city, and state" (*Examinations* xv). This positioning does not simply reside in Askew's own self-perception; it is dialogic, residing in the perceptions of her examiners, readers, historians, and critics, all of whom have genre expectations informed by their understanding of sixteenth-century debate, including its malleability in following "the twists and turns of philosophical, religious, and political discussion" (Beilin, "Askew's Dialogue" 314–15) and its masterful imitation of masculine *auctoritas* (Barratt 6). Additionally, Askew's role as an "expert witness" causes Beilin to position the *Examinations* as a dialogue and Mazzola to position the *Examinations* as something between an ontology and an epistemology, where the *nature of being* and the *nature and validity of knowledge* compete for the critic's attention in every instance where Askew invites speculation about the cause of her arraignment

(Mazzola 161). Its demonstration of both an "orderly discussion" and a "conversation" reflects the dual attributes that Roger Deakins notes in his own argument for Tudor dialogues as simultaneously reflecting "genre and anti-genre" (5).

While Beilin and Mazzola have offered two possibilities for classifying the *Examinations*—as either a dialogue or a polemic—Joad Raymond's sixteenth-century confession pamphlet offers a third. Though it is not properly considered a pamphlet, the *Examinations* also functions like the English vernacular literacy forms that Raymond historicizes in several ways: it promotes the creation of alternative models of authority; it was edited, published, and circulated by a prominent male figurehead; and it was intended to reveal the aspirations and attitudes of a marginalized person or group (Raymond 277). Pamphlets worked ahead of the manuscript tradition in terms of circulation and commercial capacity and were sometimes used to advance political propaganda (Raymond 15); more often, however, they were associated with slander, social tension, and a vernacular "loosening" of both classical rhetoric traditions (Raymond 8, 11). In many respects, the *Examinations* functions like a Tudor prose dialogue for what I would call its *extendedness*—its quality of being a continuous performance that "recapitulat[es] rather than explain[s] Askew's testimony, as if she's still defending herself before her readers" (Mazzola 159).

Reading it this way raises an agential paradox not unfamiliar to Renaissance texts authored by women. On the one hand, reading the *Examinations* as a confessional would reinforce the notion of a female subject who is in control of her own narrative. On the other hand, reading the *Examinations* as a polemic would reinforce Bale's authorship of Askew's text, since his interspersed commentary positioned the *Examinations* as explicitly controversial in scope and aim, thus turning certain rhetorical conventions to Askew's advantage and anticipating subsequent uses for the text and subsequent patterns for its authorship. Both sides of the paradox reflect how the *Examinations* could have disrupted H1 (and H2) expectations of what kinds of forensic or deliberative discourse were believed to have been available to women in the sixteenth century—expectations that were dictated not only by the feminist genres in which women writers performed but also by the masculinist genres from which women's performances were often excluded. The most resonant example of this paradox may be "Jane Anger's" *Protection for Women*, published in 1589 and preceded by two prefaces—one addressing "the Gentlewomen of England" and the other addressing "all Women in generall, and gentle Reader whatsoever" (Raymond 282). Raymond speculates that the first female pamphleteers were writing between the 1580s and 1630s, specifically in response to "derogatory writing about their sex . . . and anticipat[ing] subsequent patterns of female authorship" (277). *Protection* implies a semiprivate exchange yet accommodates a more public one in order to fulfill its own generic confounding.

This kind of disruption to categorical genres demonstrates that twenty-first-century historians of feminist rhetorics may well need Askew's performances to loosen the engendered assumptions guiding their analyses, more than her performances need them—not only to determine the grounds against which they can and do study irony in Renaissance contexts but also to question how those performances serve as "various points of entry into [unmapped or vaster] terrains, rather than reproducing trajectories from the same starting and ending points" (Bizzell and Jarratt 20). Ultimately, the critical reader's role is to become conscious of the ways in which this irony presents a disruption of *his or her own questions and expectations of genre.* Whether the stumping occurred as Askew narrates—or as Bale and Foxe have commented—is less important than what Askew and her various audiences perceive to be occurring, to have occurred, or to be possible.

Disrupting possession and promoting shared authenticity. Askew's role in the whole ironic discourse reflected in figure 1.1 is to problematize logical authority (Hutcheon 184), to reveal the limitedness of lay and expert distinctions, and to call into question multiple audiences and witnesses. As a result, the *Examinations*' narrators are multiple and complex. At the same time, this does not delimit Askew's discursive authority or negate the discursive authenticity of her text. Thus another maxim to destabilize is that rhetorical authenticity occurs only by *possessing a text,* and I counter with the argument that authenticity occurs when one successfully *inhabits a textual event* and that this inhabiting is shared. The historical making—the historical *doing*—of a case like Askew's is sought not in assumed relationships but in interpretive practices that are linked to social practice (Certeau 31).

Arguably one of the most historicized incidents of threatened textual authority is Michel de Certeau's recollection of the Loudun, France, possessions between 1632 and 1637, when several unexplained disturbances among twenty Ursuline nuns created a hermeneutic challenge for seventeenth-century theologians and scholars trying to attribute their possessed behavior to an authentic source (Certeau 244). In Certeau's historicization, possession is not synonymous with ownership; it does not so much point to a "hidden meaning that must be discovered" as it constructs a place where dominant ideologies keep other meanings at bay (264). The "somewhere" or "someplace else" that occurs within demonological discourse provokes not only the question Who is talking? but also the questions Who is *not* talking? and What evidence do we have? In turn, the question of how language becomes altered through possession is a double-edged problem for historians, because "it involves the possibility of acceding to the speech of [an absent being]" (244). Possession signifies on the one hand a presence of signs but on the other an absence of discourse. Ursuline nuns were spoken *through* and then *for*—they were mediated not only by an unknown interlocutor but also by the priests who attempted to exorcise them or who witnessed the exorcisms. Thus their "otherness" made the nuns neither the authors nor the mediators of their own text.[25]

I argue that the double-edged problem of possession is one not of historical agency but of discursive agency. In some respects, Certeau's discussion of the Loudun case both echoes and troubles the historical imperative that Renaissance women writers must tell their own stories to be considered authentic (Barratt 10). Instead of asking how one recognizes the authentic source of a mediated disturbance, Certeau equips us to recognize the "evanescent plurality of places" where the nuns' interlocutors reside (Certeau 253). Askew's text has principally been read as (in)authentic based mainly on clergymen's evidences, which report either participation in or disruption of prescribed confessional practices. In fact, her text should be read as a shaping of power relationships between historians and the histories that they re-present. The interstitial witnessing model in figure 1.1 depicts the *Examinations* as occupying an intersection between the flexible and dynamic and between the stable and static.

It would be more accurate to say that Askew *inhabits* her ironic discourse while under interrogation. By understanding Askew's *Examinations* as altered rather than mediated, and by reading her irony as interstitially significant, I raise the possibility for rhetorical criticism that Renaissance women's ironic discourse can enact alternately public roles and private identifications, beyond merely overturning rhetorical identities or circumventing the paradox of their roles. In that respect, Askew's rhetorical otherness repositions her as both author and mediator of her own text, a viable example of how Renaissance women could perform (and could be perceived as performing) in the same homogeneous contexts as their male counterparts while still causing disruption in traditionally interrogative discourse.

Ultimately, Askew's *Examinations* destabilizes the notion that historians and their subjects cannot share the same rhetorical strategies or that irony cannot be read into an event where it has not been explicitly noted before. My discursive marking of Askew's performance is intended to make new possibilities for relating and interpellating all of the elements that converge on the irony event—or, more accurately, all of the factors that converge on our making of history from the event. Thus I am examining Askew's text as both ironic discourse *and* historical record through an examination of turns that draw attention to alternatively current and provocative topoi and to how different modalities of irony work conjointly to complicate those topoi (Galewski 92). I favor Elizabeth Galewski's language that the ironic reversal of topoi can "open up spaces" in which readers question their close-range preconceptions of historical work (Galewski 95; Hawhee and Olson 91).[26]

Rather than identify stable traits in Askew's text, I note certain modalities through the blurring of embedding subjects and targets, raising such questions as *How broad does the discourse reach?*, *How broadly can we define "discourse"?*, and *In how many ways can we determine its outcome?* This is different from merely promoting a more nuanced sense of *looking back at* Askew's *Examinations* with a more enriched sense of how it functions as a Renaissance text. Discursive constraints can be reflective, promoting a deeper understanding of how we make knowledge when we do look back. Their simultaneous historicization and theorization works for *now* as well as for *then*. The questions they raise about dominant gender ideologies are not limited to historians' interpretations of *that time*, but rather include the things that either motivate or conceal our own paradigmatic disruption as we try to study them in those contexts. In the act of reexamining, then, historical audiences are repositioned as *critical* based on how little or how much they provoke the shift to a different frame.

Renaissance women writers and their political texts are best examined not as historical and temporal subjects who manage to overturn the syllogistic argument by performing subversively in a static moment, but as agents negotiating panhistorically their contingent identifications— ironist to witness, witness to target, target to context, context to history, and so on. In a way, ironic discourse positions women in a middle space between what Michaela Meyer notes as two dominant methodologies in feminist rhetorical studies since the 1960s: "writing women in" to rhetorical canons and "constructing alternative theories" to account for what they do (3, 5). While irony does not cause these problems, it simply serves as an event around which feminist critics can try to solve them. Once we do, and if we do, we will be closer to articulating that "us" in women's political discourse.

2. ON LANGUAGE AND HISTORY: Eliding Dichotomies

> Language is a part of the political and ideological power of rulers. . . . We can't just occupy existing words. We have to change the meanings of words even before we take them over.
>
> —Sheila Rowbotham, *Woman's Consciousness, Man's World*

> In any period language is a powerful signifier of position and status, as well as being the system through which relationships of power are produced and maintained.
>
> —Danielle Clarke, *The Politics of Early Modern Women's Writing*

> But every liar says the opposite of what he thinks in his heart, with purpose to deceive. Now it is evident that speech was given to man, not that men might therewith deceive one another, but that one man might make known his thoughts to another. To use speech, then, for the purpose of deception, and not for its appointed end, is a sin.   —Augustine, *Enchiridion*

Like Royster and Kirsch, I seek various "shifting[s] in operational paradigms" for feminist historical work (31), primarily to consider the tectonic shifts at which and through which irony works. This involves a good deal of what I call "historical listening." A key aspect of Krista Ratcliffe's *rhetorical listening* is that listening and understanding involve more than the mere rejection, deflection, or appropriation of truth claims. Inspired by Alice Rayner's "ethic of listening," Ratcliffe makes it understanding's goal to listen to discourses "not *for* intent but *with* intent" (28), and she makes it listening's goal to affirm the "desire to be heard" (29). In these terms, *understanding* does not describe what occurs when the reader finally "gets" the message inscribed in and carried out through the text or "gets" a message that aligns with his or her own intent for listening. Rather, it describes what occurs as a result of realizing claims and the

cultural logics within which they function (Ratcliffe 26). This concept of
"understanding to listen" contributes to my reading of irony in women's
texts in two particular ways: it challenges those interpretive methods that
privilege intention over reception, illuminating irony's "tropological function," its quality of being both representative and generative at the same
time (Ratcliffe 9); and it makes a verbal study of ironic discourse possible
without essentializing or implying that a subject's use of irony is unified
and coherent. In fact, *understanding to listen* reflects the contradictory
and paradoxical nature of feminist theorizing because it is based not in
postmodern notions that authorial intent and "textual realism" in any
way trump "readerly idealism," but in collapsing "the real/ideal dichotomy
into a strategic third ground" (Ratcliffe 27).

By revealing the cultural logics in a given discourse society, irony
constructs a critical distance from—while also drawing attention to the
possibilities in—various listening audiences. Of the tactics she describes
for moving beyond culturally dysfunctional silence, Ratcliffe proposes
"listening metonymically" (78) as one trope by which audiences would
recognize that a text or a person could be identified as part of a group
without being necessarily representative of "an entire cultural group" (78).
Instead, metonymic listeners would "assum[e] the presence of common-
alities and differences and actively engag[e] both" (99), and they would
work to disrupt the cultural logics that often mask group identification,
such as the logics that cause us to generalize about "women" by keeping
only "white women" in mind (88).

I like the contention that metonymy provides for describing what I do
when I read Anne Hutchinson's political discourse interstitially, because
it enables me to look at the residue of what assumed or expected relationships *could be there*, on the way to disrupting historical cultural logics
guiding how we use and valuate that discourse. This contention prompts
two vital questions for feminist historiography: What is involved in the
reconstruction of irony if it relies on both linguistic *and* extralinguistic
evidence? and How fluid, contingent, epistemic, or agentive can such an
act of reconstruction truly be? This chapter speaks to the challenge of
meshing positivist philosophies about language with rhetorical and humanistic needs by focusing on how language *moves historically through*
Hutchinson's Colonial controversy and on what cultural logics *could have
been*, rather than by measuring her discourse for tacit expressions of what
is, what was, or what seems to have been. More important, this chapter
seeks a new logic of identification for the ironists I study, marking what

Kenneth Burke calls irony's "strategic moment of reversal" and its "un-resolved symbolic tension" without reinscribing the primacy of language (Burke, *Grammar* 517; Olson and Olson 27).

One distinct challenge of studying women's political discourse across historical time and space is settling on a logic of identification that is both flexible and concrete, is not purely temporal, and does not rely only on temporal status markers such as being the first to speak, write, or do—or rely on recouping a "nostalgia for lost origins" (Jarratt 195). What enables us to not just take over but also to "change the meaning of words"—to transform those propagandistic "bundles of assumptions" about feminine communication or femininity writ large (Rowbotham 32)—that we still carry with us, even into twenty-first-century examinations of prior work? Most analytic and historical methods for irony still support a dichotomy between *concealing a linguistic truth* and *diverging from that truth*, and this is especially significant for Hutchinson's controversy, which has been contextualized in a persistent "lye." Yet in historical studies of women's discourse, the task of analyzing instances and uses of irony need not preclude a more critical understanding of *irony* as a phenomenon that reveals how audiences and readers access it across texts. In fact, my motive for studying Askew's, Hutchinson's, and Gougar's ironic discourse is to demonstrate how they support a metalinguistic consciousness that does more than simply reorient its linguistic features toward the reader or simply point to irony as a semantic failure for one audience or another, based on the way it either reveals or conceals the truth claim at its center. Critical discourse studies can and do emerge from a theoretical linguistic space, even in a postmodern world where the relationships among "things, thoughts, words, and actions" transcend the realistic principles of any given period (Ulman 2).

As a result, the so-called semantic failures that we now know as the Antinomian controversy—the semantic occurrences of misunderstanding due to unshared contexts between Anne Hutchinson and her examiners—can actually restore agential identification to her trial discourse by eliding a dichotomy between feminine private experience and masculine public performance that often prevented early American women from being viewed as legitimate participants in intellectual debates. Narrated accounts of Hutchinson's struggle to connect her private and public religious experiences have provoked a lingering memory of her performances as conflicted, given that her adjudicators' responses during the trial effectively denied her a legitimate blending of public with private theology.

Whereas Amy Schrager Lang observes that the New England colonists already "struggled to bring together citizen and saint, to establish a connection between private and public realms of experience" (*Prophetic* 6), I maintain that it is Hutchinson's *inability* to separate public language from private experience that forms the center of the Antinomian controversy. In the troubling disembodiment of principles that she articulates, Hutchinson represents an intriguing possibility for Colonial women's rhetorical histories: that these two realms of experience do not operate so distinctly from one another.

This is important for two reasons. First, such failures help historians be mindful of the incompleteness of women's rhetorical histories by considering what they can retrospectively examine as topoi or available rhetorics, especially in the absence of rich archives of their work (Romano 454–55). And second, these failures promote a rereading of whole discourses that tend to memorialize women rhetors as *divisive* in figure or text, of which Hutchinson is a prime example. In the same way that Lindal Buchanan's regendered fifth canon "acknowledg[es] the constraints and compensating strategies of both women and men" in antebellum America (*Regendering* 109), irony offers a necessary and alternative historical positioning for Colonial women writers.

In this chapter I examine the ironic nature of Hutchinson's responses, reappropriate Hutchinson's great "lye" (Caldwell 363), and consider how that reappropriation constructs new or varied agents in the reading and writing of feminist Colonial histories, working eventually toward what James Berlin calls rhetorical *histories* that "reveal us to ourselves" (Octalog, "Politics" 12). As Buchanan ultimately redefines what counts as "rhetorical delivery" (including the terms on which such definitions can be constructed for antebellum rhetors), I redefine what counts as power, participation, and controversy in Hutchinson's Colonial trials, to rethink what it means for discourse to be "gendered" in the early American church and to reconsider what ironic empowerment can mean for seventeenth-century women's texts. My task here is not to prove or disprove a lie, overturn existing interpretations of Hutchinson's defenses, correct false assumptions about her intentions, pinpoint the anatomy of her "strategies," or identify the mechanism underlying her response. Instead, my aims in this chapter are to rethink whole tendencies to historicize Hutchinson's trial discourse as gendered male-female (or gendered "prophetic"), and hence gendered divisive, and to demonstrate how irony enables this rethinking.

REREADING COLONIAL HISTORIES

The "trials" of Anne Marbury Hutchinson consisted of a two-day examination before the General Court of the Massachusetts Bay Colony in November 1637, followed by a period of house arrest during which Hutchinson miscarried her fifteenth pregnancy, and culminating in a two-day trial before the Boston Church in March 1638, initiated by the minister and governor John Winthrop. Winthrop's initial charge centered on Hutchinson's alleged creation of rumors about the church ministers, but by the second day of the second examination, little had been established beyond the fact that she spoke often and fervently of her assurance of salvation.[1] Still, the results of the trial did not turn in Hutchinson's favor; eventually she was excommunicated from the church and expelled from the colony.[2]

After three years in Boston, Hutchinson eventually broke with John Cotton—the English minister whom her family had followed from England to America—because of their differing opinions about the possibility of immediate revelation in a Puritan worldview that relied on rigorous self-examination. Thus Hutchinson simultaneously was caught in and provoked a complex disagreement represented in the divergent opinions of John Cotton and John Wheelwright, another Puritan leader who had left England to establish a new church in the ideal community of Boston. Both men had been Hutchinson's clerical allies until the trial provided Cotton with an opportunity to dissociate himself from what was becoming popular Puritan doctrine (Hall xiii). The persistent claim that the Hutchinsonian controversy "divided" the Puritans on matters of immediate revelation, or that Hutchinson has been "an apostle of separation" (Caldwell 353), relies on a rhetorical positioning that is in turn characterized by the following assumptions, which an irony paradigm can critically disrupt:

- the assumption that words are the vehicular expression of faith and works, and that "faith" and "works" are separate acts, rather than inward and outward expressions of the same act;
- the assumption that "permission" and "commandment" can be conflated in the discourse of Puritan women;
- the assumption that civic conflicts are distinct from ecclesiastic conflicts for Puritan women and are resolvable by isolating arguments to matters of doctrine; and
- the assumption that "private" and "public" are separately and situationally defined.

Rather than rewriting or reasserting its historical value, I suggest re-examining the controversy for its *historicity*—looking more closely at the temporal and spatial interventions in which we recognize irony as having been performed, interpreted, or perceived as a kind of early American *dissoi logoi*. It is possible to value Hutchinson's responses as "seventeenth-century text" while also thinking differently about the centrality of these linguistic concerns in seventeenth-century feminist discourse. We do have other options for memorializing Colonial women when they have left behind no textual or material artifacts other than our own commonplace assumptions. Ultimately, the value in Hutchinson's ironic discourse is not in what we think were her strategies or intentions or dogmas, but rather in those circumstances that she did not try to control. Hutchinson's irony acts as a lens by which to view her positioning as a legitimate coproducer of the cultural economy; this lens had historically belonged to the elders she critiques and now belongs to us.

Several historical accounts influenced William Sheffield's 1888 description of Hutchinson as a woman who argued with a "well sustained rational and logical force" ("Persecuted"). In an unpublished sermon, Sheffield presented New England's long history of reformation efforts as a fortification of state over individual moral forces, ultimately constructing an account of Antinomianism that emphasizes Hutchinson's role as an exceptional feminine force who knew "'when to speak and when to hold her tongue.'" I propose rereading the Antinomian controversy as something other than an ecclesiastical and rhetorical schism and rereading Hutchinson's role as something other than gender-subversive. I suggest reading Hutchinson's ironic positioning for her principal *historical placements*: evidence that language both represents and complicates her representation; accommodation of both the abstract and material dimensions to language in her argumentation; and disruption of her historical traceability as a Colonial female speaking authentically, who either deflects or capitulates to women's religious roles. For Hutchinson and her historians, irony *disambiguates*. It promotes a more agentive reading, not only of the disagreement that sparked the controversy but also of the way the whole controversy has become so inscribed.

Such a characterization of ironic political discourse can signal the interdependence of language and history, enabling historians to interpret linguistic evidence without assuming its purely rational (Ulman 10–11) or purely symbolic (Ulman 187, 193) nature and enabling historiographers to valuate ironic communication without privileging definitions of irony that bifurcate essence and phenomenon or form and function (C. Lang 3). At the same time, they must be able to realize Candace Lang's "ironic critic" (5) without resorting to what Linda Hutcheon calls a "regression to the ironist as sole semantic guarantor" of the speech act (123) and without being stymied by what H. Lewis Ulman refers to as the "problem" of language in post-Enlightenment rhetorical theory (10). I see four ways that irony equips historians to reread Hutchinson's history via an informed feminist consciousness, paying special attention to how her responses elide the public-private dichotomy that pervades historical narratives and occludes women's participation in intellectual debates: arguing beyond "words" and "works"; engaging a topos of difference; repositioning "ecclesiastic" as "civic"; and accepting a hybrid conscience.

Arguing beyond "Words" and "Works"

One important step in advancing feminist consciousness of Hutchinson's trials is in realizing that the retrospective formation of a "Colonial" civil liberty need not rely on a woman's dichotomous existence between words and works. Near the end of the first lecture day of the 1638 church trial, Cotton delivered a lengthy censure in which he clarified which of Hutchinson's words likely stemmed from his own teachings, ultimately differentiating his stance on immediate revelation from hers (Hall 371–72). Hutchinson then interjected the statement that the charges for which they accused her in 1638 did not reflect statements she had made or beliefs she had held six months prior, during the 1637 General Court examination—in fact, that the charges were not a valid basis for her trial in the first place:[3]

> HUTCHINSON. I desire to speake one word befor you proceed: I
>   would forbar but by Reason of my Weakness, I fear I shall not
>   remember it when you have done.
> COTTON. You have Leave to speake.
> HUTCHINSON. All that I would say is this that I did not hould any
>   of thease Thinges before my Imprisonment. (Hall 372)

In the rest of the trial, neither Cotton, nor Winthrop, nor any other minister succeeded in falsifying Hutchinson's statement. Instead, the conservative Thomas Shepherd admonished Hutchinson for offending her inquisitors by interrupting Cotton and asking him a question while "in the midest of her Censure" and by "Impudently affirm[ing] soe horrible an Untruth and falsehood in the midest of . . . such an Assembly as this"

(Hall 373). In turn, Hutchinson's adjudicators responded as if she had told a "publik lye" (Caldwell 363) or had made a calculated error of judgment.

This moment has been historicized in several ways in order to situate Hutchinson within Colonial religious discourse and to gender her discourse as distinctively female, and I think it worthwhile to review their genealogy here. Scottish minister Robert Baillie's criticism of American Puritanism, in his 1645 "A Dissuasive from the Errours of the Time," helped historicize Hutchinson's verdict as a product of "her grosse lying" (64). Yet Michael Winship argues in his narrative history of Hutchinson's *Times & Trials* that this particular controversy began well before and lingered well after Hutchinson's expulsion from the Boston commonwealth, pinpointing its central conflict in questions of evidence of justification and grace (How can one be assured of his or her justification? and How is it divinely given?), rather than in questions of Antinomianism proper (3).[4] Winship argues that the nuances of this "controversy" were actually centered on *how* "the free grace of God converted and saved sinners," not on *whether* it did: "Did it transform them? Overwhelm them? Leave its traces mainly in signs of holiness or mainly in rushing joy?" (1).

Caldwell has called the controversy at its core a "monumental crisis of language" over theology (346), which ended not because Hutchinson's alleged "errors" were resolved or because of the uncompromising fact of her sex, but because of Hutchinson's irreconcilable statements about the nature of language and of the "serious language vacuum" that contextualized her trial (347, 366). For example, Hutchinson delivered her inquisitors to the point of linguistic irreconciliation several times throughout the trial by distinguishing between "to preach under a covenant of works" and "to be under a covenant of works" (Hall 324–25).

David Hall understands gender as a principal factor in, if not the sole cause of, Hutchinson's inquisition (18, 152), either because of Winthrop's beliefs that women could do irreparable damage to personal and public intellect by expounding on scripture or because of a common belief that women could not be trusted to discern it (Buchanan, "Study" 241). It was, for Hall, a "'mis-called' controversy . . . not about matters of doctrine but about power and freedom of conscience" (11). Ultimately, it was centered in the common lore that Hutchinson claimed to have received divine revelations (Hall 311; E. Morgan 675). Some historians deny that this contradiction was a mistake at all. Ann Withington and Jack Schwartz describe several ways in which Hutchinson showed tactfulness well before the first General Court examination, ultimately asserting that her

discussion of immediate revelation must have been a calculated abandonment of the law (235–36). In the preface to his documentary history of
The Antinomian Controversy, Hall frames this early Colonial conflict as
a schism between the "dispersal of the 'Antinomians' and the reassertion
of 'orthodoxy'" (ix), with a woman conveniently at its center.

Lyle Koehler also frames the Antinomian controversy as a social movement (56), while Amy Schrager Lang argues that the controversy offered
Orthodox Puritans a personal vendetta over their dissenting counterparts, something that the inquisitor Thomas Welde broadly justified as
a penalty for the colonists' complacency in allowing "unsound and loose
opinions" to pervade the new American church (*Prophetic* 53). Responding to Nathanial Hawthorne's 1830 essay entitled simply "Mrs. Hutchinson," Lang argues that a new or "literary" history of Antinomianism needs
to be written, one that demonstrates how Hutchinson's "religious heretic
of the 1630s" had been "reincarnated in the female sentimental novelist of
the 1830s" (1) and how several narratives—including Winthrop's, Welde's,
and Cotton Mather's, among them—had contributed to this reincarnation
as a principally female trait (70).[5]

Lad Tobin and Lindal Buchanan further encourage critical readers to
understand Hutchinson's trials as a feminist project, arguing that these
readers have either disregarded the implicit misogynist conflicts raised by
these trials (Tobin 254) and not seen the gender-based rhetorical styles
fueling the debate (Tobin 255), or overlooked the explicit "gendered ob-
stacles" that the ministers constructed by framing Hutchinson's public
participation in terms of fertility and malformity (Buchanan, "Study" 239).
Both Tobin and Buchanan are explicit in their suggestions that after 350
years of historical work on Antinomian texts, we are afforded many more
options for understanding her civil trial than simply chastising her for
"failing to honor the 'fathers of the commonwealth'" (Tobin 253), including
reading the ministers' reactions as fearful, angry, and jealous (Tobin 254).[6]
Buchanan usefully pinpoints the charges against Hutchinson as arising "at
the junction of maternity and public discourse" and causing a discursive
exploitation of Hutchinson's body, a kind of provision of gendered means
of persuasion ("Study" 239–40).

I review these claims to show that a central question driving their
histories is one of *cause*: How could an interrogation of Hutchinson's
private beliefs (that was initially prompted by hearsay) have escalated into
a trial that not only reinforced an alleged "publik lye" as a near certainty
but also made her the scapegoat for a controversy in which she did not

actively take part? This question of how Hutchinson became a rhetorical scapegoat is not precisely my question, however. I am interested in how this dichotomy affects feminist readings of the histories constructed around the Hutchinsonian controversy, especially those that recognize Hutchinson as a proponent of civil liberties without acknowledging the paradoxical tensions that are often raised for the early American church. Throughout the trial, Hutchinson's language is both transparent and material enough to demonstrate—for immediate and distant audiences—its inadequacy for condemning her on any set charge (including blasphemy, prophecy, or heresy). Yet her legacy as an early American rhetor has been tied to a divisiveness attributed more to her femaleness than any other factor.

The entire exchange between Hutchinson and the General Court, as well as the briefer exchanges between Winthrop and Hutchinson, reflect the same disambiguation as in the *Examinations* discussed in chapter 1: the ministers assumed that when Hutchinson told this "lye," she was revealing her tendency to "bend the Word to support her own presuppositions" (Caldwell 363). It seems to have been based on whether she was sufficiently endowed with talents of faith so as to overcome Cotton's claim that she had strayed publicly from orthodoxy or whether she was sufficiently endowed with talents of spirit so as to logically evade Winthrop's claim that she held privately blasphemous beliefs. Yet for Caldwell, this "bending" represents an important motive other historians had previously overlooked—that Hutchinson was telling the truth according to her reading of the controversy (361) and that any perceived inconsistency, either between her statements at the beginning and end of the trials or between her scriptural interpretations and those of her elders, merely justifies Hutchinson's "suspiciousness of human language" (351). Caldwell argues that Hutchinson's sense of language was in fact less divine, less consensual, and less trustworthy than that of her ministers (350–51). Unlike her Boston ministers, Hutchinson does not conflate words with deeds or utterances with beliefs and notes the limits of mundane verbal expressions for trying to convey prophetic principles. For Hutchinson and her examiners, then, language may be too complicated and too fallible to adequately convey expected nuanced differences between communal and individual revelation and between deeds and words.

Engaging a Topos of Difference

Another important step in advancing feminist consciousness of Hutchinson's trials is being aware of how her discourse reflects an inadequacy of historicized, individual language to express communal principles—its symbolic inducements—while her interlocutors rely on its stable properties as evidence of individual theological beliefs and where she notes discursive contradictions in the trial. Postmodern linguistic identifications rely not on the stable properties of signification but on its *instabilities*; they signify while also transcending signification, as gendered subjects might clash with the conditions of their own social collective (I. Young 714). Where Caldwell notes a "broken connection" between Hutchinson's sense of language and the consensus required for scriptural interpretation (351), the greater irony event reveals her awareness of the communal burden that language could be when relied on to reach consensus. Hutchinson's claim about the tenuousness of linguistic expression directly reflects the puzzlement that she may feel about the uncertainties of judging one person's spiritual state based on the words or works of many persons. In short, Hutchinson inscribes *language* with an individualistic rather than a communal agency separate from *belief.* Language is neither a vehicle for moral truth, nor a one-to-one signification of the deeds the ministers perceive her to have done. As a topos for theorizing, it involves rejecting cause, accepting paradox, and leaving unresolved the contradictions their discourse helps reveal.

The lingering problem surrounding the Antinomian controversy is not that Hutchinson's Puritanical "divisiveness" has been consistently linked to her femality, but that her femality has been linked to an agency that, historically, could not be anything other than divisive. Ironically, her divisiveness is rooted in several aspects of Puritanical discourse that remain dichotomous because they are assumed to be opposing aspects of single entities—individual and collective. Instead, I propose that they are separate entities that can be read together by engaging a topos of difference, so that historians do not limit their own ways of encountering this discourse. By approaching her irony as a contingent phenomenon in which multiple agents participate, I raise the possibility for Colonial American discourse to enable alternatively public roles and private identifications, beyond overturning rhetorical identities or circumventing the paradox of these roles for women in the early colonies.

The greatest discursive value in Hutchinson's "errors" is not in how they deny the connections between verbal expressions and ideas but in how they cast doubt on the nature of language itself to solve epochal dilemmas (Burke, *Rhetoric* 2). This doubt lends new meaning to what would become an intellectual problem regarding the precise nature of

understanding in the linguistic and discursive traditions ushering in Enlightenment rhetoric. If language could be manipulated through rhetoric to obfuscate rather than clarify, then language was too limited—"so
scanty in respect to that infinite variety of thoughts, that men, wanting
terms to suit their precise notions, will, notwithstanding their utmost
caution, be forced often to use the same word in somewhat different
senses" (Locke bk. 3, ch. 11, par. 27). It is possible that Hutchinson reflects
this dilemma when naming her "mistake" (Hall 359, 361), choosing words
that would enact the revelation she professes to have received. In this
exchange, her words reflect an *asignification* that operates distinctly from
the Puritanical aim of reaching the realm of absolute truth through the
articulation of concrete ideas, even as her exchange denies a separation
between one and the other.

During the 1637 General Court examination, Hutchinson's ministers
are upset by a statement she had made during a private meeting that they
were "not sealed," by which she meant they had not undergone the necessary transformation to "preach a covenant of grace clearly" (Hall 321).
While we learn that Hutchinson had made the statement in the presence
of a single church member when called on to give her opinion of the
church elders (Hall 324), the charge still becomes inflated to a criticism
that the elders were "not able ministers of the gospel," and Hutchinson's
criticism becomes conflated with the sentiment that they "preach[ed] a
covenant of works" (Hall 320–21). As the examination continues and the
governor and deputy governor question her denial, Hutchinson aligns her
motives with their own by clarifying how one statement is not necessarily
cause for another:

> DEP. GOV. . . . . You said they preached a covenant of works and that
>   they were not able ministers of the new testament; . . .
> HUTCHINSON. No Sir it is your conclusion. . . .
> DEP. GOV. . . . . it appears plainly that you have spoken it, . . .
> HUTCHINSON. That I absolutely deny, for the first question was
>   thus answered by me to them. They thought that I did conceive
>   there was a difference between them and Mr. Cotton. . . . Then
>   I said I would deal as plainly as I could, and whereas they say I
>   said they were under a covenant of works and in the state of the
>   apostles why these two speeches cross one another. I might say
>   they might preach a covenant of works as did the apostles, but
>   to preach a covenant of works and to be under a covenant of
>   works is another business. (Hall 324–25)

This response supports the historical bifurcation of *preaching* into speaking and doing, and it implicitly distinguishes between asserting and responding and between speaking plainly and speaking obtusely. From an ironist's perspective, language confounds the clear-cut representation of truth claims in its inability to prove authentic motives, reflect authentic judgment, or deliver statements carrying truth value, as Hutchinson argues in an exchange with Cotton later during the 1638 trial by separating "experience" from "judgment":

> HUTCHINSON. . . . . If Mr. Shephard doth conceave that I had any of
> these Thinges in my Minde, than he is deceaved. It was never in
> my hart to slight any man but only that man should be kept in
> his owne place and not set in the Roome of God. . . .
> I confes my Expressions was that way but it was never my
> Judgment. . . .
> COTTON. Thear is 2 things to be clerd, 1. What you doe now hould.
> 2ly what you did hould.
> HUTCHINSON. My Judgment is not altered though my Expression
> alters. . . .
> I confesse I have denied the Word Graces but not the Thinge
> itself. (Hall 377–81)

Similarly, during the 1638 church trial, Hutchinson deflects the charge that she has "shut [her] Eyes agaynst the Truth" during an exchange in which she argues that because the "soule" and the "spirit" are distinctive, the performance of one need not conform to the other (Hall 354). Hutchinson insists that this distinction is linguistic, if not ontological—in fact, that some linguistic inadequacies are ordained and unresolved: "The holy Ghost makes this Distinction between the soule and Body and not I" (Hall 355). Tobin already notes the discursive differences between Hutchinson's testimony and that of her jurors, each employing "radically different metaphors to explain the world in which they live" (256). Irony reveals these metaphors at work by illuminating not only what the church elders may have heard in Hutchinson's language as "intimacy, inspiration, and moments of light" (Tobin 256) but also how Hutchinson's examiners and historians may regularly overlook her pluralistic understanding of language when it had to accommodate the beliefs of a commonwealth.

Finally, Hutchinson realizes a contradiction between her apparent discomfort at saying the words "God speaks" during the 1637 General Court examination and her continued reliance on wanting to "see Scripture speake" (Caldwell 350):

HUTCHINSON. . . . . I will propound my mayne scruple and that is
   how a Thinge that is Immortally miserable can be immortally
   happie.
COTTON. He that makes miserable can make us happy.
HUTCHINSON. I desire to hear God speak this and not man. Shew
   me whear thear is any Scripture to prove it that speakes soe.
   (Hall 355)

This series of definitions and redefinitions reflects both the tenuousness of choosing any words at all and the need to read metonymically. This
is most clear when the elders continually interpret Hutchinson's use of
the word "Light" ("I thinke the soule to be nothing but Light") as "Breath,"
"immortall," and "blamless" (Hall 356–58), initiating a dispute between
Hutchinson and Cotton and extending the controversy beyond their original charges. Hutchinson finally alludes to Mr. Davenport's enactment of
the principle that she struggles to define and they struggle to understand:[7]

HUTCHINSON. If Error be the Thinge you intend, than I desire to
   know what is the Error for which I was banished for I am sure
   this is not, for then thear was no such Expression from me on
   this. . . .
DAVENPORT. A soule may be Immortall and not miserable. . . .
   Immortalitie was a Gift to the Spirit in thear very Beinge. The
   soule cannot have Immortalitie in itselfe but from God from
   whom it hath its beinge
HUTCHINSON. I thanke the Lord I have Light. And I see more Light
   a greate deale by Mr. Damphords [Davenport's] opening of it.
   (Hall 358–59)

As Caldwell suggests, the elders probably thought Hutchinson was
lying "because they [were] committed to connections which she [had]
severed" (357). Yet in this exchange, the severing does not occur between
mortality and immortality, but rather between linguistic expression and
proof, and this is evident in the way that she justifies her "mistake" as
the inadequate expression of a principle already upheld by the church:

DAVENPORT. You must distinguish betwene the life of the Soule
   and the Life of the Body. The Life of the Body is mortall but the
   Life of the Soule is immortall Ecclesiastes 12. thear the Spirit
   signifies the soule, in Isaiah 53.10.11 he shall make his soule an
   offering for sine.

HUTCHINSON. I am clear in this sense now. . . .

DAVENPORT. You doe than consent to the two first Questions that *the Coming of Christ in Thessalonians to the soule is not ment of Christs Cominge in Union but of his Cominge at the day of Judgment.*

HUTCHINSON. I doe not acknowledge it to be an Error but a Mistake. I doe acknowledge my Expression to be Ironious but my Judgment was not Ironious, for I held befor as you did but could not express it soe. . . .

COTTON. If you meane thay have 2 bodies one of sine and another of death, and one outward body and an Inward Body of Graces.

HUTCHINSON. I meane as that Scripture meanes 1 Corinthians 2.16. (Hall 357–61)

Hutchinson's distinction between sign ("the soule") and signified ("divine assurance") may well reflect an accommodation of both virtual *and* material dimensions of language. It is not clear from this transcript whether her "language emerges from her religious conceptions, or vice versa" (Caldwell 348), nor is it clear whether that is a historically productive question to ask. However, in reading the whole discursive event, historians can argue that Hutchinson uses one to exemplify the other. In other words, in Caldwell's analysis, the principal difference between how Hutchinson and her examiners use language is that for the elders, "the theological ideas [were] inseparable from the basic verbal 'ideas,'" while for Hutchinson, theological ideas could not be perfectly conveyed through language, and she often demonstrated this by separating words out from their referents (353), by "divid[ing] speaking from being" (354), and by distancing herself from her own words and from those of her ministers by using the passive voice (356).[8]

Consequently, irony also reveals the paradoxical assumption of Hutchinson's ministers that whereas physical/mortal elements should be made *more* distinct from divine/immortal elements, civic and ecclesiastic goals should be made *less* distinct from one another. Again, if we accept Caldwell's argument, then Hutchinson's responses reflect the ontological limits of all discourse, while the elders place logocentric value on plain speech. In this case, and especially if Hutchinson has realized that difference at some point during the trials, her deferment strategies (e.g., saying, "I am not clear in the poynt" or deferring to claims as they are already written in 1 Corinthians) accommodate the audience in those circumstances only by deferring to their belief that language carries moral judgment. What this demonstrates about a topos of difference is the frequency with which such accommodations are historically embodied or assumed.

Repositioning "Ecclesiastic" as "Civic"

This quasi-accommodation makes Hutchinson a convenient figure for demonstrating her own and others' struggles to experience religious and secular spheres together, as women's personal relationships were often presented in contrast to their allegiance to the state (Tobin 260). By the time the elders reconvened on the second day of Hutchinson's trial, their intention was to forward some proof of her unwomanly conduct before turning to her "dayngerous and damnable" New Testament readings on the topic of salvation (Hall 358, 375). And by the time her trials had been narrated by Winthrop, Baillie, and others, the accusations had expanded "to embrace her entire nature as a woman" (A. Lang, *Prophetic* 65), albeit her nature as part of a female collective rather than as an individual woman.

As such, Colonial Puritanism became widely known as "the Massachusetts disciplinary project" (Winship 21), a logical enactment of the American Puritans' extreme confidence in the reformation of manners and in the socially unifying function of scripture (Hall 16; Caldwell 360). Historically, the religious and the secular are two highly integrated ways of appropriating discursive power toward the realization of Colonial citizenship, not merely a way of bending judicial and legislative power to support erroneous ecclesiastical decisions or vice versa. This in turn enables a rereading of the Antinomian controversy as a vital disagreement about what role the ecclesiastic could play in logically establishing and maintaining civic discipline. While the Massachusetts Body of Liberties did align democratic with theocratic ideals in its early governing practices (Finkelman 55, 979), the Bay Colony still adjudicated both perceived and actual conflicts as if they were exclusively ecclesiastic offenses.

The duration of Hutchinson's house arrest, the number of charges that the ministers brought against her, and the number of counterarguments the ministers in turn brought to one another all reveal that a singular notion of "self-discipline" was vigorously and narrowly debated in the Boston Church. Thus a third way that Hutchinson's ironic responses reveal how a historicization of Colonial women might elide a gendered dichotomy is in Hutchinson's treatment of *commandment* and *permission* as terms that simultaneously complicate the role of the collective in disciplining the individual and the role of the individual in attaining collective spiritual fulfillment. In the eighteenth century, an American minister's individual calling was paramount to his ability to learn and preach (Backus). Yet a paradoxical relationship between individual and collective obeisance is notable on the second day of the 1637 examination when Governor Winthrop and John Endicott engage Hutchinson on the subject of propriety in teaching women.

Hutchinson claims this "rule" is a legitimate public practice affirmed in the book of Titus, but Winthrop claims it is a colloquial custom contradicted in the first letter to the Corinthians. Both parties to this debate offer textual evidence as proof of the viability of teaching women as a "rule" rather than a custom, even as both parties attest to the ironic nature of Hutchinson's appearance before the Boston Church assembly:

> HUTCHINSON. . . . Do you think it not lawful for me to teach women and why do you call me to teach the court?
>
> GOV WINTHROP. We do not call you to teach the court but to lay open yourself.
>
> HUTCHINSON. I desire you that you would then set me down a rule by which I may put them away that come unto me and so have peace in so doing.
>
> GOV WINTHROP. You must shew your rule to receive them.
>
> HUTCHINSON. I have done it.
>
> GOV WINTHROP. I deny it because I have brought more arguments than you have.
>
> HUTCHINSON. I say, to me it is a rule.
>
> ENDICOTT. You say there are some rules unto you. I think there is a contradiction in your own words. What rule for your practice do you bring, only a custom in Boston.
>
> HUTCHINSON. No Sir that was no rule to me but if you look upon the rule in Titus it is a rule to me. If you convince me that it is no rule I shall yield.
>
> GOV WINTHROP. You know that there is no rule that crosses another, but this rule crosses that in Corinthians. But you must take it in this sense that elder women must instruct the younger about their business, and to love their husbands and not to make them to clash.
>
> HUTCHINSON. I do not conceive but that it is meant for some publick times.
>
> GOV WINTHROP. Well, have you no more to say but this?
>
> HUTCHINSON. I have said sufficient for my practice. (Hall 315–16)

This passage shows unresolved differences between obeisance and willful doing, in turn pointing to a dissonant understanding of the collective in Colonial religious discourse. In the scenario for which Hutchinson argues, she perceives her own willful doing (i.e., teaching Cotton's doctrine) as a public custom for the individual attainment of obedience, yet this custom clashes with Winthrop's and Endicott's expectations that she should not act individually unless permitted to do so by a publicly confirmed rule. Furthermore, Winthrop censures Hutchinson for allegedly "dishonouring" the fathers of the commonwealth by entertaining in her home members who petitioned the General Court in 1637 (Hall 313–14), and in response, Hutchinson notes his conflation of honoring the "fathers of the commonwealth" with honoring "thy father and they mother." By Winthrop's rationale, all matters of authority, countenancing, and honoring are not matters of free choice but are compulsory acts, but by Hutchinson's rationale, it is the individual's willing submission to the communal belief in preaching that distinguishes birthright from church membership and permission from obeisance, making her a willing and faithful participant. After establishing the circumstances under which Hutchinson can and should be expected to open her home to non–church leaders, Hutchinson asks for an equivalent rule by which she should know when to "put [visitors] away":

> HUTCHINSON. What law do they transgress?
> GOV WINTHROP. The law of God and of the state.
> HUTCHINSON. In what particular?
> GOV WINTHROP. Why in this among the rest, whereas the Lord
> doth say honour thy father and thy mother.
> HUTCHINSON. Ey Sir in the Lord. . . .
> In entertaining those did I entertain them against any act (for
> there is the thing) or what God hath appointed?
> GOV WINTHROP. You knew that Mr. Wheelwright did preach this
> sermon and those that countenance him in this do break a law.
> HUTCHINSON. What law have I broken?
> GOV WINTHROP. Why the fifth commandment. [Do not worship
> other Gods.]
> HUTCHINSON. I deny that for he saith in the Lord.
> HUTCHINSON. What breach of law is that Sir?
> GOV WINTHROP. Why dishonouring of parents.
> HUTCHINSON. But put the case Sir that I do fear the Lord and my
> parents, may not I entertain them that fear the Lord because
> my parents will not give me leave?

GOV WINTHROP. If they be the fathers of the commonwealth,
and they of another religion, if you entertain them then you
dishonour your parents and are justly punishable. (Hall 313–14)

Several of Hutchinson's responses are ironic in their spoken context, because she overlooked asking permission to fulfill what she says she had in some sense been commanded to do. What this exchange reveals to a contemporary reader is a constant positioning and repositioning of the commonwealth ministers as being suspended between civic and ecclesiastic concerns, individual and collective transgression, and two goals of attainment for which Colonial Puritans should have aimed: first, to please the church fathers as they would divinity, and then to adhere to church rules as they would honor the rules of their parents.

We can understand this suspension as ironic in its historicization in several ways, especially in light of eighteenth-century understandings that the church would become separate from the state in matters of individual action. To be able to reposition Hutchinson and other Colonial women as operating comfortably *within* these two goals rather than *against* them means creating new possibilities for defining *commandment* and *permission* as conjoined traits. Quaker apologist George Keith used *commandment* over *permission* to justify the calling of women preachers in the seventeenth century. More than three decades after Hutchinson's trials (Gordon 5: 322), Keith published a ministerial treatise in which he expounds on "The Woman-preacher of Samaria," a character derived from the fourth chapter of the Gospel according to John. Keith articulates distinct traits, comparing women and men preachers in the following ways, here drawing a fine line between prophesying and pulpit oratory: women were called internally to preach (or prophesy), rather than called by men; women often spoke briefly and with words given by God; women were not often conventionally educated or taught; and finally, women's preaching was inspired by the Holy Spirit, as it often had an observed positive effect on their listeners. Although Keith's exposition makes no direct reference to Hutchinson or to the Antinomians, it does reflect the simultaneous ease and difficulty with which he felt an individual would relate her moral will to the civic responsibility of the church.

In a postscript to his argument, Keith alludes to Paul's admonition against women speaking in church before asking ministers why, then, was it appropriate to "command Whores and Adulterous Women to speak in publick?" (20).[9] Keith's treatise and other similar arguments make the distinction between justifiable and unjustifiable preaching an unavoidable issue in Hutchinson's episteme:

> If they would contend, that Women ought not to speak in the Church, all that they can pretend with any shew, or colour of Reason, at most is *That women are not to speak in the Church by permission*: if they speak, they are not to do it by permission, but by commandment, whereas it is permitted unto Men, at times to speak in the Church by permission, when not by commandment. (Keith 23–24)

Keith's logic also echoes the irresolvable conflict with which Hutchinson describes her own positioning in the commonwealth church: she was positioned *either* as one who failed to seek permission *or* as one who disobeyed commandments. Thus the charge during the 1638 trial that Hutchinson had disobeyed because she had ultimately "stept out of [her] place, . . . rather bine a Husband than a Wife and a preacher than a Hearer; and a Magistrate than a Subject" (Hall 383) becomes both easier and more difficult to justify. It is easier to justify by affirming that commonwealth custom was not to employ women in the pulpit, yet it becomes more difficult to justify because of Keith's exegetical evidence that women were empowered to preach in ways wholly consistent with the lay mission of the Puritan church. By associating "permission" with external calling and "commandment" with internal calling—something that the Boston Church elders did not explicitly deny but did find offensive about the Hutchinsonians—Keith enables distant and critical readers to consider how a *collective subject* (e.g., "women in the Puritanical tradition") complicates their historicization of rhetorical and linguistic agency in Colonial religious discourse.

Hutchinson's concession that she would "cross a rule" in publicly instructing a hundred men in the will of God but that she thought it "lawful" to do the same for a hundred women provokes a contradiction in Winthrop's accusation: at no time during the trials can the ministers demonstrate that Hutchinson had committed an unlawful act, although they do argue that she subverts her appropriate role at trial, which is to confess (out of obedience, servitude, and earnestness); yet this same obedience, servitude, and earnestness are what motivate Hutchinson not to turn away discussants from her home. Just prior to their dismissal on the first day of the General Court's examination, Hutchinson clarifies her position:

HUTCHINSON . I acknowledge using the words of the apostle to the Corinthians unto him, that they that were ministers of the letter and not the spirit did preach a covenant of works. . . . He said that was the letter of the law. No said I it is the letter of the gospel. (Hall 326)

Following Endicott's question about who should be teaching men in public meetings, Hutchinson replies that "not preach[ing] a covenent of grace clearly" and "preach[ing] nothing but a covenant of works" are not equal statements (Hall 318). Her statement that civic and ecclesiastic rules should not be conflated to prove wrongdoing, and that no alleged ecclesiastic wrongdoing could be justified civically, ultimately put an end to this debate:

HUTCHINSON. I say prove it that I said they preached nothing but a covenant of works.

DEP. GOV DUDLEY. Nothing but a covenant of works, why a Jesuit may preach truth sometimes.

HUTCHINSON. Did I ever say they preached a covenant of works then?

DEP. GOV DUDLEY. If they do not preach a covenant of grace clearly, then they preach a covenant of works.

HUTCHINSON. No Sir, one may preach a covenant of grace more clearly than another, so I said. . . .

DEP. GOV DUDLEY. I will make it plain that you did say that the ministers did preach a covenant of works.

HUTCHINSON. I deny that.

DEP. GOV DUDLEY. And that you said they were not able ministers of the new testament, but Mr. Cotton only.

HUTCHINSON. If ever I spake that I proved it by God's word.

COURT. Very well, very well. (Hall 318–19)

Public trials such as Hutchinson's would become opportunities for speaking out against a perpetual double standard. On the one hand, if Colonial women were not suitable for public positions because of an alleged superior moral nature, then disallowing them to take part in moralistic activity on any stage—parliamentary or otherwise—went counter to the aims of maintaining a strong civic society (Raymond 305–06). On the other hand, if Colonial women had been barred from pulpit teaching because of an alleged moral frailty, then relying on their public testimony to settle charges of personal transgression went counter to the aims of

building a strong ecclesiastic society. Hutchinson's trial—like Askew's—
was ultimately resolved only when the governors isolated her civic arguments to matters of faith doctrine, and it was in those arguments that
Hutchinson finally "incriminat[ed] herself" (Buchanan, "Study" 248).
Rereading Colonial histories through this lens usefully complicates Carol
Gilligan's historicization of Colonial women as "viewing moral problems in terms of 'conflicting responsibilities rather than from competing
rights'" (qtd. in Tobin 257). Yet how different might our analytic practices
be—for both distant political historicizing and more recent—if we asked
ourselves why the "civic" should matter in light of historical paradigms
that have not traditionally or explicitly acknowledged it. In bridging
past with present political histories, the "civic" matters for histories like
Hutchinson's, and early America's, because it recasts engendered disputes
in an antecedent tradition that values the political narrative for its "formal
re-presentation of historical content" (Munslow 25), rather than as its
deconstruction of linguistic terms.

Accepting a Hybrid Conscience

The fourth way to affect a feminist consciousness in rereading the Antinomian controversy is by illuminating the ministers' discomfort with
Hutchinson's hybrid conscience—a conscience simultaneously informed
by both private and public motives. Those same semantic failures that David Hall reports as "strange" or "erroneous" claims[10]—and that Caldwell
says mark the conflicted relationship between "thinking and speaking
. . . about the nature of language itself" (345)—may reveal Hutchinson's
inability to separate public and private behaviors, and hence her inability to definitively gender her own text. For Hutchinson, words may not
have symbolized what Caldwell calls a "systematic linkage between the
imperceptible and the perceptible" (355), but they did reflect the cultural
confusion that ensued.

The distinction between public and private venues for sixteenth- and
seventeenth-century women is likely less stark than the "spectrum of
social spaces and activities" that have been applied to them retrospectively (Raymond 277).[11] In *The Puritan Origins of the American Self,* Sacvan Bercovitch characterizes American Puritanism according to how it
had evolved as a "rhetoric of inversion," demonstrating a strong interchangeability of "private, corporate, historical, and prophetic meaning"
(114). And in his *Historical Sketch of the First Church of Boston* (published posthumously in 1812), William Emerson portrays the Antinomian

controversy as a series of incidents involving the irrational behavior of the Hutchinsonians (A. Lang, *Prophetic* 122). Amy Schrager Lang notes that Emerson was unable "even in imagination, much less in language, to empower the 'infatuated female.' His account of Hutchinson refuses the possibility that the *private* opinions of a *married* woman (and these are the operative terms in his description) could have public consequences" (113). Emerson depicts the trial as a clash between social parties, with the Hutchinsonians clamoring for democracy and the Bay Colony Puritans preserving "reason over fanaticism" (qtd. in A. Lang 112).

While I do approach Hutchinson's trial responses as evidence of some interchangeability between the corporate and private, and while Hutchinson claimed no intermediate form of expression between herself and a deity, this is not the same thing as saying that Hutchinson believed language could immediately and accurately convey the prophetic position. Neither the examination nor the trial produced any clear evidence that Hutchinson's "errors" had been caused by her confusion of private devotion with public ministry, and yet that accusation against her remains.

At one point in the trial, in his response to Baillie's criticism of the American Puritan church in the *Dissuasive*, Cotton differentiates himself from Hutchinson regarding his ability to keep those spheres distinct (and thus her inability to do so), as well as his expectation that she should have done so consistently: "Three things I told her, made her spirituall estate unclear to mee. 1. 'That her Faith was not begotten nor (by her relation) scarce at any time strengthened, by publick ministery, but by private Meditations, or Revelations onely'" (Cotton 413). On the contrary, Hutchinson's perceived errors stem partly from her own documented testimony that public and private spheres are not concerned with different revelations at all, revealing a double standard in the ministers' valuation of public over private conscience. Yet ultimately, in this exchange, Hutchinson enacts the only kind of hybridity that early American historians can understand. The hybridity comes in blending present with past and acknowledging the inequities of questioning given her status as a woman and a layperson. She differentiates speaking before a public magistrate from speaking with a friend privately, as did Anne Askew when she performed on the basis of what the bishop's councilors charged her of not doing. "I thinke it is a Breach of Church Rule," Hutchinson later testifies, "to bringe a Thinge in publicke before thay have delt with me in private" (Hall 352).

Earlier in the 1637 General Court examination, when it is revealed that the ministers understand her utterance that they were "not sealed" to mean that the Gospel was "a covenant of works," Hutchinson neither affirms nor denies either charge. Instead, she points first to her examiners' motives, and then to the demands of the examination itself, as a principal cause for the ministers' perception that she is withholding information:

> DEPUTY GOVERNOR. . . . . It is well discerned to the court that Mrs.
> Hutchinson can tell when to speak and when to hold her
> tongue. Upon the answering of a question which we desire her
> to tell her thoughts of she desires to be pardoned.
> HUTCHINSON. It is one thing for me to come before a public
> magistracy and there to speak what they would have me
> to speak and another when a man comes to me in a way of
> friendship privately there is difference in that. . . .
> DEPUTY GOVERNOR. This speech was not spoken in a corner but in
> a public assembly, and though things were spoken in private yet
> now coming to us, we are to deal with them as public. (Hall 319)

If Hutchinson had been acting from a public conscience in critiquing the ministers, even in private, then they might find fault with her critique. If she had been acting from a private conscience in a public assembly, then they might find fault with her behavior. However, in both cases, Winthrop claims that the ministerial inquisition gained rightful public access to ideas that were expressed only through private channels, which reflects the difficulty of valuating the role of individual discourse in the Puritan Assembly. The governor's need to "deal with things [in private] as public" causes Hutchinson's actions to be perceived as either one or the other, rather than as having been performed from an undivided conscience. Even Winthrop realizes this fact at some point during or after the trial. In his 1644 narrative *Antinomians and Familists* (later published as *A Short Story of the Rise, Reign, and Ruine of the Antinomians, Familists & Libertines*), he notes that Hutchinson essentially framed a new way of conversation that typically distinguished between public covenant of works and private revelation of the spirit (65).

Hutchinson's historicized response suggests a way to rethink contemporary historicizations of Colonial discourses: historians can read an articulation of the difficulties that Shephard and Winthrop (and other ministers) had in accepting a hybrid conscience. For instance, even William Coddington, a General Court deputy who speaks up in Hutchinson's defense near the end of the second day of her 1637 examination, insists on a separation of private from public matters, thus employing a fairly limited discursive frame. His defense of Hutchinson rests on the fact that "she spake nothing to them but in private," and because "secret things ought to be spoken in secret and publick things in publick," he says, "therefore I think they have broken the rules of God's word" (Hall 346). Historians can also realize that the trial conveyed a ministerial disbelief in rhetorical difference, since Winthrop accused Hutchinson of first speaking freely out of her *own* conscience and then justifying it with scripture, rather than assuming that Hutchinson's own and collective conscience could function as one and the same (Tobin 262): "this was spoken not as was pretended out of private conference, but out of conscience and warrant from scripture alledged the fear of man is a snare and seeing God had given her a calling to it she would freely speak" (Hall 326).

Contemporary repositionings of Colonial discourse as *hybrid* are important for expanding the discursive frame applied to women's political performances in all periods and genres. Whereas Tobin argues that Hutchinson may have been choosing private over public experience in emphasizing free and direct grace, I argue that Hutchinson enacts the messiness of merging the private with the public self in her responses throughout the trial. Moreover, her language reflects crises that the young church had already been experiencing, rather than introducing new ones that would begin the dismantling or dispersal of the church's center of authority. Where irony supports such a re-presentation is in illuminating how Hutchinson's responses were likely informed by her wariness of the corporal expression of individual language—the tension that occurs in realizing that "society was only one of the myriad expressions of the self" (A. Lang, *Prophetic* 66) and not the only expression of self.

OVERCOMING CONFLICTS OF MEMORY

In the introduction to this book, I mentioned that one challenge of rereading women's performances at particular historical junctures is doing so without implying that those performances necessarily speak for others. Still, an important parallel can be drawn between the ironic performances of Anne Askew and Anne Hutchinson. In much the same way that Betsy Verhoeven finds Revolutionary-era women's rhetorical strategies to be effective only as they are inscribed into "kairotic moment[s] of larger social change," rather than at the time of their performances (28), the significance of Askew's and Hutchinson's performances is best understood in those moments that signal *when and how one narrative gives way to the next.* For Hutchinson, these moments include the occasion of

Winthrop's rebuke, Nathaniel Hawthorne's characterization of that rebuke, Patricia Caldwell's and Amy Lang's raising of the language problem
in the Antinomian trials, and Lad Tobin's and Lindal Buchanan's discussions of Hutchinson's trials as feminist texts. Irony inhabits each of these
moments by allowing me to ask not only how Hutchinson's discourse
can be reinscribed as something other than *divisive* but also how this
reinscription can be historicized as something other than "Colonial." It
invites historians to rethink (or imagine alternatives to) *periodization* in
their attempts to classify women's rhetorical traditions, promoting a classification of their discourses according to other principles and practices.

When they are used to position Hutchinson within another rhetorical
inscription, period identifiers such as "Colonial" may occlude rather than
illuminate the material evidence that causes us to privilege Hutchinson's
waywardness over her truthfulness. This occlusion occurs whenever conflicts of memory hide their own mechanisms for remembering. Lang's
Prophetic Woman begins with such a conflict of memory as it occurs in
Nathaniel Hawthorne's "Mrs. Hutchinson," which was first printed in
the *Salem (Massachusetts) Gazette* in 1830 and expresses his concern
that sentimental domestic fiction would soon undermine the national
literature. His was likely an androgynous accusation, but Hawthorne
frequently attributed his concern to the works of those female authors
coming "after Hutchinson" in the American tradition, perhaps because
Colonial interpretations of John Winthrop's *Short Story* made Antinomianism largely a narrative of Hutchinson's demise, rather than an account of conflicted and shifting loyalties within the Bay Colony church.
Winthrop's first account of *Antinomians and Familists* drew parallels
between eight events coincident to Hutchinson's banishment and her
friend Mary Dyer's stillbirth, before arguing that Hutchinson went so long
unnoticed in her anti-orthodoxy because she had infiltrated the hearts of
her community as a competent midwife (A. Lang, *Prophetic* 64).[12] As a
result, when Thomas Welde wrote the introduction to Winthrop's book,
he historicized Antinomianism as a story of husbandry, temptation, illicit
sexual attraction, and God's punishing intentions (A. Lang, *Prophetic* 58),
enabling Hawthorne to suggest that—from a nineteenth-century perspective—both Antinomians and sentimentalists were principal examples of
"feminine ambition," whose "ill-judged [female] incitements" would in
due time outnumber the male (Hawthorne, par. 1).

A similar conflict of memory occurs in Cotton Mather's 1853 narrative of *Magnalia Christi Americana*, in which he recasts Antinomianism

as "the victory of human (that is, male) reason and order over unreason" (A. Lang, *Prophetic* 68), likely influenced by the Reverend John Cotton's historical work. Buchanan argues that the Puritans' charges of malformity and monstrosity arose at the uncomfortable juncture of "maternity and public discourse," dictated by pre-Enlightenment beliefs about the overly active transmission of female traits and genes ("Study" 239–40). The most explicit example of this is Cotton's description of Hutchinson's multiple births as bearing "twenty-seven lumps of man's seed without any alteration or mixture of anything from the woman." If I consider Cotton's whole exchange via frame shifting, the chain of embedding subjects in his recollection proceeds from fecundity → unreason → disorder. Ultimately, promoting Hutchinson as the fulfillment of Antinomian dissent becomes more viable when she is rendered as "fecund seductress" and, ironically, when she is absorbed into nineteenth-century traditions of "Woman as [fecundity's] ideal form" (A. Lang, *Prophecy* 134–35), whether or not her writings appropriately locate her within those traditions.

Similar metaphoric representations lingered well into Revolutionary American discourse, especially in textual traditions that relied heavily on allegorical representations of Christ's covenant with the church, such as Isaac Backus's 1756 "A Short Description of the Difference between the Bond-woman and the Free," where "bond-woman" stands for instituted moral law and "free woman" represents "the gospel-church in her pure standing" (8).[13] In a sermon delivered at the Philadelphia Baptist Meeting House in 1781, Elhanan Winchester reminds the eighteenth-century reader that the "Seed of the woman shall bruise the serpent's head," by which he meant "Power . . . must be bruised in every Man" (15). In Winchester's account, Adam's first intended mate is portrayed as *virginal*, a label that could be applied only retrospectively, after traits such as wisdom and virtuosity had been sexed or gendered in seventeenth-century discourse, rather than applied as an originary or value-neutral term.

Finally, in early twentieth-century depictions of the controversy, Hutchinson's prophetic status is reflected in arguments about her unprecedented role in the development of independent citizenship and the forwarding of human progress, both of which rely on a phenomenology of self that C. Jan Swearingen has traced from Cicero to Christa Wolf, specifically to problematize its role in literacy scholarship (235). For example, a 1904 historical-biographical sketch in the *New York Times* portrays Hutchinson as "ahead of her time," arguing that her ousting from the Boston Colony and her emigration from Rhode Island to modern-day

New York resulted in her "founding" a "real colony" and in enacting numerous qualifications as a social leader. The writer of this sketch speculates that in spite of Hutchinson's reputation as a "good and serviceable" neighbor of "'profitable and sober carriage,'" it was the prejudices against her—rather than pure matters of doctrine—that caused her to be drawn into a conflict with the church elders. In what seems fairly typical of *fin de siècle* rhetoric, the writer makes an argument *for* gender as the cause of Hutchinson's ambitions, yet argues *against* gender as a factor in her ultimate banishment:

> If fortune had cast Anne Hutchinson's lot in the twentieth instead of the seventeenth century, she would have won the world's applause. She was a born social leader, fully equipped with every qualification needed to sustain such a position. . . . Her misfortune was that her ambition tempted her to essay the impossible, to lead what Mr. [Charles Francis] Adams characterizes as "a premature revolt against an organized and firmly-rooted oligarchy of theocrats." Her failure was not due to her sex, for Roger Williams had equally failed. Both were simply in advance of their times, and both deserve measureless honor as the harbingers of principles now recognized by the civilized world as the bulwarks of human progress. ("Tragedy")

And more recently, Buchanan reveals a "theological dismissal" of Hutchinson's participation in the controversy by seventeenth-century men ("Study" 249) by looking to Colonial fecund rhetoric for its mechanisms, arguing that Hutchinson could not be perceived as responding from any other positioning but that of a faithful midwife. Hutchinson's maternal body "continued to circulate as argumentative evidence" long after her banishment from the Boston Church in 1638, and even after being killed by the New Netherland Indians in 1643, not only in arguments opposing Antinomians but also in arguments supporting them ("Study" 255).

At best, these portrayals present historical agency as a kind of causality that is based on perturbation and response (Cooper 438), supporting Robert Baillie's 1645 criticism that the Boston Puritans suffered potential confusion about the power of ecclesiastic jurisdiction and whether jurisdiction belonged in the hands of individual believers or in the presbytery as a whole (181).[14] Baillie may have been the first to memorialize Hutchinson's several miscarriages as divine punishment and to describe her expulsion and eventual death as merciful acts in which God finally "let loose his hand, and destroyed her, sending in upon her a company of the Savages, who burnt her self, her house, and all that she had" (63). Yet he is clear that the church was being punished at Hutchinson's expense, and he argues that her reputation among the members was "much mistaken and wronged; . . . a most pious woman, [whose] Tenents [sic], if well understood, were all true, at least very tolerable" (64).

In order to complicate these historiographic remembrances of Hutchinson's early "Republican Motherhood" (Kerber 11) and to liberate discursive portrayals of the Colonial woman as a cultural novelty, it is necessary to understand how Hutchinson deflects both political *and* historical expectations on logical grounds. Instead, she can be justified as a producer of intellectual and cultural economies that extend beyond her expected moral or cultural roles. The prevalence in Colonial histories of metaphors that portray both Hutchinson's fecundity and her rhetoricity may conflate nationalist discourse with female ambition, and this conflation in turn may actually impede the rehistoricization of Hutchinson's trial as part of a feminist rhetorical tradition. Instead, a more compelling historical positioning can be achieved for Hutchinson in the contingencies of these remembrances, rather than in the novelty of their first-time occurrence.

By "contingencies," I mean something similar to Elizabeth Galewski's theory of "shifting modalities" in her analysis of Judith Sargent Murray's 1790 publication of "On the Equality of the Sexes." For Galewski, what was unique about Murray's capacity to reason was how she enabled her various audiences "to recapture [through irony] a sense of the discourse's contingency and uncertainty at the time" (89). When I consider Hutchinson's trial as a precursor to discourses of sexual difference, rather than *an enactment* of them, then Colonial periodization becomes less concerned with codified behaviors, such as social or familial stability, and more indicative of fluid and shifting loyalties.

To return to Ratcliffe's framing of this chapter, metonymic listening *would have occurred* for Anne Hutchinson if John Cotton had acknowledged how much his own doctrinal stance toward American Puritanism had changed since his earliest conversations with her, rather than insisted that Hutchinson's stance represented a dangerous minority. It might have occurred if Robert Baillie had refocused his critique on Governor Winthrop's failure to conduct trials in accordance with commonwealth law or to prove and resolve either of the original charges against Hutchinson. (None of the charges was definitively resolved.) Finally, it may have occurred if the *New York Times* had historicized Hutchinson separately from Roger Williams's legacy, as a Colonial woman *of* her time rather than "in advance" of it.

An agential interpretation of irony does not ignore but instead reveals the contextualized concerns and constraints of speakers' sex, class, and rhetorical privilege. It does not favor only specific aspects of presentation to the exclusion of others. Both what the author is able to say *and* what her audiences are able to hear (or see) are reciprocally determined, because neither the "ironist" nor the "interpreter" need be bound to a single subject position or temporal context (Hutcheon 11) where conflicts of memory are concerned. Even the *inference* of irony allows scholars to explain how such exchanges could be retheorized as sophisticated devices for discursive positioning when they are employed—and interpreted—by women across the centuries. Obviously, this describes a more kinetic, dynamic process than merely asking what other rhetorical positionings are possible for Hutchinson in her immediate context, besides those that the governor and deputy governor insisted on during her trial. In fact, it involves a process of remembering that reflects how reading controversies like Hutchinson's causes us to continually assimilate and reassimilate our own fundamental beliefs about gendered history and engendering language.

FINDING PANHISTORICAL AGENCY

If retheorizing and regendering are panhistorical acts—emergent, enacted, and viewable in the contexts in which critical readers engage with their subjects metonymically—then for the Antinomian controversy, agency is both complicated by and distributed across different vantage points. Ultimately, this exchange is a study in historical and critical agency—in allusions to "extra-scriptural moments," whose results were not lost on Hutchinson's audiences, then or now (Ditmore 372, 382).

Near the end of her trial before the Boston Church on 22 March 1638, Hutchinson responds to an argument in which Hugh Peters accuses her of identifying with the "dayngerous," heretical, and unrepentable actions of the "Woman of Elis," who allegedly preached, baptized, and lectured in Lincolnshire, Holland, and other parts of England. Hutchinson replies, "I sayd of the Woman of Elis but what I herd, for I knew her not nor never sawe her" (Hall 379–80). In the full exchange, Peters takes issue with Hutchinson's spoken testimony, implying that she is being implicated for her critique of "what was spoken," not of "what was written." This is significant for two reasons. First, John Cotton's overarching condemnation of Hutchinson throughout her trial was based on the ministers' perception that she had been ideologically motivated to imitate canonical text, and in that act she had abused the privilege of speaking, even when the speaking was nonagential ("I could only speak what had already been conveyed to me"). Second, since the ministers assumed Hutchinson's theological agency in speaking (and therefore in abusing that privilege), the realization of Hutchinson's discourse as theologically nonagential is a critically distant one operating apart from the assumption that Hutchinson is an actor in her own trial. This distinction between agential and nonagential speaking is important, given Marilyn Westerkamp's reminder of how unremarkable the notion of lay leadership was among the New England Puritans, and thus how unproblematic Hutchinson's actual lecturing had been prior to the ministers' suspicions that she used her lectures to usurp their authority in private contexts ("Anne Hutchinson" 487).

The resulting compatibility or incompatibility of author and audience expectations—as they are witnessed across various historical and circumstantial narratives—enables a fourth context for reading irony, which I ultimately call "panhistorical agency" and from which historiographers can work. The fourth context occurs at the realization of multilayered expectations of author(s) and audience(s) in what is often historically treated as a singular, temporal exchange, and in realizing that both historical and circumstantial narratives must be accommodated. I map these expectations and narratives onto the whole discourse represented by the controversy as working across agential interactions. The visualization in figure 2.1 shows three ironies: one that is perceived to have occurred in the temporal space of Hutchinson's trials by any audience, immediate or distant; one that is perceived to have occurred at the intersection of historical and cultural assumptions applied *retrospectively* to the controversy by more distant audiences, then and now; and one that is realized as a critical agency by which a distant or critical audience understands how the coexistence of the first two ironies can complicate stark analytic divisions between textual and contextual understandings of discourse.

Between Discourse and Metadiscourse

Two factors make this complication possible. First, both the physical and metaphysical (or factual and reflective) dimensions of language must be accommodated by the analysis in the first two ironies, promoting irony as a *system that signifies* according to broader discursive needs, rather than a mere *system of signifiers*. If ironic discourse has epistemic and communicative value beyond the simple incongruity or disruption of

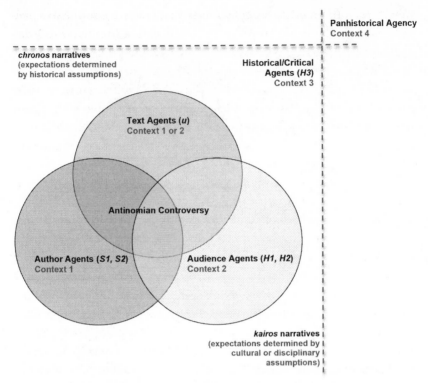

Figure 2.1. Panhistorical agency model for irony, depicting how agency is complicated by and distributed across vantage points in the rereading of feminist colonial histories.

felicity conditions for a single audience, it is because of a host of factors other than how accurately it represents truth values (Rorty, *Contingency* 76, 82). In lieu of analyzing text to arrive at a set of universal aspects that irony comprises, it seems more productive to consider irony's contextualized features and account for the various ways in which those features are conveyed, noted, interpreted, or used.

The second factor making this panhistorical reading possible is an understanding that irony analysis identifies but does not guarantee how irony was or will be read. It does identify the discursive characteristics that become visible when critical readers position themselves as interpreters of and participants in ongoing histories of discourse according to their disciplines. In the same way that critical readers devise a more emergent set of interpretive constructs for understanding irony's impact in Hutchinson's discourse, Hutchinson's irony becomes apparent in, but is not limited to, the interactions that critical readers can note between linguistic and extralinguistic constructs, what I refer to elsewhere as "language politics" (Graban, "Toward" 32). It reflects the simultaneously disruptive and representative nature of language, and the reciprocal nature of historical work, by posing alternatives to the various rhetorics applied to Hutchinson's trial discourse during the Antinomian controversy. These rhetorics have historically resulted from our viewing Colonial women's civic and ecclesiastic duties as functioning separately or as being at odds in their discourse, and they historically have functioned as separate layers, rather than as a multidimensional screen.

In Multilateral Views

In a panhistorical understanding of irony as critical agency, I make fewer stark distinctions between the dialectical subject and object and define irony as *a discourse that invites multiple uses, actual and perceived, depending on how users and recipients see a host of factors coalescing to make the irony event.* In arguing for a critical paradigm for irony that functions separately from humor, I face the same challenge as Amy Lang: arguing for more concrete differences without simplifying or reducing the heuristic potential of useful abstractions (*Syntax* 16). As well, we take different approaches to posing solutions to recognizing in irony critical agency. Building on Kierkegaard's situational irony, Lang considers how the trope can be incarnated in order to provoke interpretation (37), whereas I consider how the discourse can be reconceived to promote paradigmatic disruption. Both *chronos* and *kairos* dimensions of time must be at work in the processing and interpretation of irony. Just as Schilb notes the enduring value of a rhetorical refusal, even when *chronos* time has changed the context in which it is so recognized (*Rhetorical* 114, 139), I note the ironic qualities of Colonial religious discourse that invite vital questioning in what Giora might call an unfamiliar context (echoing her "unfamiliar ironies"), or a context in which meaning is constructed as a result of the expectations that have formed over historical time and within critical space. This is the best and most that language can do for historiographers of feminist discourse.

The model I develop in figure 2.1 is intended to move our studies of Colonial discourse from a unilateral view of history to a multilateral one, by deconstructing various problems of interpretation and their replacements. Hutchinson's responses have historically been valued as lore, largely because of her talent for "insinuat[ing] her selfe into the hearts" of the people of Boston in private and public gatherings (Winthrop, "Short"

308), even though Hutchinson argued for these gatherings as a fulfillment of her own civic duty.[15] The year that Hutchinson died in America
marked another year of circulation for mock petitions and pamphlets in
England, most notably the 1643 *Mid-wives Just Petition* and *The Petition
of Wives and Matrons, for the Cessation of these Civill Wars* (Raymond
304). This is significant to the episteme in which Hutchinson is often
read, because these petitions have served to contextualize Colonial female agency in any number of ways—as a subversion of a monarchical
government (Raymond 304) and as an attainment of authentic religious
experience or political aptitude.

These pamphlets illustrate that American Antinomianism was a problem not simply of authority, but of language in a new nation and church.
There had been a vocabulary for gender disempowerment in "the language of the New Israel" that Antinomian historians employed, but there
was not an equivalent vocabulary for historicizing civic disputes or disputes among class or status (A. Lang, *Syntax* 54; Royster and Kirsch 51).
Hutchinson need not be positioned as a more active agent in historical
rereadings of her own trial, let alone a Puritanical divisive agent. Instead,
I recommend alternatives for studying her whole discourse situation more
fundamentally apart from feminine *dissoi logoi*, and I recommend alternative identifications for Hutchinson and other Colonial women apart
from the various metaphors of prophecy, maternity, and fecundity that
have circulated to help us read them.[16]

Apart from Cause

Takis Poulakos's "strategic historiographer" is one who notices the movements in signification as politically derived by herself and her motives
("Human" 65), not by the motives of her subjects. Framing Hutchinson's
ironic discourse as a series of denials or rhetorical refusals seems insufficient for reading Colonial histories, just as it is insufficient for reexamining Renaissance texts, because it places compulsory expectations on
intentionality and participation that Askew's and Hutchinson's responses
do not always warrant. Rather than look intently at meaning and impact
for the various critical audiences of a rhetorical refusal and how they migrate (Schilb, *Rhetorical* 118), I look intently at the ways in which feminist
historical methods get politicized—embedded or dislodged in the dichotomous thinking that these refusals reveal. Hutchinson's repositioning
involves destabilizing certain Colonial tropes: those that identify Hutchinson and her audiences as principal causes in their own historicization,

rather than as critical agents through whom, and by whom, various other historical narratives can be realized.

Unfortunately, causal tropes abound. Given her training in apologetics, Hutchinson's brother-in-law, John Wheelwright, attributes to her a "remarkable force of character, intellectual power, and acquirements" (Wheelwright 7), which ultimately were linked to the Antinomian agenda of questioning ministerial doctrine (Hall 7) even though Hutchinson had not engaged in the political protesting of that party (Hall 10). John Winthrop's 1644 *Short Story* narrates Hutchinson as an impostor who "insinuated her selfe" into the hearts of those who attended her parlor talks, being drawn to her "godlinesse and spirituall gifts as they looked at her as a Prophetesse, raised up of God for some great worke now at hand" ("Short Story" 308). Thomas Welde's preface to the second edition of *Short Story* lends Winthrop's narrative an "order and sense" by which to portray Hutchinson and the New England Antinomians as the "new Israel," denying them a narrative identity as spiritual pilgrims and constructing them instead as "harbingers of Satan's downfall" (Hall 201; A. Lang, *Prophetic* 55). In fact, by positing Hutchinson as Eve, Hutchinson and Mary Dyer as "monsters,"[17] the American Puritans as *inevitable* heretics, and the orthodox ministers as ultimately unsuccessful in their attempts to subjugate heresy, Welde's religious history constructs a series of linguistic agents that lack any means of identification beyond the prophetic (A. Lang, *Prophetic* 57).

Not all narratives of women's rhetorical and political participation need be divorced from narratives of how they overcame social censure. If, however, in various iterations of Hutchinson's prophetic identity, historians succeed only in affirming the ways in which she surpassed their ecclesiastic expectations for women, then the interpretive capacity of all the agents in figure 2.1 remains bound by narratives that are based in models of action and inaction. Or at the very least, the capacity could no longer be distributed or enacted across the different vantage points in figure 2.1, because this analysis of conversations, interrogations, and deferrals would reflect an overactivity, a "hyperhistoriography" that relies on our believing either that Hutchinson had no control over the outcome or that her responses were bound by the temporal and compositional limitations of her episteme (Yarbrough 108). At its fundamental level, panhistorical discourse invites some form of ambiguity that will always occur for some audiences and some purposes—some agents will always be denied some thing in the communication, though it is not necessarily the case that the agents who are *perceived* as being denied are also the agents *perceiving* the denial, just as it is not the case that those perceiving and those perceived reside in the same temporal or historical space. In Hutchinson's controversy, these "denials" enabled me to trace the way that Antinomian histories have precluded other individual and feminist accounts. These denials are agentive inasmuch as they break or shift frames, but they are not the same as tactical refusals.

Ultimately, I do not argue that Hutchinson's only and immediate response is to embody the very actions she was not supposed to embody. That is not what I see as the "irony" in her situation. Rather, I argue that she hobbles the so-called "private" nature of her individual interrogations enough to call into question the public-private dichotomy as a historicizing function at all. That calling into question—or hobbling, as the case may be—can be justified as a divisive Antinomian or anticlerical move, although my desire is to read her performances and their histories apart from this divisiveness. I develop my own approach to recovery methodologies in the next two chapters, giving special attention to how ironic discourse enables new historical attitudes toward *archive* as an epistemology by dislodging the securities of our historical methods. The case studies throughout this book all examine the same dilemma: How can their feminist rhetorical subjects reflect those inevitable struggles that occurred in their ironic contexts, rather than become historicized as the catalyst or cause for struggles yet to occur? While this may seem to deprive Hutchinson of a certain rhetorical agency that others have assigned, it aligns Hutchinson, her audiences, and her critical readers with a greater agency that challenges not only her historical traceability as a Colonial female but also historians' traceabilities in turn.

3. ON LOCATION AND MEMORY: Challenging *Ethos*

> Irony is always (whatever else it might be) a modality of percep-
> tion—or, better, of attribution—of both meaning and evaluative
> attitude.   —Linda Hutcheon, *Irony's Edge*

> Modern memory is, above all, archival. It relies entirely on the
> materiality of the trace, the immediacy of the recording, the
> visibility of the image.
>   —Pierre Nora, "Between Memory and History"

> We do not appeal to force, but to public conscience.
>   —Helen M. Gougar, "Mrs. Helen M. Gougar
>   and Robert Schilling Meet in Debate"

If anything is to be learned from an ironic reading of Anne Hutchinson's controversy, it is that language can be inhabited as a memorial site and circulated as a historical artifact, but its inhabiting and circulating are subject to severe conflicts of memory. When we overprivilege the material and archival locations of feminist texts, historians limit the possibili-ties for whether and where women's performances can be observed and block essential exclusions and amendments from view. Nevertheless, the *historical locations* of ironic discourse remain important because they raise our consciousness of how to read language in the interstices—how to read language for the multiple agents and expectations that occur when revisiting the same textual event in multiple ways across time and critical space. The language that historians trust is often framed by material and intellectual circumstances that in turn reveal how "separate oratorical, epistolary, and bureaucratic rhetorics" can work in tandem and do often work in tension (S. Miller 105). In response, Royster and Kirsch suggest "tacking in" and "tacking out" as dual methodologies for achieving a "criti-cal imagination" of what occurs in the newly emerging landscapes of feminist discourse (75, 122), arguing that no historical context is objective or detached—neither historians' nor their subjects'. Instead, contexts can be understood through relational tensions that not only are prevalent temporally and chronologically but also recur opportunistically.

An editorial appearing in the *Lafayette (Indiana) Morning Journal* the morning after Helen M. Gougar's death on 6 June 1907 observes that while Gougar was not always "logical, and not always charitable in judgment, she was always earnest" (qtd. in Kriebel, *Where the Saints* 214). The writer elucidates Gougar's strengths as drawing and entertaining an audience before making this singularly incriminating claim: "[Mrs. Gougar] was graduated into the political arena at a time when it was considered profitable to abuse one's opponents. In turn Mrs. Gougar arraigned the two old parties in scathing language that delighted sympathetic audiences. . . . Mrs. Gougar's temperament was that of the agitator; it was her mission to arouse and awaken" (qtd. in Kriebel, *Where the Saints* 215). While it is possible that Gougar herself constructed and managed this legacy of agitation, it remains historically troubling for its persistence *and* its insistence on positioning Gougar in relation to a moral characterization—something that cannot (perhaps should not) be measured through discourse or discursive uptake. There is a tendency to assume rhetorical advocacy in the kind of self-actualization that these firsthand accounts inspire. Instead, we should reorient our paradigm to accommodate surprising, transformative concepts of *ethos* that are available in feminist activist work (Pittman 46).

My desire with *Women's Irony* has been to read the whole discursive event of women's political irony so as to realize the disruptions, material complexities, and contingencies of the histories in which we place them and all other agents. In chapter 1, I argued that all agents become repositioned as *critical* based on how little or how much they provoke the shift to a different frame, while reexamining Renaissance texts like Askew's *Examinations* through an ironic lens. By assessing irony's outcomes separately from limited felicity and truth conditions, complicating what have been seen as semantically distinct roles (ironist, observer, and victim) (Kaufer, "Irony, Interpretive" 452) and recasting Askew's *Examinations* as an inhabited discourse rather than a mediated text, I demonstrated that her irony disrupts not simply the historical events in which she participated but also the interstices through which her performance has been circulated and understood, including its antecedents and its future applications. In chapter 2, I argued that rereading the Antinomian controversy ironically reflects the simultaneously disruptive and representative nature of language, as well as the reciprocal nature of historical work when it involves rethinking whether women's civic and ecclesiastic duties should function separately in their discourse. Irony's textual features can be theorized as surpassing their own linguistic limitations in Hutchinson's controversy when we realize how one female ironist, her multiple audiences, and her critical readers effectively write themselves into the discourse. In the remaining chapters, I begin dislodging the security of our archival locations, corpora, and methodologies. More specifically, I discuss *historical locatability* as a way of accounting for the frequent and plausible movements between location and memory that occur in historical rereadings of archived events, and I argue for *irony* as a way of moving archival locations toward *locatability*, by illuminating the importance of theorizing in the interstices of the whole discourse.

In Renaissance rhetoric and Colonial discourse, locatability brings into deeper relief many and significant metadiscourses, including the ways that Askew and Hutchinson speak back to limited historicizations of their church, their words, and their sex. In suffrage discourse, locatability provides a more associative model for shifting agentive paradigms of location, place, and memory beyond limit situations. (Re)writing a feminist theory of rhetoric is never without its problems of "tokenism" or its risks of essentializing women's texts within the same traditions that have delimited them. While in those earlier rereadings I challenged the various topoi with which irony had been historically associated, in the examination of Helen M. Gougar's archive that follows I challenge Gougar's archival *ethos* by challenging our own, in order to move beyond the hobbling tropes that historians may associate with Gougar's work (Kriebel, *Where the Saints*; "Helen Gougar"). In many ways, studying nineteenth-century suffragists involves studying them within an eighteenth-century feminist rhetorical dilemma, valuating suffragists' performances without relying on either the separation or the fusion of two virtues—intellect and morality—which are articulated in earlier rhetorical histories as disparate. So as not to reinscribe that separation or the "cultural supremacy" underlying it (Biesecker, "Coming" 157), I recognize that *irony* in Gougar's texts must involve more than the simple presumption that she *employs ironic responses* to overturn a system in which she still participates. I invite historians to understand the critical questioning of irony as a practice that involves *both* focusing on how our accession of a discourse outside the constraints of location or memory makes a difference in the questions we ask of it *and* realizing the range of questions that we are enabled to ask, not just for archival work but also for other areas of feminist theorizing. When read *through* history and not merely *in* history, these ironic performances provide historians of rhetoric with alternative ways of (re) defining feminist projects and using archives in that (re)definition.

My goal is to do this without necessarily reifying intellectual categories or historical figures in such as way as to "award them quasi-metaphysical status"—a phrase I carry with me from Sharon Crowley's cautionary tale of the unintended consequences of doing historical research in the 1988 "Octalog" (Octalog 7). At the time, Crowley argued that the shaping of historical phenomena should rely on intertextual proof—such as historical narratives and whole archives—and on their usability and contributions for more than just making scholarly arguments (8). Since then, her claims have been echoed by Jean Carr, Stephen Carr, and Lucille Shultz in *Archives of Instruction*, and they resonate throughout the second and third "Octalogs" in regard to feminist historical work. Ultimately, they point to the ways in which archival remembering through figures, locations, or texts can contribute to the political agency of those being remembered. But most significantly for *Women's Irony*, Crowley's claims explain the factors guiding historiographers' inclusionary and exclusionary impulses when they construct their histories only figure by figure or text by text.

These impulses are as important as the narratives themselves. In the specific case of Helen M. Gougar's suffrage discourse, I privilege discussions of *actual and probable attitudes toward irony* over classifications of *how the irony works in its various strategies and forms.* As a long-term practice, this has encouraged me to seek out archives, first, for their potential to shift episteme and redirect the ways that historians structure their knowledge, and second, for their potential to contribute to material recovery. For example, Karlyn Kohrs Campbell's landmark examination of early suffrage texts briefly positions Gougar, alongside Clara Bewick Colby, Laura Clay, Abigail Scott Duniway, and Jane Gray Swisshelm as "sisters"—relative unknowns primarily because "their work was regional" (*Women* 8) or had its roots in "frontier" states such as Indiana, Kansas, and Nebraska (Lomicky 103).[1] Campbell's statement offers Gougar an important archival positioning, but this positioning may direct historians' attention away from the best places to observe her performances or the best questions to ask of her work. Rather than focus on who has done the action, who has received the action, or where certain actions have been performed, we might examine *who* or *what else* complicates the acts of doing and receiving, making archival texts more of a site for the transmission of shared pasts. A truly revisionist and heterogeneous history of women's rhetorical practices will challenge the underlying logic of canon formation and the uses to which it has been put (Biesecker, "Coming" 157), rather than uphold a logic of individual identification "that monumentalizes some acts and trivializes others" (159).

UNFLATTENING HISTORICAL RELATIONSHIPS

At a February 1880 meeting of the Indiana Woman Suffrage Society in Indianapolis, Helen M. Gougar delivered the first of many lectures she would write over a fourteen-year period calling for explicit revisions to state legislation regarding women's right to own property, earn a taxable income, and hold public office ("Law and the Ladies").[2] The meeting was held in the Plymouth Congregational Church building on Circle Park and drew the most attendants of any of the society's meetings to date, among them homemakers, suffrage and temperance workers, school administrators, and social philanthropists ("Law and the Ladies"). Gougar's speech was written up as alternatively brilliant and agitative, though in my view, her topoi on this occasion were not altogether unique. She argued that according to the US Constitution—which at that time specified neither "male" nor "female" in its proviso for citizenship—Indianan women were now counted as taxable, censurable, and punishable representatives of the state, yet in current enactments of state law, they were still disenfranchised "as the slaves were a few years since; counted but not voted. . . . A verification," she said, "of the Mohammedan law 'that women, mules, dogs, and other animals shall not enter the mosque.'"[3] However, even if it was not unique, Gougar's argumentative strategy was ironic in how it challenged Indiana's identification as a swing state, its ability to raise gold-standard politicians, and its willingness to resist postbellum efforts toward southernization; it also challenged archival assumptions about the styles and genres in which Gougar's performances took hold.

This ironic realization is agential—for Gougar, for her audience at Plymouth Church, and for others accessing her work—because it invites a dialectical examination of women's historical *ethos* through the archive. Many of Gougar's lecture or speeches were evidenced in public opinion or contextualized in *endoxa*, rather than noteworthy in their argumentative strategies. For example, in her 7 March 1884 address before the US Senate Committee on Woman Suffrage in New York, Gougar mentions the large number of men from "asylums, penitentiaries, jails and

poor-houses" being released "upon our shores, and within a few months
. . . are entrusted with the ballot" and seated in legislative positions (qtd.
in Stanton et al. 4: 37). From the 1884 congressional hearing transcript,
we read:

> Political parties would have us believe that tariff is the great question
> of the hour. It is an insult to the intelligence of the present to say that
> when one-half of the citizens of this republic are denied a direct voice
> in making the laws under which they shall live, that the tariff, the civil
> rights of the negro, or any other question which can be brought up,
> is equal to the one of giving political freedom to women. . . . While I
> would not have you take this right from those men whom we invite
> to our shores, I do ask you, in the face of this immense foreign immi-
> gration, to enfranchise the tax-paying, intelligent, moral, native-born
> women of America.

Gougar ended her speech by presenting a petition signed by five thousand reputable schoolteachers asking for the woman's ballot. The commonality of her performances is what I find most useful to study; the
lingering emphasis on "agitation" as a rhetorical stratagem in as complex
and common a discourse situation as Gougar's is insufficient because it
is deeply entrenched in traditions, acts of memory, and locations that
privilege a *reactive* view of recovery—a notion of recovery based on assumptions about who should be *authorized* versus merely *enabled* to
speak and based on what is heard within a limited set of speech acts or
communicative outcomes.

Over her entire career, Gougar performed in multiple genres, including lectures and speeches, columns and articles, books and monographs,
legal arguments and lawsuits, and business correspondence, most of which
Robert Kriebel notes in his comprehensive biography. Although Gougar
was delivering noteworthy essays as early as 1871 at Young Men's Christian
Association (YMCA) literary reunions, Kriebel points to the First Annual
Conference of the Social Sciences Association of Indiana, held on 15 October 1879, as Gougar's earliest entree into public activism (*Where the Saints*
54). There Gougar delivered a speech that earned her renown for being an
"elegant, forceful, and sprightly" speaker and put her in great demand as a
public speaker for the next twenty years (*Where the Saints* 54).[4]

Because of her high visibility as a social reformer in Indiana, Gougar
carried a reputation for being a "born politician," delivering a characteristic two hundred lectures per year ("Biography"; Colby, "Helen"), writing

regularly to Chicago's *Inter Ocean* about the domestic conditions of the Irish working class in Europe, addressing the US Senate, and speaking before the state legislatures of New York, Wisconsin, Indiana, Kansas, and Iowa on behalf of the woman's vote ("Biography" 637; Stanton et al. 3: 702). Additionally, the *Woman's Standard* featured twenty-three prominent articles or mentions of her activity in a ten-year period, and because of her foundational work with the Equal Rights Association (ERA) and Woman's Christian Temperance Union (WCTU), Gougar appeared as a regular subject in *Progress, A True Republic, Daughters of America,* and *Arena.* She wrote regularly in her "Bric-a-Brac" column for the *Lafayette Daily Courier* and also for the *Voice,* the *Lever,* and the *Arena,* as well as for her own temperance paper, *Our Herald,* before selling its assets to Elizabeth Boynton Harbert in 1895.[5]

As both a writer and a publisher, Gougar's rhetorical challenges were no different from those of other Suffrage or Temperance leaders: catering to hybrid audiences, reaching disparate crowds (potential converts to suffrage as well as committed suffragists), and appealing to both public and private intellectuals. As well, her performances were no less varied, given that her own allegiances and alliances were multiple and shifting. By 1897, Gougar had become a "Bryan Democrat" (Kriebel, "Suffragist" D1), having broken with Prohibitionists, Republicans, and Populists. By the time of the 1900 presidential election, Gougar had withdrawn from the National Prohibition Party to campaign on behalf of Democrat William Jennings Bryan, recasting herself as a staunch critic of the kind of "polite" midwestern activism that led to inconsistent movement on women's suffrage or privileged deference to "custom over law" (Gougar, *Constitutional* 4).

Her political allegiances after 1900 remained complex, making it difficult to discern whether she was informed by post-Populist or post-Democratic sensibilities or was exercising an early brand of social progressivism.[6] Kriebel notes that Gougar changed her political affiliations several times—most notably, that she identified as Republican through the 1884 election (Kriebel, *Where the Saints* 114), allied with the National Prohibitionist and Populist Parties from the 1888 to 1896 election (Kriebel, *Where the Saints* 142), began the 1896 year pro-Bryan and pro-bimetallism, and finally became "a guest of the Democrats" through the 1900 election (Kriebel, *Where the Saints* 179, 163). Both Kriebel and Jerry historicize Gougar's movement as "party hopping" (Jerry 269), although Gougar's path from the Prohibitionist to the Democratic Party is also archivally reflected in her shifting concerns from labor to economics.[7] Working primarily from Kriebel's book and other documents housed at the Tippecanoe County Historical Association (TCHA), Jerry suggests that Gougar aligned more closely with the National Woman Suffrage Association (NWSA) than with any other organization (268). However, a panhistorical view of Gougar's involvements call most of these alignments into question, given Gougar's frequent movement among major parties and organizations while she was president of the Indiana chapter of the NWSA, and especially in light of correspondence between Susan B. Anthony and May Wright Sewell, in which Anthony insinuates that Gougar was a frequent barrier to the NWSA's plans by fusing the mission of the Indiana movement too much with the agenda of the Temperance leagues (Gordon 5: 231).[8]

Like Kriebel, Jerry considers Gougar's work unfinished mainly because of a "fanatic zealot" character that "alienated those with whom she was attempting to serve. Her failure to accomplish more as a reformer was probably caused as much by the internal conflicts she engendered in the movements as by any difficulties she had with liquor traffickers or recalcitrant legislators" (Jerry 277). Jerry goes so far as to invoke Edwin Black's "second persona" to describe Gougar's rhetorical philosophy as "not particularly interested in adapting to her audiences, especially those who opposed her" (Jerry 270), a claim that I find undertheorized for how it limits historians' understandings of "audience" and "adaptation" on the American Suffrage scene. Both Kriebel's imagery and Jerry's assessment of Gougar's efforts as zealotry require a more critical examination. Gougar's locatability reflects an expected alignment with the NWSA after its split with the ERA and a subsequent alignment with diverse organizations and causes while working for suffrage. Yet her alignments were more complex and should be studied in multiple layers.

At times Gougar's message seems overtly simple: rather than continue to amend existing laws, she often admonished citizens to better apply and "re-understand existing laws" (Gougar, *Constitutional* 5). She argued more often from the standpoint of justice than from expedience (Campbell, *Man* 8) and otherwise avoided the rhetorical construction of "separate spheres" that grew from Alexis de Tocqueville's *Democracy in America*. Perhaps Gougar felt that the "separate spheres" argument offered too limiting a metaphor to conform with what Linda Kerber calls "the new [postrevolutionary] politics that valued autonomy and individualism" (Kerber 20).

Perhaps, however, her texts are simply characteristic of the American Suffrage movement: diverse, complex, and ideologically conflicted. Her earliest published column appeared under the title "Bric-a-Brac: Literature, Sciences, Art and Topics of the Day" in the *Lafayette Daily Courier* on 2 November 1878. "Bric-a-Brac" was aimed at the domestic or casual reader, and it hosted most of Gougar's explicitly moral and polemical arguments, including her condemnation of the miscreant use of tax money to support saloons and "rum traffic" (25 January 1879) and her complaint that the American suffragist did not have license to neglect her personal appearance or housekeeping (11 October 1879). The column ended in September 1880 without clear explanation (Kriebel, *Where the Saints* 67), but by December 1888, the *Lafayette Morning Journal* reported that Gougar was serving in some capacity as an "associate editor" at another Prohibition publication, the *Chicago Lever* (Kriebel, *Where the Saints* 119). She also wrote frequently on behalf of the WCTU (Goldberg 95) and the Indiana State Suffrage Association, and a number of her essays were published in edited literary collections and periodicals on social reform. Her lectures, letters, and legislation were often reprinted in the *Daily Inter Ocean*. Later, Gougar wrote weekly columns for the *Lafayette Evening Call* under the title "Weekly Chat with the Call Readers" from November to December 1903, and again briefly in February 1904, until the paper renamed itself the *Weekly Call* and eventually dropped the columns.

Kriebel notes a later period of "disillusionment" for Gougar, after Bryan lost the 1900 presidential election and a series of editorials brought Gougar some criticism by the *Lafayette Morning Journal*, severing her long-standing relationships with some of the newspapers for which she had written in the past. Writing of her later columns in the *Evening Call*, Kriebel described the prose as "tired" and said, "Some of the columns lacked unity; it was uninspired 'hack work' which bore little reflection of the mind and talent behind it" ("Writings" D6).[9] I do not disagree that Gougar's *Call* articles read differently than her earlier work or that Gougar was preoccupied with compiling an international history of women's suffrage at the time she wrote them.[10] However, I do think that Kriebel's history oversimplifies Gougar's motives by assuming a narrowly defined career path—one that was unified, coherent, and conforming to a kind of rhetorical mainstream that feminist scholarship continues to disrupt. In fact, Gougar's activist career confounds many genres and classifications, then and now.

Methodologically, then, this chapter challenges those relationships alleging that Gougar necessarily spoke and wrote in agitated style or under cover of either obscurity or popularity—not because I contend that they are historically wrong, but because they are too historically *flat*. Paradigmatically, this chapter considers other uses for suffrage archives in rhetorical studies besides the construction of new, or the dissolution of old, narratives. Instead, it considers how ironic delivery can transform the historical discursive space with its "complex interplay among a speaker, an audience, and a plethora of social and ideological factors" (Buchanan, *Regendering* 3). Ironic delivery can act as one of several filters for classifying the dialectical possibilities in suffrage archives, as a result of more complex interactions between rhetors, audiences, and historians—then and now. Ultimately, Gougar's full range of ironic performances and our full range of interpretations and uses are best understood through a realization of how the irony reconstructs—rather than merely provokes or responds to—each persuasive occasion and what historical relationships it inspires beyond the archival (re)inscription of suffrage ideals. Gougar's *whole ironic discourse* helps create the knowledge conditions for multiple persuasive occasions; these occasions in turn result in a typology of attitudes based on how her political discourse has been delivered, interpreted, and critically disseminated through interstitial witnessing—not based on how she has allegedly negotiated her own subject position as a female rhetorician.

From Archival Inscription to Discursive Attitude

My argument for including Gougar in feminist theorizing on the basis of her diverse rhetorical activity echoes more fundamental claims made by E. Claire Jerry and Jennifer Adams that, while there is compelling enough evidence to include her, Gougar's inclusion relies as much on complex understandings of our processes of chronicling as it does on the availability and visibility of her work. Consequently, I do not just argue anew for Gougar's archival reinscription, but I also examine the mechanisms by which such inclusions or exclusions can signal the reconstruction of archival attitudes. In figure 3.1, I illustrate an assemblage model of the various *attitudes toward preservation, representation and recovery of suffrage discourse* that occur within an "archive," broadly or narrowly defined. Because these attitudes occur as a series of unstable relationships among the various outcomes that archival work often comprises,

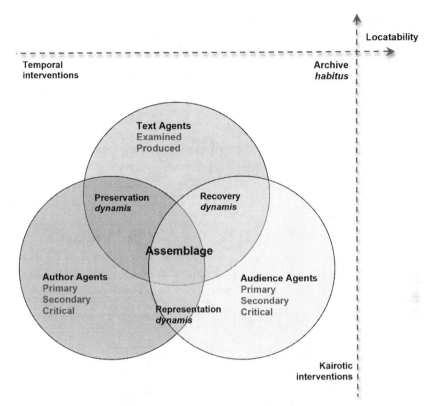

Figure 3.1. Assemblage of motives for feminist archival work, depicting frequent and plausible movements between archival agents, temporal and spatial properties that characterize women in discursive spaces, and agential properties of feminist irony, when readers reflect on their practices of historical remembering.

the whole assemblage signifies totality and absence and tries to account for disciplinary implications of studying suffrage texts as locatable and not just located.

In such a model, preservation, recovery, and representation are not necessarily individual actions, but potential relationships among agents that raise questions and inspire methods for research, whether those agents are archivists, archival subjects, archival researchers, or historiographers of archives. When I apply it to Gougar's suffrage discourse, it reveals a typology useful for defining the *archive* according to the *dynameis*—the historical and affective faculties, or leanings—that various agents share and exchange. In figure 3.1, temporal interventions represent the links among past, present, and future interests of archival subjects, archivists, and researchers, while spatial interventions represent the links among the placements or locations of archivists, researchers, and documents (or texts). The whole interaction illustrates the fact that examined ironic discourse provides a critical motivation or lens through which historians can approach archives and archiving as *habitus*—that is, through which they can see that archival documents are read and valuated across time and space, read ahead, anticipated, recirculated, and received, all in some way residual of one another. The whole interaction illustrates the reciprocal process of forgetting and remembering that goes into the construction of any archive.

Figure 3.2. Early carte-de-visite of a young Helen Mar Jackson, undated but circa 1860, the year she arrived in Lafayette, Indiana, to teach in the newly reopened free schools. By 1863, Jackson had been appointed principal at the Jenks School on Eleventh and Elizabeth Streets. The photograph was taken by S. D. Phillips and A. N. Pierce of Lafayette. From the Helen M. Gougar Collection, Tippecanoe County Historical Association, Lafayette, Indiana; item 84.94.1

Figure 3.3. Card-mounted photograph of Helen M. and John D. Gougar in their study at Castle Cottage, at 914 Columbia Street in Lafayette, Indiana. Undated, though taken after 1897, when the cottage was completed. Helen regularly read to John, who suffered from chronic eye inflammation and ocular disease (Kriebel, Where the Saints 20, 39). From the Helen M. Gougar Collection, Tippecanoe County Historical Association, Lafayette, Indiana, item 84.241.

As it turns out, Lafayette, Indiana, was an appropriate backdrop for both remembering and forgetting Gougar's career in writing, activism, and law at the turn of the century. It was a hub for intellectual conversation and social reform until Prohibition, and it remained a center for experimental education in the lower grades before World War I. When she was still Helen Mar Jackson, Gougar moved to Lafayette from Hillsdale, Michigan, in 1860, presumably to earn a living wage in the city's newly reopened free schools and help finance the college education of her younger sisters. Within her first year of employment, she earned accolades for her teaching, and within three years, she was appointed principal of the Jenks Public School ("Biography"). By December 1863, she had met and married a young lawyer by the name of John Gougar, whom she frequently assisted and represented during his periods of illness over the course of their marriage.

Moreover, Lafayette has been something of a smoke screen for historians of midwestern suffrage because of its presumed political swings

(Gray) and because it was the legislative center of the Tippecanoe County seat. Through her own activism for Prohibition and social reform, Gougar became an expert in Constitutional law and eventually authored legislation for municipal suffrage in several states, including Kansas, Utah, and Indiana. She authored resolutions at four women's congresses between 1888 and 1896 and participated in five (recorded) lawsuits during her peak years. Most significantly, on 10 January 1895, Gougar was sworn in as the first female member of the Tippecanoe County bar, in order to make an unprecedented test case against the county election board for denying her a voting ballot during the 1894 general elections ("Mrs. Gougar's Test Vote," qtd. in Kriebel, *Where the Saints* 151).

The resulting transcript of *The Constitutional Rights of the Women of Indiana* earned a reputation for rhetorical and stylistic clarity that revealed Gougar's mastery of the law and thoroughness of argument (Stanton et al. 4: 622). Two years later, on 19 February 1897, Gougar appealed the 1895 verdict to the Indiana Supreme Court and argued sixty-three additional points. This also marked the first time a woman had addressed both the Tippecanoe Superior Court and the Indiana Supreme Court on a single issue.[11] The Democratic *Columbus Press-Post* later memorialized her as "one of the world's most important factors in its better and higher civilization," whose name "belongs with those of Harriet Beecher Stowe and Mary Livermore" ("Helen M. Gougar"). The case still circulates as a cultural artifact within the state of Indiana,[12] which makes incorporating Gougar into the "suffrage conversation" as challenging as determining the parameters of that conversation post hoc, let alone measuring their impact.

Recognizing Gougar's performances according to the various attitudes in figure 3.1 makes it clear that she could be categorized as either "confusing" the efforts of suffrage with temperance or focusing too much on Prohibition and moral causes at the expense of alliance building, and it also helps explain why she was often introduced primarily as someone whose "chief work is in the temperance cause" and whose belief was that "impartial suffrage would result in repressing the evils of the liquor traffic" ("War on the Wabash"). Gougar's earliest admission of public activism appeared in the context of securing suffrage for immigrant wives and other married women whose property rights or livelihood were controlled by an alcoholic spouse. But her earliest activities seem to have been as consistently motivated by economic accountability ("Mrs. Gougar Lectures"; "Bloody Record"), expansion of the middle class, and ensurance of welfare (Gougar, "Plea") as they were by moralistic causes.

Figure 3.4. Card-mounted photograph of Helen M. Gougar standing in black lecture attire with taffeta overlining and rose at the bodice. Albumen print by Phillips and Company of Lafayette, Indiana, in 1905, two years before Gougar's sudden heart attack. From the Helen M. Gougar Collection, Tippecanoe County Historical Association, Lafayette, Indiana, item 85.94.8.

Whether or not she was motivated by Prohibition, Gougar was more consistently motivated by the economic and social inefficacy of keeping saloons.[13] She frequently argued that alcohol was among the principal causes of poverty in working-class homes (Edwards 98), and her earlier writings for the WCTU often declared a crusade against "the three corrupting elements of social and political life—the saloon, the brothel, and [the] gambling den" (qtd. in Goldberg 95). And labor economics was a consistent theme throughout Gougar's varied career, often linked to other causes. During her 1899 YMCA lecture circuit, Gougar promoted municipal ownership and public service systems, and she invested with John in the Joplin, Missouri, ore mines (Kriebel, "Mining" D1). In a chautauqua

Figure 3.5. Front page of the Portland, Oregon, Woman's Tribune *on 29 June 1907, under Clara Bewick Colby's editorship, reporting the recent passing of Helen M. Gougar. The portrait accompanying this obituary was taken circa 1885 (Kriebel,* Where the Saints *21). Colby edited and produced the* Tribune *from 1883 until 1909.* From the Helen M. Gougar Collection, Tippecanoe County Historical Association, Lafayette, Indiana, item 75.17.26a.

talk during August 1904, Gougar argued that the country's $1.7 billion debt from 1903 could have been better spent if it had "diverted into the legitimate avenues of trade in building and furnishing homes, churches, schools, etc." (Kriebel, "Gougar"). To simply say that she went from temperance to suffrage to law presents too flattened a landscape, not only of Gougar and the attitudes that motivate her recovery, but also of the other women and men who frequented multiple causes.

FORMING A TAXONOMY OF RESPONSES AND TYPOLOGY OF ATTITUDES

Instead, Gougar's archive underscores a rich rhetorical career that considered politics to be a socially transformative and pragmatic power, principally realized through persistent individual action. What Kriebel calls Gougar's penchant for morality, and what Jerry calls Gougar's moral doggedness and second persona (Jerry 270), may be better understood as an overarching drive toward labor reform and social progress. Gougar's movement among major parties—and her ultimate decision to reject them—demonstrates this drive, as do her outspoken criticism of the class privileging of the gold standard in 1895–96, her interest in bimetallism as a national currency prior to 1900, and her interest in affecting international laws that governed suffrage and immigration.[14]

What results is a taxonomy of historical responses emerging from several ironic features in Gougar's whole discourse that is neither stable nor absolute (see table 3.1). The processes and practices by which feminist ironic discourse is historically recovered should capture both its actualities and its potentialities, and in Gougar's archive, it is especially worthwhile to illuminate possible reasons for her responses and why they get historicized the way they do.[15] It is also worthwhile to illuminate the potential relationships among female suffragists, the organizations to which they belonged, and the genres through which they performed in order to understand the myriad factors bearing on the success of their work.

This taxonomy has both historical and metahistorical functions. It reflects a range of analytic possibilities for Gougar's hundreds of speeches and writings in different forums between 1878 and 1907, given that those dates are as broad as her archive currently extends (Graban, "Emergent" 213; Graban, "Toward" 37). It relies on archival genres as invitations to analyze the ways in which suffragists negotiated discursive attitudes through performances that seem inconsistent with each other. It also illuminates a set of discursive attitudes based on how a historian might understand irony's role in the delivery, interpretation, and critical dissemination of Gougar's known and potential performances that are not date-range specific. These *attitudes* represent potential relationships among archival agents that raise questions and inspire new methods for research. Both the taxonomy and the typology are flexible; when more of Gougar's archive surfaces, the contents and range of each category change, and some categories merge or expand. At the time of this writing, I have identified five *strategic responses* to account for the frequent tensions and patterned relationships among the multiple agents implied in Gougar's archive: (1) provoking women of means into action and reprimanding social leaders for their faltering efforts toward suffrage; (2) appealing to social pragmatists by demonstrating the domestic and economic benefits of their political participation or pointing to the perils of class discrimination; (3) appealing to public intellectuals by repositioning midwestern suffrage efforts as politically rather than morally progressive; (4) undermining arguments against suffrage by using condescending regional stereotypes of suffragists in order to overturn them; and (5) criticizing US policy makers by showing the disparaging effects of immigration laws on state suffrage and highlighting the progress of women's suffrage abroad.

Table 3.1. Taxonomy of five strategic responses and resulting typology of three discursive attitudes that historians might notice among archival documents held in the Helen M. Gougar Collection to date. Documentary information appears below as it does in archival records.

Taxonomy	Typology		
	Discursive attitude 1: Reading peer-to-peer	Discursive attitude 2: Confounding suffrage genres	Discursive attitude 3: Unsettling transnational identifications
Strategic response 1: Provoking women of means into action and reprimanding society leaders for their faltering efforts toward suffrage *1871–1901*	"Accepting Criticism," "Bric-a-Brac" column, *Lafayette Daily Courier*, 27 Mar. 1880 "Ass-Toot," "Bric-a-Brac" column, *Lafayette Daily Courier*, 7 Feb. 1880 "Campaign of 1888: Mrs. Helen Gougar Replies to Anna Dickinson," *Lafayette Daily Courier*, 6 Nov. 1888 "Christ and the Liquor Seller," *Arena: A Journal of Religious Reform*, Mar. 1893 "Criticism vs. Gallantry," "Bric-A-Brac" column, *Lafayette Daily Courier*, 6 Dec. 1879 "'I Have All the Rights I Want,' A True Story," n.d. (possibly printed in *Our Herald*) "I Have All the Rights That I Want," "Bric-a-Brac" column, *Lafayette Daily Courier*, 25 Jan. 1879 "Mammie Smith," "Bric-a-Brac" column, *Lafayette Daily Courier*, Dec. 1879 "On Behalf of the National Republican Ticket," *Our Herald*, 15 Nov. 1884 *Our Herald*, inaugural issue, 13 Aug. 1881 "Pimples," YMCA literary reunion lecture, 24 Mar. 1876 "Place for Saloons: Mrs. Helen M. Gougar Suggests the Church Vestibule," *The Daily Inter-Ocean*, 1 Jan. 1894 "Prudence Crandall," *The Daily Inter-Ocean*, 29 Jan. 1887 "A Reply to Ms. Anna Dickinson," *Lafayette Daily Courier*, 6 Nov. 1888 "Shirks," YMCA literary reunion lecture, 15 Dec. 1871 "Thinks Men Will Go to Heaven," *Lafayette Morning Journal*, 29 July 1901 "Woman in the Home and in the State," lectured delivered Apr. 1880 "A Woman's Plea: Mrs. Helen M. Gougar on the Rawson Case," *Inter-Ocean*, 9 July 1888 "Woman Suffrage in New York, *Voice*, 31 May 1894 "A Word to Women," "Bric-a-Brac" column, *Lafayette Daily Courier*, 21 Feb. 1880 Untitled article on women's constitutions ("alligator skin"), "Bric-a-Brac" column, *Lafayette Daily Courier*, 9 Feb. 1879		

Strategic response
2: Appealing
to social
pragmatists by
demonstrating
the domestic
and economic
benefits of
their political
participation or
by pointing to
the perils of class
discrimination

1879–1900

"Bric-a-Brac" column Nov. 1878; reprinted as "Indiana Social Science Association" in *Daily Inter-Ocean*, 9 Nov. 1878

"Christ and the Liquor Seller," *Arena: A Journal of Religious Reform*, Mar. 1893

"Criticism vs. Gallantry," "Bric-a-Brac" column, *Lafayette Daily Courier*, 6 Dec. 1879

"The Girls of a Household," "Bric-a-Brac" column, *Lafayette Daily Courier*, 22 May 1880

"Industrial Training for Women," lecture given for the Tippecanoe County Home-Makers Association, 29 Jan. 1900; reprinted in *Lafayette Evening Call*, 3 Feb. 1900

"Influential Women," *The Daily Inter-Ocean*, 23 Apr. 1881

Introduction to *Women Wealth-Winners; or, How Women Can Earn Money*, 1893

"The Law and the Ladies," *Kendallville Standard* or *Indianapolis Journal*, Feb. 1880

"Making Money for a Family" and "Holding Executive Session," "Bric-a-Brac" column, *Lafayette Daily Courier*, 28 Feb. 1880

Our Herald, inaugural issue, 13 Aug. 1881

"Prudence Crandall," *The Daily Inter-Ocean*, 29 Jan. 1887

"Reply to 'J. H.' of *The Leader*: 'After Suffrage What?,'" "Bric-a-Brac" column, the *Lafayette Daily Courier*, 26 June 1880

"Self-Culture: One of the Duties of Motherhood," *The Daily Inter-Ocean*, 9 Oct. 1880

"Suffrage Her Theme: Mrs. Helen M. Gougar Addresses the Federal Club" and "Reception to Mrs. Gougar: Many Suffragists Assemble in Honor of the Woman's Rights Champion," *The Daily Inter-Ocean*, 17 Jan. 1895

"Temperance and Religion," "Bric-a-Brac" column, *Lafayette Daily Courier*, 10 Apr. 1880

"Where Is the Blame?," "Bric-a-Brac" column, *Lafayette Daily Courier*, 17 Jan. 1880

"Where Rests the Blame?," *The Daily Inter-Ocean*, Mar. 1893

"A Woman's Plea: Mrs. Helen M. Gougar on the Rawson Case," *Inter-Ocean*, 9 July 1888

"Woman Suffrage in New York," *Voice*, 31 May 1894

Untitled article on rejection of separate spheres and moral clarity, "Bric-a-Brac" column, *Lafayette Daily Courier*, 23 Nov. 1879

Table 3.1. (continued*)*

	Typology		
Taxonomy	Discursive attitude 1: Reading peer-to-peer	Discursive attitude 2: Confounding suffrage genres	Discursive attitude 3: Unsettling transnational identifications
Strategic response 3: Appealing to public intellectuals by repositioning midwestern suffrage efforts as politically rather than morally progressive *1877–1903*	"Address by Helen Gougar at the Indiana State Assembly on February 15, 1881" "Campaign of 1888: Mrs. Helen Gougar Replies to Anna Dickinson," *Lafayette Daily Courier,* 6 Nov. 1888 Clarks Hill Speech, delivered at annual meeting of Tippecanoe County Sunday School Union, mid-Aug. 1878 "Congressional Hearings and Reports of 1884," 7 Mar. 1884; reprinted as "Speech of Helen M. Gougar to the Senate Committee on Woman Suffrage, March 7, 1884" in *History of Woman Suffrage* *The Constitutional Rights of the Women of Indiana,* transcript of her four-hour defense on 10 Jan. 1895 "Defends Woman Suffrage: Mrs. Helen M. Gougar Replies to Rev. W. Q. Ryan of Denver," *Journal,* 20 Dec. 1900 "Discuss Drink Evil: Mrs. Helen M. Gougar and Robert Schilling Meet in Debate," *The Daily Inter-Ocean,* 19 Feb. 1896 Editorial, *Lincoln (NE) Journal,* 7 Sept. 1882 Letter from Helen M. Gougar to B. Wilson Smith, *Esquire,* 18 Oct. 1882 "Making Money for a Family" and "Holding Executive Session," "Bric-a-Brac" column, *Lafayette Daily Courier,* 28 Feb. 1880 "My Ideal Man," lecture delivered for the Lafayette Parlor Club c. 1877 "Place for Saloons: Mrs. Helen M. Gougar Suggests the Church Vestibule," *The Daily Inter-Ocean,* 1 Jan. 1894 "Post-Office Muddle: Mrs. Gougar Appealed to by the G.O.P. to Let Go Her Prohibition Grip," *Lafayette Morning Journal,* 3 Jan. 1890 "The Present Outlook for Woman Suffrage," "Bric-a-Brac" column, *Lafayette Daily Courier,* 15 May 1880 "Prudence Crandall," *The Daily Inter-Ocean,* 29 Jan. 1887 "Reply to 'J. H.' of *The Leader:* 'After Suffrage What?,'" "Bric-a-Brac" column in the *Lafayette Daily Courier,* 26 June 1880 "A Significant Scene: Mrs. Helen Gougar at Albany," *The Inter-Ocean,* 26 Apr. 1884 (an account of her address before the General Assembly of New York) "Suffrage Her Theme: Mrs. Helen M. Gougar Addresses the Federal Club," *The Daily Inter-Ocean,* 17 Jan. 1895		

"Taste in Companionship," "Bric-A-Brac" column, *Lafayette Daily Courier*, 3 Jan. 1880

"Thinks Men Will Go to Heaven," *Lafayette Morning Journal*, 29 July 1901

"Unrestricted Suffrage," *Joliet (IL) News*, Nov. 1887

"Weekly Chat with the Call Readers," *Evening Call*, 1 Dec. 1903

"Welcoming Address of Mrs. Helen M. Gougar, Delivered before the Woman's Suffrage Convention," 16 June 1880

"Women before the Law," address given at National Suffrage Convention of 1884

Strategic response
4: Undermining
arguments
against American
Suffrage by
conceding
to regional
stereotypes of
suffragists in
order to overturn
them

1879–1903

"Ass-Toot," "Bric-a-Brac" column, *Lafayette Daily Courier*, 7 Feb. 1880

"Bric-a-Brac" column, *Lafayette Daily Courier*, 12 June 1880

"Defends Woman Suffrage: Mrs. Helen M. Gougar Replies to Rev. W. Q. Ryan of Denver," *Lafayette Morning Journal*, 20 Dec. 1900

"Female Politicians: A Conversation with James G. Blaine," *Lafayette Daily Courier*, 1888

"Female Politicians: Mrs. Helen M. Gougar Exchanges Trenchant Ideas with James G. Blaine," *Lafayette Daily Courier*, 1888

"Girls of a Household," n.d.

"Gougar's Sarcasm," *Indianapolis Journal*, 15 Aug. 1882

"Man's Rights," "Bric-A-Brac" column, *Lafayette Daily Courier*, Dec. 20, 1879

"The Man Who Blows," "Bric-a-Brac" column, *Lafayette Daily Courier*, 22 Nov. 1879

"Mrs. Gougar's Joke," *New Albany (IN) Public Press*, 29 Aug. 1882

"Parnell the Irish Agitator" "Bric-A-Brac" column, *Lafayette Daily Courier*, 31 Jan. 1880

"A Plea for Woman Suffrage," 1894 campaign pamphlet

"Present Outlook," n.d.

"Self-Culture: One of the Duties of Motherhood," *The Daily Inter-Ocean*, 9 Oct. 1880

"Some of the Idiots," *Our Herald*, n.d. (1882 or later)

"Suffrage Her Theme: Mrs. Helen M. Gougar Addresses the Federal Club," *The Daily Inter-Ocean*, 17 Jan. 1895

"The Thick of the Fray: Mrs. Helen M. Gougar Reaches England during the Excitement of the Campaign," *The Daily Inter-Ocean*, 21 July 1886

Table 3.1. (continued*)*

	Typology		
Taxonomy	Discursive attitude 1: Reading peer-to-peer	Discursive attitude 2: Confounding suffrage genres	Discursive attitude 3: Unsettling transnational identifications
	"Weekly Chat with the Call Readers," *Evening Call*, 1 Dec. 1903		
	"Welcoming Address"		
	"Will Reply to Mr. Stead: Mrs. Helen Gougar to State Some Facts about British Pauperism," *The Daily Inter-Ocean*, 8 Dec. 1893		
	"Woman in the Home and in the State," lectured delivered Apr. 1880		
	Untitled article on why/how men vote, "Bric-a-Brac" column, *Lafayette Daily Courier*, 3 May 1879		
Strategic response 5: Criticizing US policy makers by showing the disparaging effects of immigration laws on state suffrage and highlighting the progress of women's suffrage abroad *1881–1907*	"America in the Philippines: A Conversation with Helen M. Gougar," *Arena*, Apr. 1906		
	"Among the Evicted: Helen M. Gougar on the Wretched Scenes She Witnessed at Bodyke," *The Daily Inter-Ocean*, 9 July 1887		
	"The Bill Drawn Up," *The Inter-Ocean*, 14 Apr. 1881		
	"Labor Day in Lafayette," *Lafayette Morning Journal*, 5 Sept. 1899		
	"Last Article Written," *Lafayette Sunday Morning Leader*, 16 June 1907		
	Matthew Peters: A Foreign Immigrant, 1898		
	"Shall Educated Chinamen Be Welcome to Our Shores?," *Arena*, Nov. 1906		
	"The Thick of the Fray: Mrs. Helen M. Gougar Reaches England during the Excitement of the Campaign," *The Daily Inter-Ocean*, 21 July 1886		
	"Wall Street's Bold Threat," unpublished essay, 28 June 1896 or 1898		
	"Weekly Chat with the Call Readers," *Evening Call*, 1 Dec. 1903		
	"Weekly Chat with the Call Readers," *Evening Call*, 24 Feb. 1904		

To be clear, these categories represent possible rhetorical situations that we can identify by looking at Gougar's texts, their social contexts, and her audiences, as well as persuasive occasions that are constructed in and accommodated throughout various phases of recovery. I still do privilege the word *strategic* for classifying these situations, but *strategy* need not apply only to Gougar, nor is it a one-way expression of agency. Instead, I see *strategy* as a broadly productive explanation for how the archive—the *assemblage*—has emerged as a "corrupted . . . repository of human memory" whose processes of selection and interpretation are unstable and reflect complex ways of representing social memory (Blouin 105–06). In much the same way as antebellum styles of delivery gave rise to six contingent topoi in Lindal Buchanan's study of how social context "exerts itself subtly but insistently" (*Regendering* 159), these strategic responses have emerged from Gougar's ironic discourse *as it is recalled, co-constructed, and used.* They do not signify generic or textual features; they merely account for the interpretive capacities and gaps made possible for the historical or critical reader, ultimately revealing a set of discursive attitudes for typological examination of other suffrage archives. In fact, they present new ways of using Gougar's archive.[16]

Table 3.1 organizes these responses and their discursive attitudes according to the kind of historical reflection they make possible—for Gougar's work in particular and for suffrage archives in general—where the reflections occur at various intersections of space, time, expectation, and memory. And yet, in order to move beyond archival (re)inscription, I emphasize three things. First, I call the typologizing that I do "emergent," not to prove anything absolute about Gougar's archive (or about archives in general), but rather to demonstrate that *attending to archives discursively makes it possible to consider their historical and critical value in terms other than origination, preservation, or personification.* In fact, we can consider their purpose or function in terms of other attitudes or potentialities that reflect their locatability. Second, I demonstrate the consciousness-raising potential of what might be construed as Gougar's most "agitative" styles without necessarily describing agitative properties. Finally, I privilege Campbell's "consciousness-raising" as irony's most important outcome for writers and readers, then and now ("'Rhetoric'" 140); at the same time, this raising of consciousness can be further extended toward realizing how we, as critical and historical readers, cope with our own role in historicizing and preserving women's performances. Neither their performances nor our historicizations of them are unified, coherent, or safe from occlusion.

This kind of discursive locatability allows me to reflect on the opacity of Gougar's few official introductions in suffrage literature as the result of expected, perceived, or desired involvement in the inner circles of Elizabeth Cady Stanton and Susan B. Anthony. As Carol Mattingly writes, and for circumstances that revisionist historians have already identified, Stanton's and Anthony's histories have—for better or for worse—usurped others. Without alternative histories to replace them,

they remain the center through which all other rhetorical activity is recovered and assessed, in spite of the "inconsistencies and accuracies" that
recur throughout their interpretations of national and regional suffrage
events (Mattingly, "Telling" 101). Mattingly mentions rival rhetors such as
Amelia Bloomer, Clarina Howard Nichols, and Mary C. Vaughan as more
rhetorically effective in promoting women's issues in the 1850s ("Telling"
101), in the same way that I have found Gougar to be more prolific in
some years than Stanton or Anthony. However, the solution may lie not
in replacing current histories, but in unsettling dominant ones.[17] Volume
3 of Anne D. Gordon's authoritative *Selected Papers of Elizabeth Cady
Stanton and Susan B. Anthony* makes one editorial mention of Gougar at
the 1880 Republic National Convention, while Gougar is mentioned on
more than a dozen pages in volume 5.[18] In these few mentions, it seems
that Gougar's principal role in Anthony's letters between 1889 and 1894
was to be portrayed as one who was "doing all she [could] to weaken the
national" movement (Gordon 5: 583). Furthermore, in Gordon's note on
the text, Gougar is described principally as "a prohibitionist who joined
the suffrage movement in 1880" (5: 67), an introduction that by now seems
opaque, and I have tried to fortify it with the first two strategic responses
in my taxonomy of Gougar's texts. In these contexts, much of Gougar's
rhetorical provocation and many of her appeals served to reveal her low
tolerance for partisanship in any form, especially when it was disguised
as moral progress in midwestern states.

In September 1893, that reputation followed Gougar on a return trip to
Kansas to speak in support of a referendum that would grant full suffrage
to women in that state. Laura M. Johns, then president of both the Kansas
ERA and the Woman's Republican Club, refused to let Gougar speak because of what she perceived to be a "radical Prohibition stance." Gougar's
response, as printed in the *Lafayette Morning Journal* on 11 September,
was scathing and self-congratulatory: "This association cannot muzzle
or gag me. I have been at work in the interest of suffrage too long to allow
some unknown suffragist to switch me off the track. I propose to say what
I please about Prohibition every speech I make" ("Mrs. Gougar Returns
to Kansas," qtd. in Kriebel, *Where the Saints* 141). A decade later, that
reputation followed Gougar on her trips off the continent. An interview
that ran in the *Honolulu Independent* on 2 February 1901, capturing her
reactions to Hawaii's "Francis Murphy craze,"[19] unfortunately positioned
her as a "temperance apostle," rather than a critic of partisan behavior or
a champion of fiscal accountability:

While I am always in favor of any conscientious effort which is being made against intemperance, I can consistently say that I am not in favor of Mr. Murphy's plan. . . . He is in for the side of the question that has the most money in it, every time. . . . I have heard Mr. Murphy speak about three times. I would not go to hear him again because I could not endure his monkey-shines in the pulpit.

Temperance work certainly is serious enough to call for some dignity, and Mr. Murphy not only lacks dignity, but his actions in the pulpit are sacrilegious in the extreme and absurdly ridiculous. He has no logic and advances no line of thought. He dances about upon the platform in a silly and senseless manner and without any purpose whatever, except it be that he is playing to the gallery gods. ("Gougar on Murphy")

My ultimate goal in presenting table 3.1 is to shed light on how historiographers might discursively organize a suffrage archive as vast and varied as Gougar's, while also transcending the categorical limitations of assumed relationships and challenging the political and ideological associations underlying those relationships. In particular, there are three relationships to complicate: the relationship between Gougar and her peers; the relationship among various suffrage genres; and the relationship between national and transnational identifications. As a result, the taxonomy and typology can help historians reclassify extant performances according to *new* assumptions about the political and authorial agencies they invoke, then and now.

Gougar and Her Peers

One outcome of witnessing these various agencies is in recognizing the difficulties of comparing *ethos* models based on propriety and respectability to rhetorical contexts "whose *ethos* models may exclude [women's] lived realities and experiences" (Pittman 46).[20] Kriebel, Jerry, and Rebecca Edwards note the complexity of Gougar's relationship with other Suffrage and Temperance leaders, as she undoubtedly shifted her allegiances in response to the many ebbs and flows of political activity between 1879 and 1907. However, as historiographers usefully have refuted the idea that Suffrage was only ever a single social movement, it has become necessary to imagine subject positions and speech acts other than those that are "for the movement," "against the movement," or "hindering the cause" (Yearwood). Several possible agentive relationships can be found among Gougar, her parties, and her peers, and I argue that they are useful for challenging the assumed subject positions of primary archival figures and their audiences, including the ones I had to assume for the construction of Gougar's taxonomy in table 3.1.

These assumed relationships have caused Gougar to be too easily summarized in some venues and too easily dismissed in others. Kriebel asserts that Gougar's political restlessness may have caused her to provoke both Republican and Democratic ideals and eventually to fall out with principal leaders such as Susan B. Anthony and Elizabeth Cady Stanton ("Suffragist"). I think it is more likely that Gougar's tying of suffrage with other legislative issues and her unpopular stances on immigration and the church often led her to break with former allies and national organizations on the basis of "principle" and "conviction."[21] While Gougar often employed practical reasoning in arguing for women's political or social endowments, she did not necessarily demonstrate the fundamentalist conviction of gender-bound inequality, never had children, and was not necessarily partisan toward her female contemporaries. In 1892, she rejected the WCTU's general stance that women were more moral beings than men, and she frequently criticized gender distinction in political work on the basis of social or spiritual "evidence" (Adams).[22]

Yet Gougar, Anthony, and Stanton were often mentioned together in the press,[23] and they often shared the platform at NWSA conventions in Indianapolis and Washington ("Woman Suffrage Convention"). Of the principal Indianans working on the 1887–88 campaign for a sixteenth amendment, Gougar was listed alongside Anthony, Zerelda Wallace, and May Wright Sewall as a headline speaker who "aroused great enthusiasm and made many converts" (Harper 626). During the controversial *Gougar v. Mandler* slander suit of 1884,[24] Anthony wired strong words of support and encouragement to Gougar on behalf of the national movement (Kriebel, *Where the Saints* 79), and for a period of years, they exchanged public displays of mutual flattery ("Speech" 38). In early 1887, while still lecturing for the Indiana State Suffrage Association, Gougar announced her intentions to succeed Mary A. Livermore and begin lecturing for the Chicago office of the Redpath Lyceum Bureau. But in May 1887, at the women's suffrage convention in Indianapolis, Anthony presented a memorial to Gougar, urging her to postpone her Redpath lecture plans in order to continue lecturing on behalf of the Suffrage movement through the remaining campaign ("Great Compliment"). In informal meeting minutes representing a pivotal discussion among Anthony, Rachel Foster Avery, Alice Blackwell, and Lucy Stone in Boston on 21 December 1887,

Anthony lists Gougar as one of seven women whom she would appoint to a committee of the NWSA (Gordon 5: 64). In a letter dated 29 December of that year and sent from Rochester, New York, Anthony again mentions Gougar to Avery as a key volunteer in the "big and difficult job" of arranging reduced train fares for speakers at the first International Council of Women, to be held in Washington, DC, the following spring (Gordon 5: 64).[25] Finally, in a letter to Clara Bewick Colby dated 5 November 1888, Elizabeth Cady Stanton describes Gougar as "someone on whom [Colby] can definitely depend" to speak at a Nebraska convention on behalf of the NWSA (Gordon 5: 141).

The significance of these appointments and accolades becomes clear in Michael Goldberg's history of the NWSA: Anthony and Stone represented opposing organizations—the NWSA and the American Woman Suffrage Association (AWSA), respectively—and Gougar's presence among them acknowledged that she had been a "catalyst" for the merger of the Kansas Equal Suffrage Association with the WCTU three years earlier, in 1884, largely because of her numerous speeches and monthlong lecture circuits throughout the state urging the disparate organizations to partner together (Goldberg 86).[26] This creates multiple possibilities for how Gougar—and others like her—were instrumental in bridging the reorganization of both groups into the National American Woman Suffrage Association (NAWSA) in 1891 (Kriebel, *Where the Saints* 109; Riegel 486; Edwards 41). Yet Gougar's relationship with Anthony and Stanton was not consistent, according to more than one public critique that Gougar delivered based on the AWSA's inability to get any suffrage laws passed (Stowitzky 1; "Susan B. Anthony"). Correspondence between Anthony and Avery indicates some tension regarding Gougar's refusal to work with the AWSA prior to 1888, inasmuch as Anthony felt that Gougar was too celebrated a public figure (Yearwood). Furthermore, although the first International Council of Women was a success and helped motivate the merger of the AWSA and NWSA into the NAWSA a few years later, in an 1894 article for the *Voice*, Gougar accuses Anthony of moral cowardice and of exercising antagonism toward suffragists in the Prohibition Party (Kriebel, *Where the Saints* 148; Edwards 39).

A topical reading of Gougar's archive shows that her "undesirable" political involvements ran deep and that her recurrent ties to the National Prohibition and Populist Parties were not generally favored because she often conflated them ("Women at War"; Edwards 98). In a letter from Anthony to Rachel Foster Avery dated 25 November 1889, Anthony expresses some frustration with Gougar's "third partyism" in the following warning: "And now all agree that the success of the [women's suffrage] am't [*sic*] will depend upon whether the state suffrage [committee] can be equally successful in keeping all 3d Partism out of the state—Why Helen Gougar's last winter's Washington speech would tear things to fritters here" (Gordon 5: 221).[27] This warning corroborates others that Anthony would make over Gougar's whole range of political activity, and it continued to be a divisive issue between Gougar and Anthony for years to come.[28] Regardless, none of these instances is substantial enough to warrant that Gougar should be remembered as an NWSA party agitator without considering her concurrent interests in labor and economics, her commitments to bi- and nonpartisanism (Kriebel, *Where the Saints* 162), and how those interests have historically caused her to be positioned "against the movement." In other words, Gougar's various memorializations are a function of an archive that is based on historicized motives, yet I argue that this no longer is—or perhaps never was—a sufficient way of writing archival narratives on a movement as politically and ideologically entwined as women's suffrage.

Attempts to explain these diverging motives may lead historians to try to write a coherent narrative of working partnerships that were, at best, inconsistent or unalarming and, at worst, too challenging to define without assigning principal rhetorical agency to one party or the other (i.e., without determining who fell out of favor with whom). Indeed, in his fourteen-part series of biographical sketches in the *Lafayette Morning Journal*, Kriebel retrospectively portrays Gougar as a moral soldier whose work was unfinished and who would "be forgotten." He writes, "She would vanish from memory like the countless ranks and files of other Christian soldiers in that mighty army who, in their own ways, in their own lands, in their own times, spent their lives marching where the saints have trod, in search of a better life for all (Kriebel, "Gougar Touted" D2)."[29] In this column, Kriebel begins to justify Gougar's portrayal as a stalwart moral laborer by identifying her involvement with a number of other "failed" but significant movements. However, we do not have to understand Gougar's activity as inconsistent, her professional relationships as fraught, or her legacy as "failed." Instead, we can assess her involvements with temperance workers, Populists, and politicians as historically and interstitially salient, rather than as minor associations that need to be explained away in order to construct a more coherent narrative (Mattingly, *Well-Tempered*). Moreover, since both the strategic taxonomy and discursive typology in table 3.1 presumably measure discursive relationships and attitudes between Gougar and her peers, irrespective of party lines, we can read her nonsuffrage texts as immediately salient, rather than as merely archival evidence of her involvements with particular causes.

As a result, what historians may read as ad hominem attacks by Gougar on Anthony, by Anthony on Gougar ("Susan B. Anthony"), or by Gougar on the women's collective could be recast as historiographical failures to demonstrate a reciprocal, archival agency. Both individual and collective agency are fundamental to my naming of Gougar's five strategic responses, but each strategic response is meant to accommodate the rhetorical positioning of all its archival agents—Gougar, her close and distant audiences, and her historians. For example, in an early "Bric-a-Brac" column that I have classified in the first strategic response, Gougar acknowledges and debunks a regular justification for feminist inaction—that women (especially when married) were ill equipped for activism and hence could not be liable:

> The first thing a woman must do, if she has ambition and opportunity to do much else than wash dishes, tend babies and gossip, is to encase her sensitive nature in an alligator skin, metaphorically speaking. Unless she possess philosophy and judgment enough to do this, she will either settle down to a life of inaction, or she will spend more time in senseless grieving than in earnest thought and work. . . . If the "eating of the apple" ever brought one curse upon woman greater than all others, it is the curse of this element of female nature called sensitiveness; though more justly it should be named weakness. . . . This sensitivity must give place to common sense, this cringing fear to ambition and justice. . . . True dignity of thought and action lies not in what others say we should do, but what we know we ought to do . . . a thought as applicable to women as to men. (9 Feb. 1879)

Enabled by the first strategic response, the multilayered criticism here is not just one that Gougar makes of her peers; rather, it is the presumed ubiquity of the critique as both a rhetorical and a historical trope. In this case, the notion that what historians see when they look through moralistic, truistic, and singular conceptions of *ethos* is neither their subject nor themselves, but an assaying of the situation as stereotypically feminist. Looking interstitially, panhistorically, and strategically allows us to recognize a "matrix for understanding patterns and actions" that typically are limited by what historians perceive to be the "edges" of their subjects' landscape (Royster and Kirsch 42–43). By this logic, the justification that regularly stymies late nineteenth-century feminist action equally stymies twentieth- or twenty-first-century *in*action by pointing historiographers to the various *dynameis* of figure 3.1 and how those *dynameis* mirror one another's motives.

What results is not a revisionist or corrective rereading of how we assume Gougar related to her peers, but rather an encouragement that the amount of richness or flattening we experience in reading Gougar's archive peer to peer reflects the same disciplinary and historical liabilities we believe are in place over our practices. We are better poised to notice *both* the multidimensional contexts that critically empower any social environment (Hutcheon 91) *and* the intertextual quandary between ethical and psycho-aesthetic approaches to interstitial looking: Does the discourse community precede and make possible the historian's participation, and if so, which "community" is so defined (Hutcheon 94)?

In another example from *Our Herald*, the same criticisms resonate after Prohibition candidate John P. St. John lost the 1884 presidential election to Grover Cleveland, but this time they resonate with the vitality of masculinist inaction, when Gougar writes:

> The political campaign that has just closed makes a strong appeal to all Christian, self-respecting, patriotic women, to be up and at work to secure their enfranchisement. So immoral and dangerous has become the management of political affairs by men alone, that women must take up this work with earnestness and zeal and push forward until they have invaded every department of political life. We fearlessly assert that for women to spend their time in aimless social life, in church work that enfeebles Christian work, and to whisper their demand for the ballot, is simply criminal. The blood of the liquor traffic is today upon the skirts of cowardly women. (15 Nov. 1884)

Again, what is enabled by the first strategic response is the ubiquity of Gougar's critique as a historical trope—not as a corrective reading of her stance on Cleveland's politics or pious and capable women, but as an encouragement to rethink the usefulness of this kind of repetition in her archive. It might point historiographers to a fusion of historical qualities or archival characteristics other than those that are informed by an assumed private-public dichotomy, for example, alternative qualifications for "public" versus "counterpublic" or redefinitions of "management" or "political campaigning." Moreover, it might enable interpretations that do not try to reconstruct feminist political discourse through a resolution of the "personal as political" dilemma (Mackinnon 535). If anything, the assemblage in figure 3.1 recasts this dilemma as a *shared condition* among Gougar's archival agents—immediate and distant—because of lingering assumptions that successful suffrage performances would naturally occur in two different kinds of spaces.

As a final example, in a column for the 29 July 1901 *Lafayette Evening Call* titled "Thinks Men Will Go to Heaven," Gougar delivers a sardonic refutation to the notion that women may be more inclined toward charity but are less compelled to demonstrate it:

> Women have been told long enough that they are angels by nature. They will never see themselves in the true light until they cease hearing and teaching such twaddle. First, we would like to know by what reasoning woman is better than man. . . . Custom pushes the man out into the rush and whirl and temptations of the world, and he may be guilty of larger crimes than the sister, who is still kept under the protection of home life. Give her the same room and the same temptation . . . and we feel safe in saying that she will be equal to the task of keeping even with him in going against the laws of the right; inherent goodness is no more natural to one than to the other, and if it were so, we would be sad, on account of the extra responsibility she would be obliged to assume. ("Thinks Men")

The refutation itself is not what figure 3.1 reveals. Rather, it is the tendency for historiographers to assay suffrage discourse according to extant performances whose *new* assumptions about the political and authorial agencies they might invoke are no longer new. The promotion, almost to symbolic status, of once new ideals (what Gougar calls "custom") both hobbles social progress and hinders historical process. This is in spite of what Cristina Rodríguez calls an implausible belief among nineteenth-century women that certain infrastructures could be "forum[s] for democratic community governance" (1838). Rodríguez notes divergent beliefs among suffragists and suffrage organizations about what constituted a "female justice" (1816), yet ultimately the differences served women's rights advocates. For example, claims that women were incapable of administering justice because they could not relate to men enabled them to argue for juridical representation by women, that is, for representation by their peers (1814). I note the same divergent stances among historiographic approaches to documenting relationships between and among suffrage peers.

Suffrage and Its Genres

At best, historical recovery of archives is multilayered and unstable work; it poses obvious and nonobvious risks for historians who are making claims as contingent as the evidence on which we draw. One obvious risk is simply not doing enough critical examination of the archives that we study before proposing a snapshot of the landscape we think constitutes standard suffrage genres. A less obvious risk is that our landscapes and snapshots may reflect entrenched disciplinary expectations or portray gaps as "more complete" histories on the basis of new genres coming available, when we should be relying on archival genres as invitations to rethink suffragists' seemingly inconsistent performances. One way of overcoming these disciplinary entrenchments is to ironically complicate the relationship between genres as much as possible so as to arrive at an understanding of new or surprising cultural forms, but this requires a kind of critical distancing we may not be accustomed—or willing—to take when working with archival subjects.

The first and third strategic responses in Gougar's taxonomy (table 3.1) especially demonstrate her tendency to admonish both female and male philanthropists to conduct themselves in such a way as to be taken seriously, complicating the portrayal of socially active women by coupling together terms that represented dissonant paradigms. For example, in her 6 December 1879 "Bric-a-Brac" column, Gougar juxtaposes "newly emancipated people" with "monkeys removed from the primeval forest [who] are too troubled to know just what to do with their tails," resulting in a noticeable clash of semantic registers. The juxtaposition provides an ironic backdrop against which Gougar admonishes her female readers to accept the criticism that will likely come from their participating more actively in the public sphere:

> It is difficult for newly emancipated people to accept all things pertaining to a new sphere or condition in life, with proper grace. Monkeys removed from the primeval forest are troubled to know just what to do with their tails. . . . What we have said of man and beast is equally true of woman. . . . She has so long been used to a sort of acquiescence, a gallantry from friend and foe, that she brooks with ill all change from this, to the severer test, criticism. . . . She must cease thinking all criticism of conduct, work or opinions, as of unkindness, but must learn to look with suspicion upon the old form of gallantry that would praise and never blame. . . . In the new order of things, let woman invite, demand, and expect polite criticism, rather than cringing, humiliating, hurtful gallantry. ("Criticism vs. Gallantry")

The criticism, she seems to argue, is less fearful than the outcome where social movements are "gallantly" tolerated. Furthermore, the "newly emancipated" woman suffragist should embrace the arts of that criticism as intellectual and moral sharpening, and engage in it herself, rather than be fulfilled by the parroting, weakening behavior caused by this gallantry.

Gougar's topoi are not unique in this example or in many others—she makes an argument for the measurable gains from women's specific participation in political and economic life (Lomicky 103). However, in light of her other writings on pragmatic social action and the role of industrial training for women, these topoi read like *dissonant* genres rather than multiple examples of the same performed genre, opening up new rhetorical possibilities for both Gougar and her historians, beyond a logical expansion of the "woman's sphere" into public life for the public good. These possibilities can historiographically target the masculine and feminine styles that dictate our understanding of what women writers do and how we remember what they do, offering what Christopher Holcomb calls "cultural forms"—repetitive devices in political discourse that are intended not to reduce whole behaviors to tropes, but rather to "restore [certain] verbal devices and behaviors to those situations and contexts" (79).

For Holcomb, "cultural forms" have three defining attributes: they may or may not be conventionalized, but they must already be in circulation and thus "available to speakers and writers as they make their 'individual projects' public" (80); they must be ubiquitous and pervasive, "accumulat[ing], carry[ing], and shed[ding] cultural values and meanings independent of the content they may be used to convey" (80); and they must "organize and impose structures on social experience" (81).[30] Unlike other cultural forms, Holcomb's figures have the capacity "to organize social experience and other phenomena in highly economical and compressed" and somewhat ritualistic ways (76). Irony may well be this cultural form in historicized suffrage discourse for the way it illustrates genre formation while also transcending some of the constraints of genre.

Gougar wrote the introduction to her sister Edna C. Jackson Houk's *Women Wealth-Winners; or, How Women Can Earn Money* (published in 1893 and reissued in 1894), in which she argues for the pragmatic benefits of educating wives and unmarried ladies to join the ranks of the professional working class and to participate in suffrage. In her introduction, Gougar does not argue that women needed to be "unsexed" to be suffragists, take up mixed public opinion about whether women are frivolous in their spending habits, or admonish Houk's readers to choose certain kinds of timid careers. She does argue that need and domestic security should be blind to sex, though she frames this argument as she does many of her speeches—by calling attention to the pervasive worldview in which suffragists saw themselves as working:

> When society is at its best, men will be the bread-winners and women the home-makers. That we are a long way from such a social millennium goes without the saying. That Necessity knows no sex is shown by the large percentage of women who are forced to inquire; "How can we earn money?" . . . While the author has taken special care to answer this class of bread-seekers, she has not been unmindful of a more favored class of women, with time and some capital, who are anxious to enjoy greater luxuries of life or possess an ample bank account for the proverbial "rainy day." (Introduction, 9–10)

With some critical distancing, this passage offers several interpretive possibilities. It demonstrates one residual pattern to many of Gougar's performances. Moreover, it reflects one of several ways historians are tempted or desire to read her—either with or against the grain of what we think constituted known suffrage ideologies. And finally, it illustrates one way we might value the genre of introduction to the women's primer as a space for unsettling domestic ideals, that is, to be concerned only with the home or to redefine the home for broader societal participation.

Without that critical distancing, Gougar's framing of this remark becomes an isolated textual event, or at best, one of several related textual events, that can be treated incriminatingly. As a case in point, Renee Stowitzky cites Gougar's opening passage as evidence that Gougar "still saw women's proper place in their home" (Stowitzky 5). True, Gougar might be reassuring Houk's readers of her own femininity and thus structuring her arguments inductively "to give audiences the impression that the conclusions were their own" (Campbell, "Gender" 480). And presumably in good faith, Stowitzky puts this text into conversation with other, similar examples she reads, in order to solidify Gougar's position as an agitator in an already complex social climate. In doing so, however, the complexity gets erased. If we consider other analytic possibilities for (re)positioning Gougar among her genres—such as reading her genres discursively across a whole archive—and in turn for (re)using those genres inventively, then historians can simultaneously reexamine stereotypes of suffrage writers, their critical audiences, *and* the viewpoints those audiences are inspired to take.

Given the collaborative nature of women's discourse (Engbers; Buchanan, *Regendering* 133), it is reasonable to expect that suffragists blended genres—fusing, disrupting, or remixing them as needed—in ways still not fully accounted for by our generic labels, which is why we look to the interstices of archived events to assign their performances new meaning. It also seems reasonable that they would have innovated genre situations that historians understand as being in response or in contrast to the various audiences and contexts that they faced. By *genre situations*, I do not mean different renditions on the "feminine style" that Karlyn Kohrs Campbell has seen emerging from the tensions between women's expected conventions and actual performances,[31] or the inventional "double bind" that Campbell and Kathleen Jamieson say spurred the nineteenth-century rhetor's creativity and transcendence, "justifying their violation of taboos" while "speaking in ways appropriate to the occasion" (Campbell, "Gender" 480). I do mean the situations revealing Gougar's canonical impact and its limitations—not only how her texts were circulated, deployed, and rejected or embraced but also how historical accounts of her texts have been either lauded or overlooked in consequential ways.

Campbell's "feminine style" has itself been historicized in useful ways—most notably through the work of Carol Mattingly, Hui Wu, Nan Johnson, Shirley Logan, and Lindal Buchanan—but not always in the service of inventing new genres. Instead, Buchanan reutilizes antebellum discourse in order to redefine how delivery styles were gendered as both feminine and masculine (*Regendering* 2, 91). As a result, Buchanan articulates four gender differences that both clarify the styles we might associate with antebellum delivery (*Regendering*, 108) *and* raise the possibility that postbellum rhetors like Gougar might require a different measurement still, particularly if they addressed stratified readers, did not bear children, or took up invitations to speak beyond the modes of "correspondence, conversation, and reading" (*Regendering* 83). What figure 3.1 tries to show most clearly is that Gougar's ironic discourse best reflects the particular resources that emerge from yet *another set of demands* on women's suffrage discourses and how those resources can enable historians to reclassify her genre situations without codifying their styles.

This is possible because what I am proposing as "genre" in suffrage discourse is not recognized only through marked properties, performances, or characteristics but achieved in how it situates the rhetors and reflects the forms and topoi in which they invent and situate themselves. Irony can act (and be read) as a genre because it promotes awareness according to how it elicits desired or undesired effects and becomes a tool for taking up ideas in the minds of readers. For example, in November 1879, Gougar published the transcript of what was originally a two-hour speech as an essay in the *Lafayette Daily Courier*. "The Man Who Blows" has been historicized several ways, but never apart from circulating lore. In the essay, Gougar targets an unnamed local politician whom Kriebel indicates she had criticized (or taken criticism from) in another context (*Where the Saints* 60). Rather than write anecdotally, Gougar assigns to a third-person male subject the behaviors that were often attributed to midwestern suffragists by reusing certain published or circulated stereotypes and applying them to prominent public figures: women "acted illogically" (first stated by Justice John H. Denison),[32] acted "immodestly" (often stated by Secretary of State James G. Blaine), acted provocatively, thought too highly of their own intellect, or were morally upstanding if politically ineffective (frequently editorialized by writer Ambrose Bierce).[33] The resulting essay reveals multiple targets and embedding subjects, and it illustrates how the logical shifts that embed these ironic targets are in fact embedding an undermining of regional stereotypes—what I identify in the fourth strategic response in table 3.1 as "undermining arguments against suffrage."

In select passages, Gougar appears to caricaturize the politician by signaling a shift from understatement to excess. Here the first shift is logically absurd, occurring in the statement about knowing writers "to come in the great hereafter":

> (A) This man is not a fool. He reads pretty near everything and is a judge upon all matters of literature; knows the ear-marks of every writer who has lived, <u>and all those to come in the great hereafter</u>.

The second shift is high context, occurring in reference to a popularly circulating text:

> (B) He constantly points out plagiarism in local poets and poetesses, and "somewhere, he [*line omitted*] ed a little," but the thought and rhyme are the same. Like George Eliot's Pummel, if you tell <u>him that they cook puppies in China, that there are ducks with fur coats in Australia, or that in some parts of the world it is the pink of politeness to put your tongue out in an introduction to a respectable stranger, he replies</u>, "O, yes; I knew those things long ago; when did you find them out?"

The entire excerpt refers to George Eliot's "The Watch-dog of Knowledge," the eighth chapter in her recent and popular *Impressions of Theophrastus Such* (1879), which employs a fashionably ignorant valet named Pummel to caricaturize those men whose belief in virtues is "always requiring to be asserted in spite of appearances against them" and whose egoism "guards against itself." The underlined passage is quoted verbatim from Eliot's chapter as a way of directing criticism toward those whose ignorance shows the more they pretend to know, the less they admit they have ever been wrong, and the less they admit that an idea they have not discovered is novel to them.

A closer examination of both passages demonstrates how these shifts can illuminate a contextual inappropriateness that simultaneously represents stereotypical classifications and generates other possibilities for classification. The historical implication in (A) is that the politician presumes a familiarity with past and contemporary literary subjects, even where it is metaphysically impossible, and the context is principally informed by Eliot's text and her reader's familiarity with Pummel (and moreover, by how Pummel's description is itself stereotypical). The historical implications in (B) are that the politician claims to read more than he does—thus confusing popular and political opinion with literature—and that the reader would have an alleged knowledge of the interactions between the politician and Eliot's text, as well as between the politician and Gougar. But a third (ironic) implication is that the politician feigns recognition of authenticity in the inauthentic works of others, and a fourth is that he considers this feigned recognition a morally necessary task by borrowing a quotation from Eliot's text.

Yet the point of naming these strategic responses is not to promote simple rereadings of suffrage texts or guarantee any particular analytical outcome, but rather to offer them as critical possibilities for using Gougar's archive differently. If we archive this essay against the expectation that Gougar should have argued for enlarging the woman's sphere based on sex distinction, social mores, or gender roles, then the essay reflects some sarcasm, light ad hominem, and perhaps even caviling. As a result, its value is determined based principally on attitudes of preservation and recovery, because it either does or does not act in accordance with what we know of suffrage genres. Alternatively, if we archive the essay against the expectation that Gougar problematizes the physical and cerebral stereotypes that were often assigned to "fanatical" midwestern women and their texts, then the essay contributes to a way of classifying her archival texts apart from the lore that often determined who was authorized to speak, in what forms, on what topics, *and according to what powers of circulation*. In that case, its value might be determined based more on attitudes of recovery and representation because it either does or does not disrupt how historians approach and analyze suffrage texts. Its implications accommodate *both* what Gougar assumes the politician thinks of his female rivals *and* what a critical reader might do with those assumptions in turn. As an essay, its embedded target is the stereotype of regional women suffragists that causes politicians to disagree. As an archival genre, its ontological question becomes how to read and reclassify a range of suffrage genres as pan-historical that had been previously classified according to historically regional stereotypes.

UNSETTLING TRANSNATIONAL IDENTIFICATION

The third relationship to complicate—indeed, the third *attitude* to be discovered in the various *dynameis* of the suffrage archive—is the most significant: the relationship between historiographers and their belief systems, especially where regional identifications are concerned. In particular, a discursive typology might help historiographers realize more concretely the ways that American Suffragists' perceived "activism" is sometimes grounded in historiographers' own need to "settle" certain historical identifications that are unsettled at best. Elsewhere, I have argued for the importance of analyzing Gougar's irony in a metalinguistic sense, beyond simply comparing her performances with those of the major party leaders (Graban, "Toward" 32). I wanted to demonstrate how her ironic discourse was both dynamic enough to shift notions of "the woman suffragist rhetor" and rich enough to support a cross-disciplinary methodology for valuating her work. More important, I wanted to resituate Gougar as a "second-generation" suffragist because of how she both reflected and deflected claims about regionalism and because I assumed that her legacy was in "settling" her participation in a nationalistic movement that had neglected her in its own historicization (Graban, "Toward" 36).

In light of the work that Campbell has done on Frances Wright and Janice LaFlamme has done on Lucy Stone and Mary Haggart—both suffrage rhetors from Indiana—I argued that feminist historians were better served by recognizing this regional suffragism as transient, fluid, and tied to materialities and resources rather than to any intrinsic property of the land, given the mobile and collaborative nature of their work. In retrospect, while this methodology did demonstrate the usefulness of revisiting Gougar's archive, it never fully disrupted historicized expectations of how American Suffrage worked (or continues to work in historians' minds), and it never fully broke free of the dichotomies we often support between foreign and domestic, national and regional, or even national and transnational. It was not until I envisioned Gougar's archive as an assemblage of critical loyalties and expectations that I was able to name two particular dichotomies it more fully disrupts.

Xenophobe versus Xenophile

Kriebel and Adams each note a xenophobic quality to Gougar's work—if not in their own reading of her work, then in perceptions that circulated among Gougar's contemporaries—and the fourth and fifth strategic responses in table 3.1 reflect this fact to a small degree. However, historically, Gougar's motives for strengthening national suffrage have been inextricably tied to a number of issues surrounding immigration, given her conviction that both disenfranchised women and foreigners should be politically expedient. In Kriebel's account, these motives are discerned mainly through the lengthy letters that she composed for the *Lafayette Morning Journal* and for the *Daily Inter Ocean* while traveling abroad between 1886 and 1906. The Gougars made several trips abroad, including a world tour from October 1902 to July 1903, which resulted in her 1905 publication of *Forty Thousand Miles of World Wandering*, and an extensive West Indies trip in 1906, which resulted in her unfinished article on the progress of women's suffrage abroad, with voting and population statistics, as well as an accounting of suffrage legislation that was emerging in Poland, Russia, Sweden, Austria, Germany, Finland, Great Britain, and France ("Last Article"). *Forty Thousand Miles* gives a detailed, reflective tour of "the people, politics, land, and customs of every foreign country she had visited" (Kriebel, *Where the Saints* 198); interspersed throughout are Gougar's observations of suffrage laws and suffrage customs in nations that were publicly developing them, and interspersed throughout those observations were her political commentaries on which nations ranked more highly in the work, some of which also appeared in the few editorials or letters that Gougar circulated after 1905. By the time of her death in 1907, Gougar had traveled to every continent except South America, and she had become a noted enough authority on international suffrage that on a pleasure trip to

Los Angeles two years earlier, she was asked by fifty local Suffrage and Temperance leaders to spontaneously deliver a public lecture, which was titled "The Story of New Zealand: A Government of Divine Justice" ("Suffrage Worker").

Gougar was also interested in seeing immigrants achieve the social and economic status necessary to become good citizens, and I hope to destabilize the need to ground Gougar's involvements abroad in anti-immigration sentiments. Her 1898 book *Matthew Peters: A Foreign Immigrant*, based on the true story of an immigrant's involvement with the underground, Civil War, temperance, and missions, represents the work of suffragists and suffragettes worldwide as anti-imperialistic at best (Hoganson 10).[34] While it is neither plausible nor productive to try to discern whether she acted from xenophilic or xenophobic motives, we can critically examine historians' motives for linking her work in this way. Again, in the interest of using irony to read *through* history and not merely *in* history—to unsettle the constraints of location or memory that might limit how we access suffrage discourse—I propose that this perceived dichotomy between xenophobe and xenophile does not need to be resolved, but it can be archivally unsettled so as to amplify the parties it affects.

During Spain's occupation of Cuba in 1898, Gougar had been consistently opposed to US involvement abroad and outspokenly opposed to the United States' annexation of Cuba, an opposition that she saw as justifiably linked to her nation's inability to resolve the problem of universal suffrage on its own soil. When Grover Cleveland refused to proclaim neutrality against involvement in Cuba, on the grounds that "the United States has a character to maintain," Gougar responded by calling into question nationalist assumptions about the nation's own character and its assets:

> We have not only a character to maintain, but we must ever defend our cowardice and our lack of humanity for not having long ago spoken the word that would have made Cuba one more republic, prosperous and at peace with the world. . . .
> We have enough territory now upon which to test the refinement of a free government without annexing Cuba, Hawaii, or any other outlying territory. ("Pictures," qtd. in Kriebel, *Where the Saints* 168)

Kriebel offers this incident as one reason why Gougar advocated for immigration laws: she apparently "wanted 'no more Spanish, Creole, ignorance or foreign blood made a part of the voting, political influence in the United States until the intelligent American woman has direct political power through the ballot'" (*Where the Saints* 168). To be clear, this was a recurring theme in Gougar's arguments for fortifying suffrage laws after 1900. However, it is just as likely that Gougar's ironic critiques of the principles governing US involvements abroad were less concerned with promoting a stronger national identification and more concerned with rethinking nationalist aims according to more globally interdependent ideals—beyond the narrowly defined notions of "peace" and "prosperity" that she often critiqued in US Suffrage legislation.

The fact that Gougar's observations cannot be historicized as being completely entrenched in or free of Americanist assumptions about cultural superiority is vitally important for unsettling the xenophobic-xenophilic dichotomy. What I identify as the fifth strategic response in table 3.1 reveals that Gougar recognized abroad a civic model that she thought could expedite suffrage at home, even though she was often highly critical of the foreign governments she observed, and this tension has been underexplored in other accounts of her work. At the 1900 convention, Catharine Waugh McCulloch, president of the Illinois Equal Suffrage Association, proposed an ideological alliance between US states currently without suffrage laws and the Philippines: "They, too, feel the desire for freedom, opportunity, progress; the wish for liberty, a share in the government, emancipation" (Hoganson 18; Stanton et al. 4: 378). Together, McCulloch and Gougar made it clear that no motivation, religious or otherwise, could justify US occupation in the West Indies (Gougar, "America" 388)—a fairly significant point for understanding Gougar's ironic discourse apart from imperialist assertions and for understanding why the NAWSA did not take a universal stance against American imperialism, or why its stances against it were diverse and complex.

At the same time, Gougar did not generally accept the fundamental principle of "empire" as a necessary outgrowth of suffrage, but she often used the immigration question in her speeches to reveal the illogical terms on which citizenship was determined. For example, in a 1906 interview for the *Arena*, Gougar explicitly denounced US occupation in the Philippines for its assumptions about the Filipinos' lack of civility ("Gougarine"), based on her own observations that, in terms of music, theatre, cultural display, and public behavior, "the Filipinos are by far the superior race of the Malays" ("America" 386):

One of the sad features of our occupation of the Philippines is that
we are instructing so many, especially of our young soldiers, in a
contempt for free institutions. . . .

Ex-Governor Taft is giving [this bill to impose a Chinese contract-
labor system in the Philippines and Hawaii] his support, be it said to
his everlasting shame. Its enactment would be a crime not second to
that of African slavery, if such a measure should be adopted for any
of these islands. ("America" 388–89)

For several years prior, Gougar had offered public endorsements of
the Agoncillo municipality and Philippine independence ("Helen Blazes"),
criticizing US president William McKinley's plans to return the Philippines to Spain, praising former insurgent leader Emilio Aguinaldo, and
expressing her hope for Philippine independence from US occupation
while on her 1903 Manila tour ("Aguinaldo"). Gougar lectured on the
subject of public and political trusts when she was a speaker on the pro-
gram of the fourth annual convention of the National Good Government
League ("Good Government") in November 1900, shortly after McKinley
was elected to office.

Following the lead of Mary A. Livermore of the New England Anti-
Imperialist League, many American suffragists may have found it more
beneficial to position themselves not as benefactors to the occupied Filipinos but rather as disenfranchised alongside them, equating the US
struggle for women's suffrage with the struggle for national liberation
in the wake of the Philippine Insurrection (Hoganson 9). A rhetorical
move such as this likely had varied effects. Kristin Hoganson notes that
on the one hand, Livermore's sentiment might have provoked "white,
middle-class American" suffragists from differentiating too much between "civilized" white women and "savage" women (Hoganson 10), and
in fact in Gougar's trans-Pacific and trans-Atlantic writings, she often
praises any nationalized group for its promotion of high culture, sometimes bringing into deeper relief the perception of an anti-"savage" bias.

On the other hand, women's suffragists might have been leery of
broadening their cause too much or forming extrapolitical alliances that
would move them farther away from what had traditionally been their
centers of power (Hoganson 11, 13) and—to be fair—the concern that
granting rights to Filipino men would succeed in cementing a patriarchal
society abroad (Hoganson 15). The argument to let nations "be free to
govern themselves" while enfranchising women to achieve political aspirations was not uncommon, though the NAWSA and other American

Suffrage groups were less energetic in building anti-imperialist coalitions than they had been in building antislavery alliances decades earlier. In spite of the rapid growth of the Anti-Imperialist League, which Hoganson notes as having over thirty thousand members in its more than one hundred affiliated organizations by 1899, American suffragists did not see enough in anti-imperialism to believe it worthwhile, neither did they see that by not demanding a withdrawal of troops from the Philippines, they were strengthening the sense of empire in ways antithetical to helping disenfranchised groups become enfranchised.

In the wake of John Hay's "Open Door" policy, Gougar submitted an article to the November 1906 edition of the *Arena*, in which she refutes a recent editorial in a "leading religious journal of the East [Coast]" that argues for renewing the 1882 Chinese Exclusionary Act. Gougar quotes directly from the article in passage (C) below, before providing her own commentary in passages (D–F). The embedding subjects in Gougar's commentary are complex, making for a rich exchange that accommodates multiple presuppositions and contexts, while it also complicates the expectation that Gougar either held to NAWSA's stance on immigration or upheld an American standard:

> (C) "The request [to limit Chinese immigration to professional workers and exclude laborers] is a reasonable one. Certainly no good reason can be offered for the exclusion of Chinese professional men, and particularly traveling commercial agents. . . . We want the best of all nations to see us and know us, and it is to be and it is hoped that the present administration will make this possible." . . .

> (D) It is true that the cultivated Chinaman is a charming specimen of the human family; he is keen of intellect, tireless in energy, honorable in his dealings to an eminent degree, a law-abiding citizen; but he is also a cheap employee, a poor home-maker, superstitious in religion, holds woman in supreme contempt,—possessing the right of life and death over his wife or wives in his own country,—brutal in his punishments, and if he comes here he comes with all these qualifications as a citizen. . . . Of the two, the intellectual is a more undesirable immigrant than the coolie; the latter may undermine us with his shovel, but the intellectual would knock us on the head. ("Shall" 506–07)

Read together, the entire passage demonstrates more than Gougar's response to public opinion and more than Gougar's assertion of cultural stereotypes in the underlined passage (D); rather, it demonstrates that supporters of both the 1882 Chinese Exclusion Act and its proposed emendation went counter to suffrage goals.

Gougar argues for excluding the genteel class on the same grounds the writer of the editorial offers for excluding the laboring class. If we archive this passage against expectations of preservation and recovery, then the underlined passage (D) reflects Gougar's caricaturization of the ways in which anti-immigrant activists rationalized their choice, in turn complicating what they understood to be "keen of intellect," "honorable," "tireless," and "law-abiding." In fact, one explicit target for the essay appears to have been "the Chamber of Commerce of New York, the Merchants' Club of Chicago, and many of the leading magazines and newspapers of the country" that had endorsed the emendation (Gougar, "Shall" 506). For Gougar, "Those who demand the exclusion only of these laborers must hold that labor and poverty are twin disgraces, and by such exclusion are willing to increase the misery of those who toil with their hands and produce the wealth of the world!" ("Shall" 506). The extent of that exclusion and its ironic expression becomes evident over the next several passages:

> (E) <u>Great primeval forests wait the axe and saw of the millions of coolies and their ambition to build homes; rich mines of gold, silver and other precious metals, coal-beds and stone-quarries invite the brain of the intellectuals and the labor of the coolie to remain at home to better the conditions of the race</u>, instead of gaining entrance into this country through a sentimentalism that does little credit to the patriotism, common-sense or commercial spirit of Americans. ("Shall" 508)

While passage (E) appears to provide argumentative support for opening up immigration to China's labor class, it also reveals several embedding subjects and ideological targets, including the razing of forests, the mining of precious metals, and other economic ambitions that inspired the Open Door policy, all demonstrating that—no matter which way they vote on the issue—suffragists cannot help but discriminate:

> (F) There is but one way to settle the vexed problem of Chinese exclusion and incidentally foreign immigration, to avoid the cry of unjust discrimination.
>
> Put not less than a $500 poll-tax on the head of every immigrant not of Caucasian blood. <u>We would not only protect ourselves from the "yellow peril," but from the "brown peril" of the Orient.</u>

<u>Let ours be an Anglo-Saxon civilization wrought successfully as the world's example.</u>

<u>Under such non-discriminating law, China and the Orient would have no occasion for complaint and America's welfare and safety would be conserved.</u> ("Shall" 508)

In the underlined portions of passage (F), all phrases echo the language of the editorial that Gougar refutes and demonstrate the discriminatory nature of an alleged "nondiscriminatory" solution. As well, her suggestion of a solution that acts nondiscriminatory reflects what she has elsewhere criticized as Americans' weakened judgment in terms of how and whom to enfranchise ("Significant").

I use assemblage in this example as a way of destabilizing one assumption: that the American woman suffragist is a subject position best understood as directly proportionate to suffrage's imperialist or anti-imperialist agendas. Contrary to this assumption, Gougar's archive enables the question of whether and how nationalist definitions of woman suffragist may have required justifying one form of imperialism in order to defy another. In fact, these definitions could have reflected (and can still reflect) a principal weakness in America's foreign policy circa 1900 in that its historicization puts "too great a strain" on the notions of individual (Brooks, qtd. in George, Weiser, and Zepernick 4), individual nation, and the nation's *other*. More important, her archive enables the realization that the activist identifications of most American suffragists, and the critical identifications of those who read them, are historically grounded in a paradigm of "the other nation" that is contingent, negotiated, and unstable at best.

National versus Domestic

The (trans)national strain in Gougar's archive lends credence to the notion that a model based solely on historicizing feminist "waves" is systematically erasing certain performative possibilities from public memory projects as much as it is reinforcing others (George, Weiser, and Zepernick 3). This does not achieve the more dialectical history that feminist activism warrants. Instead, looking ironically at Gougar's responses to anti-immigration reflects the dialogic-dialectic process that I think does and should occur among historiographers and their histories, motives, and archives. It also reflects the kind of dialectical engagement that Valerie Renegar and Stacey Sowards glean from Richard Rorty's "liberal irony"—irony that provides a theoretical grounding for citizenship in a liberal society and optimally promotes a third-wave feminist ideal. More specifically, Renegar and Sowards use Rorty's "ironist perspective" as a rubric for providing the necessary philosophical position to move third-wave feminist criticism forward, in a temporal context where feminist critics might otherwise feel no clear historical belonging because they are not tied to a single unifying cause ("Liberal" 337).[35] I admire what they do because their perspective accomplishes more than just securing a philosophical position for the third wave. In fact, their adaptation of "liberal irony" *as a historical perspective* makes the kind of reciprocal locating I do in figure 3.1 more viable even for suffrage. By arguing for the ironist perspective as historically transcendent and culturally grounded, they enable critical readers to transcend the expectation that first-wave feminism emerged out of culturally monolithic assertions, in turn revealing where the suffrage archive more likely promotes a "tolerance for a plurality of subcultures" that is both productive and unproductive in our historical remembering (Renegar and Sowards, "Liberal" 341).

My goal throughout this chapter has been to explore the effects of this plurality on our remembering. It is difficult to assess whether Gougar was principally nationalist or domestic in her concerns—whether she was concerned more with US perceptions of suffrage or those perceptions *about* US suffrage that circulated abroad—and yet the assemblage usefully justifies her archive beyond even the limitations of this question. This occurs in several ways. First, the ironic employment of characters and subjects that I note throughout Gougar's archive may reflect what Julia Lee and others have already discovered: that nineteenth-century genres—fictive or not—were already laying the foundation for an early transnationalism by inventing a blended context in which to reread prose that had traditionally been read only in nationalist terms (Lee 450). This is demonstrated most clearly in the second and fifth strategic responses in Gougar's taxonomy. The assertability of Gougar's arguments for suffrage does not have to be so stably defined according to American morals, positionings, or ideals—or by historical motives that are themselves influenced by American morals, positionings, or ideals. Second, the shared recovery and representation goals depicted in figure 3.1 may signal an epistemic invitation to rethink the utility of American pragmatism as a lens by which to view suffrage histories, since Gougar's archive invites us to question whether pragmatism was necessarily a domestic imperative.

Gougar frequently argued for rethinking the moral and economic benefits of women's professions after 1900. In repeat performances of a popular lecture titled "Industrial Training for Women," she delivers part educational treatise and part commentary on the curricular obligations of public schools toward their female pupils, depicting the "modern twentieth-century girl" in the following way:

(G) It is usually believed that every girl should be trained to be a housekeeper, with no other aim. It is as fallacious to teach this as it would be to demand that every boy should be trained to plough and reap, making this his chief end in life. A woman that could write an "Uncle Tom's Cabin," that would strike the shackles from the lives of 4,000,000 slaves would doubtless fail in washing dishes and ordering the domestic affairs of a home, and she would have a justifiable right to fail. . . . The aim of all education should be to first, develop the best possible human being, be it man, or woman; then let natural tendencies and dominating tastes decide the life work of the woman as well as the man. If a man wants a wife to do his kitchen work, let him seek such an one, but he has no business to marry a Harriet Beecher Stowe, expecting to make a $3 a week domestic out of her. There will always be plenty of domestics from which to select, while there may be a "corner" on Stowes. ("Industrial")

Gougar concludes the lecture by emphasizing the importance of thrift as an individual trait, regardless of sex, and as one on which the country's political future rests. Perhaps for this reason, "Industrial Training" had been historicized as lauding pragmatic ideals in support of a strong domestic economy. It also was first delivered for the Tippecanoe County Homemakers Association at a time when the group aligned women's economic participation with national social reform, and it employs several popularly circulating tropes that juxtaposed human security and social progressivism.[36] Yet it is possible to archive this lecture against expectations that conflate national values with necessarily domestic ones.

In passage (G), Gougar draws a connection between the possibilities afforded by women's rights and an abolitionist outcome. Juxtaposing such images as "strik[ing] the shackles from the lives of 4,000,000 slaves" with "washing dishes and ordering the domestic affairs of a home" creates a striking incongruity between female and male perceptions of a woman's social potential for those readers expecting some separation between morality, economy, and profession. Those readers might conclude that any man who opposes women's rights on the basis of wanting her to be a "$3 a week domestic" is not only ignorant but also fiscally naïve and politically incompetent, since arguing for the enfranchisement of some and the disenfranchisement of others may simultaneously support and disrupt the nationalist identification that has historically informed Gougar's "industrial woman." It is the researcher's "consciousness of engagement" (Wu 87) that can re- or deemphasize Gougar's "industrial woman" as the rhetorical subject of American ideals. In Gougar's case, an ideological stance that is tied to social uplift—regardless of race, class, or ethnicity—can raise historians' awareness of certain complexities in the American experience, even during times of strong national identification. As a result, we might see the so-called "domestic" lecture as an occasion to destabilize a certain nationalist episteme that has dictated how suffrage discourse gets read and how suffrage archives are used.

One aspect of a nationalist episteme that Gougar's archive helps destabilize is the assumption that American Suffrage succeeded only when it broke from other tangential causes that historically delayed the promotion of a domestic suffrage agenda for the sake of itself. Yet Gougar reported no countries on her world tour that had achieved suffrage distinctly or even independently from central national politics. By Gougar's own admission, her suffrage career began after a series of events in 1878 raised her awareness of the particular ways in which immigrant women serving the households of Lafayette's middle class could benefit from immediate reform on wage earning and taxation. Her 25 January 1879 "Bric-a-Brac" column features an article titled "I Have All the Rights I Want," in which she describes a fictional encounter between a woman named Helen Garth and her washerwoman Mary O'Toole, who ultimately freezes to death in a blizzard while fleeing from an argument with her abusive husband. The incident so complicated the relationship between temperance and women's rights that it caused Gougar to thereafter be considered "a fanatic on both subjects" (Kriebel, Where the Saints 53).[37] Moreover, it drew Gougar's attention to the various issues faced by the families of midwestern immigrants, especially to the complexities of their economic and political identification during the Progressive Era.

As president of the Indiana chapter of the NWSA ("Noted"), Gougar's business stationery contained two printed titles: on the left side, "President, Indiana National Woman Suffrage Association," and on the right side, "W.C.T.U., Superintendent, Relation of Temperance to Labor." Her archive shows consistency, if not cohesion, among her interests in suffrage, temperance, and labor and among her introduction to *Women Wealth-Winners*, her "Industrial Training for Women" lecture, her ethnographic account of *Matthew Peters: A Foreign Immigrant*, her editorializing on Americans in the Philippines, and her campaign to deal with the questions of the domestic helper and the woman's social asylum. To either separate out these issues or expect their more cohesive arrangement is not viable given Gougar's extrapolitical involvements, and it is also not strategic from a historiographic perspective.

I see this destabilization as more than a justification of Gougar's multiple involvements, more than a statement of shared identification between Gougar and her immediate audience(s), and more than incidental recovery by her distance audience(s). Instead, I see it as the realization by historical and critical readers of a politically motivated restoration to a condition "prior": returning some rights to historicized feminist subjects who lacked them before (Wu 85). Gougar's reliance on national cultural norms has always been complicated by her extensive knowledge of both national and international law. She knew how laws could be moved to collectively provide economic agency regardless of a person's sex, moral standing, or domestic status, and she insisted that individual responsibility could be used to incite a global comparison of suffrage progress (Flower 384). While her extensive constitutional knowledge may have appealed to multiple classes of women by demonstrating the economic necessity of practicing suffrage at home, her interest in character may have reflected those processes through which suffrage and labor laws were enacted abroad long before they were ratified in the United States.

In sum, Gougar's archive does not necessarily support a clean and uncomplicated *importation* of international suffrage models to the United States, nor does it necessarily promote an *exportation* of nationalist assumptions about suffrage abroad. Neither does Gougar's archive give evidence of a clear-cut dichotomy between "nationalist" and "domestic" or "xenophobia" and "xenophilia." Such an importation-exportation dichotomy may stem more from the NWSA's and AWSA's fluctuating agendas—or from Gougar's—than from her published views about global interdependence. Rather, the archive's transnationalism occurs in its spaces and gaps among historians' perceptions of status (Royster and Kirsch 51), geographic sites (Royster and Kirsch 54), and modes of expression (Royster and Kirsch 65)—in spaces where "territories" are not bound by clearly discernible lines. As a result, her arguments for and against international comparisons of women's suffrage laws can raise historians' awareness of how suffragists could have challenged (and still can challenge, in our remembrances of them) the notion that an American Suffrage movement needs to be defined by its adherence to nationalistic ideals.

Reading across Gougar's archive to articulate a typology of discursive attitudes will not lead historians to a unified rhetorical theory at the center of all her work (Campbell, "Theory" 127), although it can lead us to find epistemic potential in Gougar's irony as more than just a trope or rhetorical strategy. The *endoxa* in figure 3.1 occur in more than just commonplace assumptions about how Gougar's archive came into being. In fact, Gougar's archive evolves according to its shifting interests and agents, and like most other suffrage archives, it functions best as a shifting series of eyewitness accounts—then and now—rather than as a set of authoritative historical records. Considering feminist ironic discourse as locatable and potential, archives as motivational assemblages, and historicity as a discursive practice enables a historical attitude toward Gougar's performances that her responses are epistemic *based on how they problematize the securities of our historical methods.* The omissions that Kriebel, Jerry, Adams, Stowitzky, and other historians note in the papers of Elizabeth Cady Stanton and Susan B. Anthony regarding their involvement with Gougar are evident not only in the absence of Gougar's mentions but also in the *absence of types of mentions alongside the prevalence of other types* and in the absence of explicit methodologies for measuring the difference.

4. FREEING THE *ARCHON*

The process of examining any topic is both an exploration of the topic, and an exegesis of our fundamental beliefs in the light of which we approach it; a dialectical combination of exploration and exegesis.   —Michael Polanyi, *Personal Knowledge*

The archive then is something that, through the cultural activity of History, can become Memory's potential space, one of the few realms of the modern imagination where a hard-won and carefully constructed place, can return to boundless, limitless space . . .   —Carolyn Steedman, *Dust*

In the thick of researching and writing pan-historiographies, we have . . . tried not to lose sight of what is rhetorical: that which moves.
—Debra Hawhee and Christa J. Olson, "Pan-historiography"

Even in the recovery of panhistorical performances, there is still a need to construct archives, though not all archives need necessarily *contain*. The discursive attitudes I proposed in chapter 3 occur as a result of tracing Gougar's archival locatability using irony as a device to unflatten certain networks and perspectives. They are not theoretical containers; rather, they signify three dimensions of recovery work: the social, historical, and methodological. They also signify different and overlapping attitudes toward archival work: preservation, recovery, and representation. In the interests of preservation and recovery, the typology identifies socially contextualized features of Gougar's texts and organizes them as constructs for rethinking suffrage performances. In the interests of recovery and representation, the typology complicates empirical assumptions about women's suffrage that might dictate how historians interpret ante- and postbellum suffrage discourse and the constraints acting on their interpretive attempts.[1] And in the interests of preservation and representation, the typology demonstrates a research methodology that enables historians to consider the theoretical possibilities in finding new ways to recover ironic discourse through the archives.

Richard Enos has suggested "rhetorical sequencing" as a kind of typology for archivally recovering women in rhetorical traditions, by "creat[ing] methods of research and analysis that will provide a more sensitive accounting of primary material" (65). It is a methodology in which Jane Rhodes, Carol Mattingly, AnDrea Cleaves, Ann Marie Mann Simpkins, and others have productively engaged and intervened. Enos realized this need for sequencing in the conflicting and confusing characterizations of Athenian ladies' hydria jugs in the British Museum (66). Mattingly realized the need for sequencing by searching among tangential causes to suffrage, such as dress reform, domestic property rights, custody battles, and domestic abuse ("Telling" 103). Simpkins recognized it in the visual fullness of newsprint pages and their ability to show how rhetorical legacies shifted from one abolitionist to another (*Professional* 47). I recognize it in the typologies that emerge from broad sweeps of performances and genres that irony challenges and that challenge irony in turn. It is also realized in the discursive gaps that appear in our extant histories as one-sided conversations. Ultimately, I (re)present the archive as an assemblage that enables historiographers to challenge what have always been best guesses or assumptions about who had access—and how they had access—to one another's work.

In this way, the typology demonstrates what Linda Ferreira-Buckley has called, more than a decade ago, history's *persuasive function* ("Rescuing" 579). It occurs between what John Brereton and Cinthia Gannett call an "archival turn" in rhetoric and composition studies (672) and what Cheryl Glenn and Jessica Enoch note as a "generational tension that opens up possibilities for what we see, value, and then leverage" in historical work for the field ("Drama" 333). It is residual of the kinds of things that historical participants—archivists, researchers, students, and subjects—discover *can occur* within and between the boundaries of traditional historical study. And it transcends what Mattingly has called the unfortunate "residue" of establishing keystone collections against which to measure all subsequent rhetorical activity by women ("Telling" 101).

As important as such collections are, Mattingly argues that they can lead to an "erasure and denigration" of important temperance figures who are not traditionally represented in the holdings, queries, or historical methodologies that drive the archive ("Telling" 101). Thus the idea of conceptualizing archives as agential constructions seems well established. One particularly useful purpose for Suffrage and Progressive Era archives is not in *finding things*, but in illuminating what compels historiographers to determine their starting places (Steedman 6) or what enables or disenables them to see epistemological gaps. History writing becomes process, ideation, imagining, and remembering (Steedman 68). This chapter articulates those new starting places and epistemological gaps in three ways: by considering new reasons for and ways of using suffrage archives; by acknowledging the analytic and philosophical topoi that emerge from this kind of archival study; and by laying claim to ontological dilemmas that can make feminist archival recovery an intellectual discovery for the third wave. With the kinds of dissociation and reassociation that assemblage allows, feminist archives—of suffrage and other events—become intellectual centers for historiographies that *move*.

USING SUFFRAGE ARCHIVES FOR MORE THAN RECOVERY

By shifting my interests to the locate-*ability* of Gougar's performances, I have initiated a series of questions that I think worthwhile both for suffrage historiography and for feminist methodologies: What are suffragists' actual and probable impacts on the way we have done history, which has often been figure by figure, text by text, and topic by topic? What are our other options for constructing, studying, and influencing, and in turn being constructed by, those histories? How do these other options bear on the function of *kairos*, or timeliness, as a concept for constructing and theorizing histories, and on the concept of topoi, or commonplace strategies, in measuring historical outcomes of women's texts? And finally, what attitudes intrinsic to feminist recovery in rhetoric and composition could contribute to, or extend toward, historical studies in other disciplines, especially the way in which those other disciplines use *the archive*?

However, *the question I am often asked* hinges on a recurring dilemma in feminist theorizing: How do I elide the dichotomies reinforced by normative methodologies for recovering women's texts without rejecting *the normative* as a useful proposition, especially in an archive where the presence of a female subject is essential to the study? My response is to consider the epistemologies that an examination of irony makes possible for archival investigations into feminist subjectivity. By considering the kinds of topoi that irony makes possible for suffrage archives, perhaps

discourse analysts, rhetorical historians, and feminist theorists can proactively determine and navigate what is present and absent in archives
with an indigenous confidence.

What I have tried to show through my mining of Gougar's archive is
that the critical emergence of topoi from ironic discourse allows historians access to an arena in which "ethos, argumentation, and epistemology
are [flexibly] entwined" rather than categorically entrenched (Janack and
Adams 223). They reflect irony's function in women's historical discourse
as an interpretive method, a historical lens, and a generic taxonomy all at
once, with archival *locatability* serving as an alternative to the synoptic
reconstruction of originary (or corrected) narratives that tend to domi-
nate historical work in suffrage. I offer this when the collection exists
mainly to narrate the subject in the past, when the narratives tend to
uphold the power-driven relationship between *arkhe* and *archon*—the
principle ruling the archive and the *ethos* that controls it—and when they
limit what should be broader or atemporal discussions of what it means
to do archival remembering for the future.

Much as Enoch argues for broadening our understanding of "rhetorical
education" in order to identify the texts, sites, and archives best suited to
its study (*Refiguring* 173), my own interest in redefining historiography for
feminist political discourse relies on that generative broadening in sites
that are typically bound by assumptions and beliefs about disciplinary ar-
chons. Gougar's suffrage archive elides the constraints of the *archon* when
its most significant contributions are not information about the subject
herself or about her elision of historical normatives, but rather approaches
for identification with and within the agents of an assemblage. Just as
Lomicky, Logan, Rhodes, Simpkins, and Buchanan have suggested more
context-rich analyses for classifying the various constituencies represented
in ante- and postbellum discourse, I propose more resource-rich methodologies for accessing the assemblage, encouraging its users to rethink its
possibilities and to reflect on ways of seeing *possibility* at all. Of course,
my own interest in Helen Gougar as a feminist subject puts me at risk of
reinstating the very things I have worked hard in this book to disrupt—the
tendency to personify her and her feminisms through the lens of what
limited and targeted evidence I have managed to gather or whose materiality I have managed to willfully overlook. As Jacques Derrida cautions
historians not to write themselves into any collection by theorizing and
organizing it (*Archive*), I caution us to avoid writing ourselves out of the
metadiscursive arrangements that emerge from our rigorous rereading.

SEEING TOPOI IN ARCHIVAL GAPS

In her book *Dust*, which is an exposition of archival remembering and
modern history writing, Carolyn Steedman expounds on the socioeco-
nomic importance of a rag rug, which she had remembered as covering
the tidy domestic parlor floor in one scene of an Elizabeth Gaskell novel.
Only after returning to the novel years later did Steedman learn that the
floor was covered with a "gay oilcloth" (114) and not a rag rug at all. The
rag rug was a memory from a different book set a century later that she
had imposed onto the Gaskell novel. Once she becomes aware of this "error of transcription," Steedman suggests looking back on that oilcloth as
a *likely* rug—a *possible interpretation* of the kind of rug she knew *would
emerge* on later parlor floors—and looking at that later rag rug as a personification of the material conditions that transpired in the early parlor.
For Steedman, the rug's absence (not the oilcloth's presence) does more to
guide historians' interpretations of the novel by illuminating the material
scarcity that prevented the rug from being there in the first place. That
absent rug is the truth of how Gaskell's novel has been dehistoricized by
cultural researchers. One or two such errors of transcription have per-
sisted to create a path forward for Gougar, even before she had been fully
embraced by the rhetorical suffrage conversation. They do not illuminate
the material scarcity of her work—she was actually prolific in her writing
and speaking. Neither do they illuminate Steedman's notion of history
writing, as the dehistoricization of material realities seems to me a useful strategy for feminist rhetorical scholars to approach the works of the
women they study, particularly when those works are limited or accessible
only via poetics or traditions that have been identified as "mainstream."

No archival paradigm is completely free from the "privileged topol-
og[ies]" (Derrida, *Archive* 3) brought about by what we perceive to be the
chain of influence on the documents in any collection. As a result, historians' best option is to continually question the usefulness of viewing
archives as instabilities rather than as stable collections, to be mindful of
the many points of origination and instants of "archivization" that occur
over its life cycle (Derrida, *Archive* 25), and to examine *archive* as a question of the future, rather than a question of the past. One outcome of such
an examination is that it allows for a redirected understanding of what
archive is and what *suffrage archive* can do—to challenge the places (and
institutions) where we look, the directionality of how we look, the kinds of
looking we do (glancing, starting, fixating, sweeping, and so on), and the

ways we measure what we see. Another outcome of examining archive as
future is that it allows Gougar's ironic discourse to function historically
and critically, which is paramount to rethinking the various processes
of inclusion and exclusion that historians perform when "writing women
into" the larger suffrage narrative and to understanding irony's potential
for shifting episteme and enabling "archival agency" (Glenn and Enoch,
"Invigorating" 20; Mattingly, "Telling"; Royster, *Traces* 274; Sharer 124).

    "Writing women into" rhetorical histories is more methodologically
demanding than simply building them into a canon, especially in feminist historiography of the late nineteenth century. It is already an interstitial endeavor. For instance, Jane Rhodes notes an interstitial gap
between archival agents and methods in scholarship about Canadian
abolitionist Mary Ann Shadd Cary, both because of the largely invisible
status of African American women journalists in the nineteenth century
("Mary" 210; *Mary*) and because of a lack of constructs by or through
which to understand biracial journalistic performances as "professional
writing" as well as "activism" ("Mary" 211). Ann Marie Mann Simpkins
and Shirley Wilson Logan argue for a similar gap while recovering the
correspondence of Cary and Mary E. Miles Bibb, as a way of discovering the gendered expectations that made their earlier historicizations
incomplete. Each historian finds that at the time of Bibb's and Cary's
recovery, rhetoric and composition had insufficient analytical practices
to measure women's historical performances in professional speaking,
technical writing, and publishing (Simpkins, "Rhetorical" 229; Logan 155)
or to form a dialectic from the quasi-public discourses of Bibb and Cary
when they did not write directly to one another (Simpkins, "Rhetorical"
229; Simpkins, *Professional* 1). It is through multiple contexts—"quasi-
public," "public sphere, grass-roots"—that Rhodes, Simpkins, and Logan
can eventually argue for methodologies we should be inventing to create
the necessary epistemological space for writing history about abolitionist
activism in Canada.

    What this means for the paradigm I am constructing is that irony's
topological significance extends far beyond simply revealing the difference between what is said and what is unsaid in each category of discourse
(Hutcheon 177). When historiographers know to seek them, new topoi
emerge in the various *dynameis* of the suffrage archive—in the "gaps" that
occur between the various agents in figure 3.1 when our methods for valuating suffrage discourse rely primarily on assumptions that women have
historically overcome limitations on female subjectivity. In this paradigm,

a "gap" is not signified by the absence or lack of women's participation (via the availability of their texts), but by the tension between local (archival) and global (theoretical) expectations and attitudes. In addition to urging feminist scholars to expand the range of texts and methodologies we use to valuate activism within these archives, I urge us to articulate these new topoi as sites for disciplinary rethinking—for overcoming historicized assumptions about the ways we should study the archival subjects that we do. In Gougar's archive, these topoi are invitations to rethink access, affiliation, and class consciousness.

Access: Gaps between Audience and Text Agents

Examining ironic discourse apart from historicized assumptions about language, gender, and memory cannot overturn normative assumptions about feminist rhetorical practices. However, it can shed light on new ways of *accessing* the normative, including the range of texts we think were required to promote social action within various discourse communities, the kinds of discursive practices we think were used to disseminate those texts, and the disciplinary memory or expectations believed to be acting on suffrage audiences at the time of recovery. Gougar's archive presents sufficient evidence that agitative was the normative in both her historical and historicized narratives. She was at times characterized differently as a speaker and a writer, remembered either as "absorbed," "bitter and dangerous," and "directed by mind not by impulse" or as "graceful and effortless," "free from affectation," "direct, fluent, original, earnest, and impassioned" ("Biography" 638–39). As an orator, she was known as "self-possessed and collected" ("Two Opinions"), able to speak extemporaneously for two hours at a time without losing the audience's attention (Colby).

Frances Willard calls her "inexhaustible and untiring . . . [speaking with] impassioned eloquence, earnestness, easiness, dignity" (Willard and Livermore 329). Of Gougar's significant work toward securing municipal suffrage in four western states, the editors of the *Lafayette Morning Journal* note that she "was graduated into the political arena at a time when it was considered profitable to abuse one's opponents" and that her "temperament was that of the agitator" (qtd. in Kriebel, *Where the Saints* 215). And although it is not evident in any reports of her activity that she went saloon smashing or window breaking, national newspapers often maligned her zeal by ascribing to her the kinds of activities that stereotypically described Carrie Nation's temperance activism at home and Emmeline Pankhurst's suffragette activism abroad ("Temperance Question"; "Example").

In short, Gougar was no more or less a participant in what might be considered a kind of standard public agitation, originating with the rhetorical careers of Sarah and Angelina Grimké (Buchanan, *Regendering* 93), adopting a fairly androgynous attitude toward justice, and being subject to criticism no more or less than either her predecessors or her peers.[2] This is especially evident in a delivery before the Indiana State House of Representatives on 15 February 1881, in which Gougar spoke about the ongoing debates on women's rights and refuted opposing arguments, eliding questions about whether women were by nature more or less just (Gougar, "Address"). The *Indianapolis Journal* later praised her speech as "arous[ing] the legislators to consider the injustices committed against Hoosier women" ("Editorial," 15 Feb. 1881, qtd. in LaFlamme 66), and the *Indianapolis Daily Sentinel* said she had "present[ed] logical arguments in a tasteful manner" ("Editorial," 15 Feb. 1881, qtd. in LaFlamme 66).

Without the assemblage, Gougar's performances would have largely lacked a critical methodology for fitting her into extant suffrage conversations or establishing the parameters of new ones apart from the standard fallacy of ad hominem. The solution is not for historians to try to analyze Gougar's ironic discourse as disinterested or neutral observers when in fact they are not, but to look beyond ad hominem and other commonplace assumptions that have historically leveled charges against suffrage rhetors for being "bitter" or "dangerous." These could be usefully replaced by the development of new topoi that are linked more to the articulation of methodological gaps than to rewriting female subjectivities or revising historians' expectations of how those subjectivities are performed.

Feminist standpoint theory postulates that what we believe counts as knowledge depends heavily on our cultural, social, and historical locations and, in fact, that those who occupy "marginalized positions in a culture acquire a 'double perspective' . . . understand[ing] the workings of both the dominant culture and their own marginal one" (Kirsch 14). Janack and Adams offer several assumptions grounded in feminist standpoint theory for why we can argue *against* considering ad hominem as a standard fallacy in feminist epistemological projects and, furthermore, for why historiographers can argue against the default "shrill" or "bitter" positioning that often results from reading ad hominem in women's texts. One assumption is that "who[ever] does the theorizing—whose presuppositions, models, and methods are used" is critical in determining whether a social scientific theory (of fallacy) should be applied at all (Janack and Adams 215). Another assumption is that taking fallacies as claims that stand universally on their own is too limited a sociopolitical viewpoint to make the best use of ad hominem in suffrage discourse. Fallacies may best inform historical and critical readers of their own epistemic dependence and responsibility, that is, reminding them in which contexts "to the man" need or need not be seen as "against the man" (216). In turn, our assumptions about what Gougar did accomplish, does accomplish, and can accomplish through her ironic discourse are grounded in *kairotic*—rather than temporal—methods of accessing normative and non-normative behaviors.

Affiliation: Gaps among Author, Audience, and Text Agents

Another topos, encompassing the first, is reflected in the types and kinds of relationships that Gougar was historically expected not to have—both local and global. Part of Gougar's national legacy rests in the alliances she formed with rising American political figures such as Henry Ward Beecher, Grover Cleveland, William Jennings Bryan, and Benjamin Harrison, as well as a number of younger philanthropists whom she mentored directly and indirectly. Her affiliations are both promising and problematic. What is promising is that the archival evidence of her involvement with public figures is diverse, ranging from a lengthy letter dated 29 February 1894 from the Reverend George W. Vaughan, an unsalaried liberal Christian preacher in Massachusetts whose causes she financed, to a brief memo dated 11 November 1900 in which William Jennings Bryan penned his appreciation for Gougar's "good work" in spite of the presidential defeat he had suffered five days prior.[3] What is problematic is that Gougar's ironic discourse helps position her as simultaneously a party affiliate and a party outsider, making her challenging to both classify and reclassify. Thus the same methodological gaps that make *access* a site for productive questioning can raise *affiliation* as a way to problematize lore about actual and potential influences on suffragists' work.

In addition to serving the interests of the national and state Prohibition Parties, Gougar was a platform speaker for the three major parties—Republican, Democrat, and Populist—over her whole career, causing several candidates from Indiana to seek her endorsement when they ran for office. In an 1882 letter to the Reverend B. Wilson Smith regarding his campaign advertisement in her Prohibition paper, Gougar advised him straightforwardly on how to attain a majority of the conservative vote if he did not wish to remain "the weakest man on the legislative

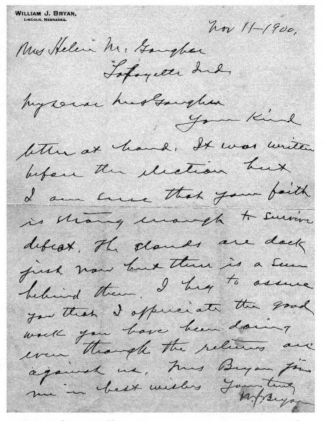

Figure 4.1. Letter from William Jennings Bryan written on the eve of his presidential defeat, 11 November 1900, in which he acknowledges Gougar's work done on his behalf. "I am sure that your faith is strong enough to survive defeat," Bryan writes. *"The clouds are dark just now but there is a sun behind them."* From the Helen M. Gougar Collection, Tippecanoe County Historical Association, Lafayette, Indiana, unnumbered item x.2056.

ticket" ("Letter"). In an 1889 letter from newly elected president Benjamin Harrison to Lafayette saloonkeeper Nathan Craigmile, Gougar was mentioned as a vital enough influence on public opinion that Harrison urged Craigmile to seek Gougar's endorsement for his bid in the 1890 election for Lafayette postmaster ("Post Office").[4] On several of these archived occasions, irony serves a kind of dissociation and detachment from main-party politics.

For example, in one event, Gougar mocks Craigmile's deductive rigor by reaching and stating a conclusion that exaggerates, rather than logically leads from, his premises, leaving the reader to infer that the Republican

Party is the target of its own stereotypes. In this exchange, Gougar positions herself as a "neutral" observer in a more systemic debate that raises critical questions about whether suffragists' party affiliations can be retrospectively determined without confining them to specific genres or looking for static demonstrations of loyalty that are necessarily fluid.

> [Mr. Craigmile] said to me, "Mrs. Gougar, . . . I have come to ask your assistance on my behalf. You have it in your power to have me appointed or you can defeat me, if you are so minded." I expressed my surprise at this statement as I was quite sure the present administration was not indebted to me, or any effort on my part for its being.
>
> He told me of the twenty seven hundred leading citizens who had endorsed him, but assured me that a grave difficulty still stood in his way. It was myself. . . . Inasmuch as the Republicans played fast and loose with the saloon . . . and at the same time crying out against us Prohibitionists as "Democratic boodlers," "Tail to a Democratic kite," "Saloon allies," etc., etc., ad infinitum, the situation is, at least interesting to a Prohibitionist. It shows that the g.o.p.'s are having a hard time to keep peace with the saloon-keeper. ("Post Office")

Gougar frequently experienced the paradox of having to borrow from tested genres and models while also reporting fluctuating political sentiments in ways other than those genres allowed. As a result, our *archival remembering* may rely on models for philanthropic and political participation that, even in the late nineteenth and early twentieth century, still stemmed from neoclassical roots. Or our archival remembering may deny suffrage figures the hybrid positioning they require at any given political moment. At the end of the post office controversy, Gougar ultimately endorses neither candidate, but she cites the incident as an opportunity to represent a "dead" party (the GOP) whose interests she had once served and that was now dependent on a woman for its success. Through this discourse, irony positions her as an activist affiliate aloof of any party line and repositions her historians and their methodologies within that aloofness.

Class Consciousness: Gaps between Assemblage and Habitus

A third topos reflects the ways in which Gougar's ironic discourse complicates historians' efforts to discern a solidly middle-class stance on women's issues. The gap between the perceived parameters of class consciousness among suffrage organizations versus the allowable parameters of class consciousness among historians signals that our analytic methods at any point in time will rely on one set of parameters more than another. This is essentially a gap between assemblage (the whole archive or event) and the *habitus* (the social and disciplinary expectations acting on the whole archive or event). According to Francis Bowen, editor of the *North American Review* from 1843 to 1854, "class" in the midcentury represented fairly neutral terms of official social description and primarily accommodated the "peculiar social mobility" of American society (qtd. in A. Lang, *Syntax* 1). It was a transient and variant designation, representing movable pathways and interests (A. Lang, *Syntax* 2), yet this transience and variance were anything but objective. Amy Lang has argued for a concept called the "language of class," or linguistic evidence of America's self-consciousness of its own rising class conflict and the difficulties in allaying inevitable tensions between still stabilizing lower and higher classes (*Syntax* 2). For Lang, this conflict meant that appropriate modes for describing new social conditions could not be made fast enough to accommodate social progress; as a result, the gaps between extant language and unarticulated needs—for example, between the expectations underlying "chattel slave" and those of the contemporary "free man"—caused a "crisis of classification" that is now rich with tension and useful for historical study (*Syntax* 3–4).

Realizing this topos especially allows me to complicate the language surrounding what is often assumed to be a middle-class lens by which to view social uplift in Gougar's work, since her "language of class" does not necessarily reflect the same attitudes assumed by the NWSA or the NAWSA in the 1880s and 1890s, nor do Gougar's arguments reflect the same "neutrality" or denial of class distinctions that Bowen says dominated American thinking in the 1850s. At best, Gougar's historicization points to an imprecise treatment of class as a *subject position in which to participate*, offering yet another way to tackle the questions I posed in chapters 1 and 3: How can historians witness women *inhabiting* their political discourse? and How can they measure irony's discursive function in historical controversies without precluding all other possibilities for that discourse?

In Gougar's discourse, the tension between the terms *domestic* and *professional* is especially rich, for it reflects an ideological conflict that is visible only when we consider their interpretability across historical time and rhetorical space: while Gougar may not have seen the terms operating in opposition to one another, readers in some dimensions of the assemblage inevitably would, making the pair of terms an ironic "end" or a tendentious contingency of the here and now (Hutcheon 184) that occurs when the historian is surprised by her own subject. Beyond simply problematizing reality, irony carries within it our historical expectations. In her contributions to both the state and national women's suffrage platforms, Gougar often rejected arguments that were made on the grounds of separate spheres and moral purity. She also often rejected woman's role as the "decoratial [*sic*] part of the human family," arguing, "We do not need loveliness so much as we need intellectual brightness and vivacity founded upon common sense," and insisting that women's rights have not been withheld by the "tyrannical spirit of men," but rather by women's own hesitancy to claim them ("Bric-a-Brac," 23 Nov. 1879). As a result, Gougar often argued in terms that challenged popularly circulating definitions of "expediency" (Campbell, *Man* 12)—the standpoint that women rhetors could be more effective public activists if they acted on the basis of their superior nature—and argued explicitly for their professional enfranchisement, yet she did not reject definitions of "domestic," nor did she delimit "professional" to its opposite term. In fact, conjoining both terms as adjectives enables a multilayered analysis of their prejudicial significance.

"Campaign of 1888" illustrates this contradiction in an interesting way, though I maintain that the contradiction is less in Gougar's performance than in its *historicization*. The speech was originally delivered on 3 November 1888 in response to a provocation by former activist Anna Dickinson several weeks prior, and it was reprinted in full in the *Lafayette Daily Courier* with the report that hundreds were turned away unable to gain admission.[5] In spite of Dickinson's presence in the title and opening and closing statements, the speech primarily delivers abject criticism to fallen parties and former suffragists by labeling their apathy as provincialism at best and self-importance at worst. Gougar begins the address by pointing to the event or challenge that instigated the occasion, first praising Dickinson's early reform work with the early Republican Party, then chastising her for leaving the work and "turn[ing] her attention to the theatre, attempting to play the part of the man, Hamlet":

> [S]he made a signal failure, as any woman will who attempts to make a man of herself; . . . She has made a failure in this line of work, and she awakens from her Rip Van Winkle sleep at the end of twenty-five years and comes out upon dead issues, a woman of the past pleading the cause of a political party of the past. ("Campaign")

In the rest of the speech, Gougar critiques Dickinson's indictment of President Grover Cleveland, whom Dickinson had called "the hangman of

Buffalo"; repudiates her language as "unjust, unwise, unchristian, unlady-like, and unpersuasive"; and chastises the major political parties for their ineffectiveness and inattentiveness to pressing social issues. ("Campaign")

On the surface, Gougar compares Dickinson to other legendary imitators, conflating "acting Hamlet" (or "playing the part of a man") with "trying to make a man of oneself" ("Campaign"). The allusion to Rip Van Winkle might represent Dickinson's ambivalence toward late political causes, it might reflect Gougar's criticism of GOP joiners after 1884 (an election year that marked her own turning away from the party), it might reflect her criticism of major parties that adopted the antics or strategies of other parties,[6] or it might ambiguate her own reasoning that party loyalists and suffragists treated acting and doing as the same.

Though she gave the speech on something like a third-party (or Prohibition) stance, Gougar critiqued each party in turn. Her audience of more than one thousand people included Democrats and "a large body of Republicans . . . with the evident intention of disturbing and breaking up the meeting" ("Campaign"). However, this syntax offers evidence of class conflicts not in the contexts in which Gougar first employs it, but in those historical and archival contexts in which her language has been disseminated and used—including appeals to demoralize suffrage, reposition midwestern suffragists as more progressive than provincial, and even relinquish a historical reliance on party or class loyalty—all possibilities that reinscribe agency to the various aspects of the assemblage in figure 3.1 and all possible replacements for the ad hominem tactics that have been ascribed to Gougar and do get ascribed to other suffragists. The expressed tensions between Gougar and Dickinson that are threaded throughout the speech echo the tensions between Gougar's class consciousness and that of the NWSA, but they also create a potential gap between historians' expectations of class and other counterdiscourses (Hutcheon 184), especially where Gougar makes these imitative and reductive stances more a problem of provincialism than of partisanship.

In columns 8 and 9 of the reprinted transcript, Gougar turns her attentions toward provincial voting practices:

> Voters are much like the little girl on a railroad train whom I met recently going from Crawfordsville to Indianapolis. The sweet-faced little body crawled up to one of the windows, and on looking out saw a picture of Mr. Harrison in a cottage window—[Applause]—I am glad to have so many Republican friends with us to night; it shows they have come to crowd the Democrats out. [Applause.] This little

girl looked out upon that picture and turning to the gentleman back of her she said, "I just hate that picture—I'se a Democrat; my pa's a Democrat and I'se born a Democrat." [Great laughter.] That child has as intelligent for her political opinion as 99 out of every 100 of you voters have. [Applause] And I do plead with Mr. Cable for more intelligent voting in this country. ("Campaign")

While on one analytic plane Gougar's syntax demonstrates the subjugation of individual intelligence and character to an argument for agency—"I do not plead the cause but do repudiate the language"—on another plane this becomes a historicization of class consciousness for the way it conjures up historians' assumptions of the kinds of tensions Gougar would have had to address between Republicans and Democrats in order to uphold the "third" party as the only party free of ambivalence, ignorance, and provincialism:

And, my friends, if you will read the two party platforms and note the spirit you will mark the unkind, the dishonest, and the partisan spirit that leads our people only to degradation. If I am to believe the witnesses on both sides, the Democrats calling the Republicans scoundrels, and the Republicans calling the Democrats scoundrels, I take it for granted neither party can be trusted, and it is time to have a new political party in the country. [Applause.] ("Campaign")

The analytic and philosophical topoi that emerge from this kind of archival study are productive for extending the archive's dialogic functions beyond repository or narrative. There is much that is transparent in Gougar's language if we study it as a panhistoriographic syntax of class, that is, a panhistoriographic realization of where Gougar's language *and ours* may be insufficient for bridging the gaps she experienced between past and present subject positions.

Finally, we might realize several possible "movements" for reconstructing the theoretical heritages that govern how to recover women's ironic discourse at all, calling into question rhetoric's tolerance for evolving definitions of "feminist" in describing this recovery. All these possibilities are echoed in Michael Leff's description of agency as movement between tradition and invention and between individuality and commonality; in Michaela Meyer's assessment that "the future of contemporary feminist theory lies in our ability to extend agency to ourselves, our subjects, and our texts" (13); and in Belinda Stillion Southard's examination of "class conscious" feminism in the 1890s suffrage rhetoric of Harriot Stanton

Blatch (133). Southard's argument especially makes new possibilities for realigning late woman suffrage in the United States and Great Britain with capitalism, labor equity, and economic emancipation, going somewhat against the grain of arguments for flattening class difference or fusing public and private spaces. Instead, Blatch, Gougar, and others of Carol Lomicky's "second-generation" suffragists might have worked hard to keep such distinctions visible, articulable, and communal (Southard 134), rather than assume that their resolution was a political problem to be overcome. All of these possibilities point to archival irony as a third-wave historical project when it is embraced as a way of looking beyond fixed constituencies or imitative genres and practiced as something other than truth telling or interventionism (Munslow 20).

DEFINING ONTOLOGICAL DILEMMAS FOR THIRD-WAVE RECOVERY

Of the three "starting places" for archival liberation that I offer in this chapter, the third one is the most significant: articulating those attitudes that are intrinsic to feminist recovery in rhetoric and composition but that can contribute to historical studies in other disciplines or reflect ways that other disciplines might use *their archives*. In the case studies throughout this book, I have tried to demonstrate various ways that a critical application of irony elides strict demands on temporality and intentionality by measuring its *historicity* instead—that is, by measuring the kairotic and spatial interventions in which historians recognize irony as having been performed, interpreted, or perceived. In fact, my analyses throughout this book rely on the notion that irony's historicity demands more from, and reveals more about, the frequent and plausible movements between historical location and memory that occur and recur. As a result, I can offer a series of questions that display the assemblage's potential for raising ontological dilemmas that reflect third-wave concerns:

- How can rethought, recast archives enable users to note the intersectionality of materiality, representation, and power, and how do they carry intellectual value?
- What are, or have been, their constituent genres, and on what processes or remembrances do these constituencies depend?
- What can be gained by placing critical distance between archival subjects and authors, objects of narration, and the acts of narrating and remembering?

Considering the ironic positionings of women in the archives can heighten an archive's sense of "merely appearing to be present in an ontic sense, as material proof of the past" (Biesecker, "Historicity" 124). Rather than merely containing expectations, archival materials can help determine the boundaries of historiographers' questions and the parameters of their involvement. In turn, the act of historical archival recovery becomes one of theoretical frame-shifting, where historiographers confront and reinvent their own epistemic values.

Julia Kristeva justifies her "third-phase feminist" as someone with a nascent subjectivity that was not marked as a linear historical project, but that grew from women's need to reconcile their collective insertion into history with their refusal to subjugate to the limitations of that history (463). Decades later, Kristeva's feminist subject still makes possibilities for a historical positioning that is determined *apart from time*, indicating that language has played a powerful role in repositioning women's texts, precisely for its ideological transparency. But even this logic of identification is not without constraints for a project like *Women's Irony*, since most historical examinations of verbal irony raise questions about how a subverted ironic meaning can be reconstructed, when they should be raising the question of whether rhetorical theories of irony need be (re)constructivist at all. This kind of examination still reinforces a dichotomy between history and language that causes historians to privilege either the chronology or the text. Yet in a study of irony that is ahistorical, extraintentional, and reciprocal, simply arguing for another analytic logic may not be enough to elide the philosophical binary between understanding discourse as "an abstract account of linguistic functionings" (Rickert 35) and understanding discourse in completely nonlinguistic terms. Language still is one of the most significant constraints in critical examinations of feminist ironic discourse for its potential to both codify and disrupt.

I prefer a situating logic that offers typologies for identifying and classifying women's discourse according to patterns that are not strictly historical (Donawerth, *Rhetorical* xix), encourage us to rethink the linguistic flattening of gender (Merrill, *Social* 107), and promote rhetorical "counterdiscourses," in order to bring forward "interpretive frameworks that permit their achievements to be acknowledged and valued" in a more dynamic way (Royster, "Sarah's" 49). For example, my rereading of *Examinations* in chapter 1 is not theoretically useful unless it draws as much metacritical attention to the historian's reflexive purview as it does to how women's irony carries the dual properties of logic and imagination—of "represent[ing] that which already exists" while "generat[ing] that which does not yet exist or is not yet named" (Ratcliffe 9). Throughout Askew's various quests, words such as "conscyence," "questyon," and "utterynge" function rhetorically rather than descriptively, which is to say they suggest multiple, contextualized, and unstable remembrances that shift across time and place and reveal contingencies in a community's logics of identification, whether that community is composed of Askew's immediate examiners or her historically distant readers.

Such remembering evokes what Sharon Crowley has called the seeming "impossibility of writing history" without clear expectations that it would also tell the story of the intellectual methods driving it (Octalog, "Politics" 13). I articulate three of these methods, but I prefer to think of them as *dilemmas* or *contradictions* in the same vein as Renegar and Sowards have described contradictions in third-wave feminist literature to mean "internally inconsistent or oppositional positions" ("Contradiction" 5). "Contradictions" are agentive because they are used to realize emergent identities, develop new ways of thinking, and imagine new forms of social action. I also call them "ontological" because of their potential to disrupt and reinvent categorical realities and their potential to direct feminist recovery toward an ethic of pluralization, (im)materiality, globalization, and reciprocity.

Exchanging Metaphor for Process

The first dilemma exchanges historical metaphors for historiographic process. Where spatial metaphors such as *landscaping* and *mapping* can limit potential rewritings of feminist rhetorical positioning—either by binding women's subjectivity to resistance (Glenn, "Remapping" 289) or by limiting the possible ways for historiographers to choose their subjects (L'Eplattenier 137)—they might also be employed as sites for agential flourishing according to how they enrich historians' abilities to think, act, react, and imagine.[7] Even alternative metaphors for historical landscaping such as *placement* and ecological *location*, tend to privilege a legitimation of location as territory, fortifying borders and boundaries between agents rather than making them more fluid in order to chart new epistemologies for historical work (Royster, "Disciplinary" 149, 163). If they do not provide the same richness or texturedness as Royster calls for in exhorting us to note the contexts out of which we landscape, they at least help reflect the ways in which those contexts limit our discernment and vision.

In the same way that Nedra Reynolds articulates "dwelling" as a reciprocal action between those who are rooted in time, space, and material conditions and those who are learning to read the palimpsest in which they reside (139), I have suggested *locatability* as a reciprocal geography for irony's agentive relationships throughout this book because it is not bound by singular intention nor by stable time or static space. I understand it best as a process through which historical work is done, rather than as a metaphor for historical work. In the case of Askew and Hutchinson, archival *locatability* accounts for what their historical locations do not, and in the case of Gougar, it accounts for what her archival location cannot: the various slippages and movements of figures, audiences, and texts that occur when critical readers reflect on their own practices of historical remembering—of tracing how a text, memory, or transcript moves between various points, how its interpretations differ at each point, and how those points in turn take on significance as the discourse situation in which they are involved either shifts or expands.

To be clear, place *is* important to feminist historiography in rhetoric and writing. This is apparent in the growing number of archival histories that draw significant conclusions from lesser-known corpora of texts and about the disciplinary methodologies that specifically originate in (rather than merely change to accommodate) the places where these texts circulate as they become available. For example, Jessica Enoch's *Refiguring Rhetorical Education* and David Gold's *Rhetoric at the Margins* were made possible by the deliberate mining of obscure primary source material in obscure places in order to present a more nuanced picture of the feminist teacher and feminist rhetorical education in nineteenth- and twentieth-century North America. Their archives included local historical associations, administrative histories, and institutional collections of schools whose ties to the development of rhetoric studies, writing studies, or antebellum literacy had not yet been established.[8] Glenn and Enoch return to this argument again, almost full circle, as they consider how various archival moves enable and disable, that is, how archival researchers in rhetoric and writing can "le[t] go of the disciplinary ideal of the kinds of materials that constitute primary and archival material" and rethink what counts as viable and legitimate "locations" ("Invigorating" 15–16). Feminist historiography should continue to focus on making more robust its theorizations of location as ecologies of place.

However, the rendering of these locational ecologies as metaphors may diminish—rather than heighten—the vital role of location in the analysis of feminist political discourse, implying coherences where they do not or, as L'Eplattenier might argue, should not reside (139). To more fully appreciate the messy, complex, agentive relationship among authors, audiences, and texts in ironic discourse, it seems more beneficial to understand these relationships as processes for rethinking what Susan Miller might call "textual imaginar[ies]" (105). I borrow this term from Miller's *Trust in Texts* to indicate the overarching narrative that occurs when historiographers realize those "ad hoc, often unexpected relationships" between texts and the materialities and economies that are involved in their dissemination (105), as well as to recognize the precise factors that cause new analytic methodologies to emerge. Even shifting notions of space, place, nearness, location, and positioning—while they may challenge what we think of as the fixed historical record—are not transparent or without material shifts. In this way, locatability in the study of ironic discourse can be justified both as resource and as restraint, a process that acts on critical readers but that critical readers act on as well.

Exchanging Spaces for Strata

The second dilemma arises from the first. The analysis of women's ironic discourse reveals that their historicity—particularly when it involves archives—is best represented by an *assemblage* rather than by a location, because of how *assemblage* makes it possible to understand their locatability according to interventions in space and time and according to the numerous agents who had a hand in putting them in those archival spaces. Glenn and Enoch argue for the limitedness of viewing archival locations as centralized or empowered spaces in their own research into ancient perceptions of women and into Mexican education, respectively ("Invigorating" 16). Sometimes, they note, more apt "beginnings" or "endings" of archival inquiry occur not only in what Robert Connors calls the archive without the "upper-case-*A*" (qtd. in Glenn and Enoch, "Invigorating" 16) but also in the realization that the terms we think drive our archival motivations are fairly underformed (e.g., "political," "ancient," "ethnic," and "diverse"). Our challenge is in acknowledging that the other agents who drive our work—the other researchers who make possible these multilayered paths to discovery—legitimately operate on other historical dimensions than just our own. There are primary, secondary, and even tertiary audiences for the archives we consult; for the archivists themselves, whose "various material processes . . . affect the corpus of records on which we . . . construct diverse and subversive narratives" (Sharer 124); and for the material processes that, if known by researchers, would give them a better understanding of the dimensions of archival materials they study (Morris and Rose 51).

Even Carolyn Steedman argues for archives as spatial and historical *processes*—as constructions of consciously chosen documentation as well as their unintended fragmentations—rather than as places where the researcher or historian goes to be alone with the past (*Dust* 68). For the purposes of locating women in rhetorical histories, then, an archive is best understood as what Gilles Deleuze and Félix Guattari recognize as "lines of articulation or segmentarity, strata and territories; but also lines of flight, movements of deterritorialization and destratification"; lines on which readers can see "relative slowness and viscosity, or, on the contrary, . . . acceleration and rapture" (3). In this arrangement, actors can be subjects or objects, social meaning becomes one of several categories, archives become systems of cultural activity that can and do operate panhistorically, and archival documents or texts become discursive locations. The discursive locations of Askew, Hutchinson, Gougar, and others invite reconstructions based on multiple sets of decision making. Their ironic placements are highly intertextual and therefore highly disruptable.

Exchanging Memory for Habitus

The third dilemma exchanges memory for *habitus*, in direct response to how so many archives of women's political performances challenge commemoration and commemorative devices, especially where circulating material artifacts are few or where their remembrances are hobbled. When texts are unavailable, this work becomes almost a rereading or realigning of public memory projects in whatever forms they are available, leading to range of questions about agency that Ekaterina Haskins has usefully summarized in asking, "Which past is identified and worthy of remembrance? Who carries out the work of recalling it? What forms does commemoration take?" ("Between" 402). To some degree, these extant decisions enable us to rethink serendipity—to understand archival discoveries as the realization of how groups of texts *could have functioned together more broadly*, how the circulation of specific texts *could impact the valuation of others*, or how prescribed reorderings and arrangements of vast quantities of information *can help new archival relationships emerge* by highlighting exclusion or inclusion and outcome. Assemblage moves us beyond the paradigm of containment.

The disruptions at work in ironic discourse—those overlapping territories depicted in figures 1.1 and 2.1 that denote reflective, interpretive contexts—offer at best nascent answers to the questions of *What could the writer(s) (have) mean(t) in various historicized contexts?* and *What factors convey this meaning?* Irony's interstitial witnessing both reveals and occludes the continuous and participatory nature of making the transmission of shared pasts a distinctly feminist project. In this sense, *habitus* is intrinsic to human memory without being bound by it (Bourdieu). Barbara Biesecker tells us that such a practice is already denotative and ontological ("Historicity" 124), where the "present/absent" nature of the historical space enables researchers to name what they observe and to observe what they name, further acting as a scene of collective invention for the way it invites the constitution of an evidentiary "we" (126). Both concepts—*habitus* and habit—rely on the notion that certain behaviors or beliefs eventually become socialized into the individuals of a particular culture when the originary source of that behavior or belief has been forgotten or misplaced. The significance of *habitus* for my own project is that it enables me to posit archival remembering as an active social practice that fulfills the desires of knowing the *already*, while anticipating the questions elicited by the *not yet. Habitus* better accounts for the myriad decisions and circumstances—both personal and institutional—that can raise historians' consciousness of the various acts of exclusion, omission, inclusion, and inscription that are committed in archival remembering.

As Seyla Benhabib argued in the 1990s and Gesa E. Kirsch has reminded us more recently, what feminist subjects believe counts as knowledge depends heavily on their cultural, social, and historical locations and, in fact, on an acceptance that those who occupy "marginalized positions in a culture acquire a 'double perspective' . . . understand[ing] the workings of both the dominant culture and their own marginal one" (Kirsch 14). A principal question driving this book has been how historiographers can and should analyze ironic discourse in a theoretical milieu that understands history, language, memory, and rhetorical identification as contingencies rather than stabilities. The answer I have tried to construct is that in irony, historiographers find a complete framework for feminist rhetorical history, given that it invites or compels them to come to terms with intellectual assumptions about how, when, and where to recover one another's texts—to question who is authorized to narrate rhetorical history about and alongside whom. It invites us to question not only Who are all the agents? but also How are they more or less visible in ironic spaces? and When does that (in)visibility become a shared endeavor?

5. TOWARD AN IRONY PARADIGM

> A theory that incorporates the dialectics that exist between
> feminists and feminisms into an ongoing conversation has the
> potential to unleash a great deal of transformative power.
> —Valerie R. Renegar and Stacey K. Sowards, "Liberal
> Irony, Rhetoric, and Feminist Thought"

My desire for *Women's Irony* is that it will help feminist historians find new "places to stand"—new places from which to "expand [the] constitutional scene" and rhetorical impact of certain discourses or texts that are believed to have limited circulation (Olson 78). Whether or not they promote a Burkean framework that understands history as *scenes*—as occurring among texts, agents, and attitudes—feminist historians can rely on these expanded circulations to push the limits of their own and others' disciplinary, scholarly, or geographic perspectives. As a result, they might recoup both the imaginative aspects and the activist desires of historiography to make new possibilities for women's political performances—for what women have done, can do, and could be seen as doing in various contexts. Such aspects and desires need recouping.

To illustrate, I return to the critical wake of former Israeli prime minister Golda Meir's well-circulated, well-politicized ironic statement of cultural disidentification that opens this book. Part of its ironic persistence is that it reflects a simultaneously nationalistic and antinationalistic logic. This particular statement could have merely echoed what Meir thought was a popular claim, alluded to by other political leaders in her own temporal context:

> There were no such thing as Palestinians. When was there an independent Palestinian people with a Palestinian state? It was either southern Syria before the First World War, and then it was a Palestine including Jordan. It was not as though there was a Palestinian people in Palestine considering itself as a Palestinian people, and we came

and threw them out and took their country away from them. They
did not exist. ("Golda Meir Scorns Soviets")

Or her controversial statement could have underscored a stance she believed Israel should actively and collectively promote, in both past and
future contexts: that Palestinian Arabs had denied their own separatist
existence and administration when protesting the Balfour Declaration
of 1917 (C. Smith 77). However, since I have avoided discussing ironic
intentions throughout this book, a more critically nuanced approach to
Meir's statement would note that it simultaneously promotes and defies
its own historicization—its own quality of being historical or perceived
as historically actual—because accepting its logic requires accepting a
particular conviction, acting out a cultural belief, or taking a political side.

It is difficult in any century to historically valuate political performances that are this blatantly and painfully charged, especially when they
are performed by women whose identifications are too closely tied, or not
tied enough, to the regions in which they perform. For this reason, and
especially in times of historical revolutions or historicized conflicts, I
embrace an irony paradigm that philosophically recognizes the complex
involvements in any *revolution*, challenges accepted historical responses
to statelessness or postconflict identifications for women, and recasts disciplinary assumptions about what is appropriate in rhetorical work. In
so doing, I re-present feminist rhetorical analysis as a historical practice
that can take up certain "signposts of memory" without seeming to deny
others (Benvenisti 230). Whether one agrees or disagrees with Meir's assertions or mine, this statement demonstrates the need for a figurative site
to theorize *both* the rhetor *and* the forms and topoi in which she has been
remembered to have performed, while also building knowledge about how
to theorize at all. A more critically nuanced approach, then, would promote
both optimistic and skeptical readings of this historicized statement.

Such an approach would raise to consciousness those terms in Meir's
statement that are more widely politicized than others, signal *felt* versus *perceived* statehood, reflect both linguistic and culturally diasporic
experiences, and provoke a stratified response. Most important, such
an approach would rely on textual properties and reception evidence as
twin determinate moments in the irony, recognizing the multiple factors
that make "ironic discourse" historical. In sum, such an approach would
enable a reimagining of all the ways Meir's irony is valued by, or commu-
nicates to, multiple agents across interstitial contexts, beyond the mere

acceptance or rejection of Palestinian statehood or Israeli nationhood. A more critically nuanced approach would move historians toward an expanded understanding of all the agents being implicated or harmed.

At this juncture in feminist theorizing, historians do not need a model for irony that requires time and delay in order to strengthen certain interpretations or soften others (Giora, *On Our Mind* 66). Historians need a model that demonstrates critical empathy and enables them to argue for irony as agential—as aiding the invention of new relationships between discourse and meaning for feminist rhetorical projects. In such a model, textual markers such as Meir's understated identification of Israel as being "efficient at" military acts or Palestinians as being historically "nonexistent" do not have to reify particular tropes. Instead, they might reflect more fundamental questions about *how to historically interpret national identification by pointing to something beyond language—beyond the textual marker itself.*[1] If our irony theories have formed, by and large, on the basis of expecting a coherent and orderly universe in which each discursive act is dictated by a single intention, then studying how each text's "metafacts" invite an understanding of what gives them communicative force is both disruptive and useful. In the cases examined in the previous chapters, ironic discourse becomes a critical process.

Throughout this book, I have worked to dissociate irony from *humor* in critical readings of women's political performances, from *gender* in the performances of women's histories, and from *agitation* in the historicization of women's archives because these are necessary steps in liberating irony from theoretically limiting conditions. As Cheree Carlson argues, rhetorical conceptions of irony need not arise from (Kenneth Burke's) comic frame (310), which has traditionally flattened its complexities and framed women's performances alongside or against an ideal of "true womanhood" (311–12). It is more telling to realize that Gougar's quips arise from a critical attitude, rather than a passive one, and that she makes her references to body and self in order to shift focus from her sex as a target to the stereotypes or social order she elides, and not to fully accept or reject a social order (312). I do not mean to imply that Burkean dramatism necessarily precludes (or prevents) a way for us to theorize more complex uses of irony than by target or subject. I do acknowledge—along with Carlson—the limited uses to which the Burkean comic frame has been put in classifying women's nineteenth-century discourse and in measuring women's wit according to how women are framed against the ideal of "true womanhood" or against her rejection of it (311–12).

This is especially pertinent for reading whole archives, because it allows for the fact that not all social or political positions represented in the archive are derived from literary personae or dramatic attitudes. Moreover, "whole" archives are rarely complete, as they reveal tangible gaps in articulating what irony means for *analysis*. In this final chapter, I articulate these gaps by describing what tenets they call into question and explain their importance for helping historiographers find new places to stand.

QUESTIONING HISTORICAL PRACTICE

Wherever possible, I hope this project enables feminist historiographers to consider irony's critical disruptions. In the introduction, I stated that irony's greatest critical function in rhetorical studies of women's texts is not empowering historians to recast narratives of what women *do* or *have done*, but providing a discursive site for raising questions about historical practices. In my own historical practice, I have come to favor dialogism as a principal methodology; thus, in many respects, this book calls into question the stability of location and time as placeholders for historical activity. *Women's Irony* has been guided by a conviction that it is possible to study irony *both* as a historically situated act *and* as an ahistorical system of discourse, based on the inventive potential of women's texts for helping others recreate themselves as rhetorical theorists and for transcending historical tropes.

As such, feminist historiography's reliance on location and memory as interpretive tools is both promising and problematic. It is promising because *location* and *memory* are useful abstractions that can contain multiple processes, but it is problematic because they sometimes privilege the found and the extant over the absent and the obscure, or they promote some materialities (the archivist's, the researcher's, the reader's, the subject's) over others. Even enriching the narratives of their recovery and making their contexts more transparent cannot guarantee women's theoretical (re)presentation if those narratives are trying to address or correct a lack. While there is an undisputed lack of accessibility to records of women's writing from before 1600 (for example, the *Old Bailey Proceedings Online* begins with records dated 1674, more than a hundred years too late for Anne Askew to be represented as a primary text or mentioned in eyewitness accounts), a bias for the familiar also affects the processes by which certain records are overlooked and others get promoted once they are accessed. This same bias causes certain *categories* of primary texts that have been miscatalogued to be brought forward while others remain obscure, and still others are limited in function according to what we perceive to have been their limited circulation.[2] Instead, to better understand historicized political performances, we need a committed paradigm that does more than construct historical narratives figure by figure, text by text, or even topic by topic, since these approaches may paradoxically reinscribe textual traditions that are incomplete.

I am also calling into question the nature of historical evidence because, as Hui Wu reminds us, historical facts are knowable only by revealing how historians take up, use, or abandon them (86). In fact, *abandonment* is useful to observe because it causes us to reconsider how we trace women's subject matter and events of the past in the face of new theoretical orientations and cultural logics. If it is possible to "see" irony in situations that other readers might not (Hutcheon 123), then irony may well create the kinds of additional conditions by which abandonments can be witnessed. By additional conditions, I do not just mean Sean Zwagerman's "indirect illocutionary acts" (22), Linda Hutcheon's "psycho-aesthetic" intentionalism (119), Natalie Zemon Davis's "fictional" elements that encompass the writing of historical narratives (3), or even Salvatore Attardo's "multiple narrative levels" that one must account for in judging irony's appropriateness conditions (*Humorous* 81). I do mean those conscious moments that occur when we recognize how the descriptive phenomena in feminist texts can help us access the empathetic mechanisms in women's ironic delivery. Historical evidence no longer resides only in observable facts, but in perceived absences of information and methodological gaps as well.

In questioning these things, I establish feminist historiography's reliance on *reflection* and *dialectic* to provide a more optimal theoretical paradigm for mining the gaps that emerge from archival work. I have turned to irony to call into question what we consider to be the sources of our interpretive evidence (Octalog, "Politics" 15), making it possible for rhetorical historians to reject or counter each other's methods while still arriving at the same goal (Octalog, "Politics" 17). When they are done well, dialectical studies of women's irony can effectively raise questions about the worth and efficacy of studying gendered collectives at all, making visible the "collective fantasies" that mobilize historians and merge their searches with their "subjects' quest for wholeness and coherence" (Scott, *Fantasy* 19). In turn, the acts of historicizing and being historicized become part of the same quest for identification. For Kirsch and Royster, this quest has already led to innovative ways of evaluating feminist topographies and methods—indeed, to the very foundations of what constitute "feminist practices" ("Feminist" 644).

All historical work is to some extent a mediation of language and a dialogic shifting of power from one to many. The intersections of history and language in Askew's, Hutchinson's, and Gougar's ironic discourse form a kind of dialogism that reflects what historians bring to the task based on what shifting power relations can be observed through interstitial witnessing. As a result, it becomes possible to valuate feminist performances—politically, socially, and otherwise—apart from the perspectival limitations of location and time, challenging "who is using/attributing [the irony] and at whose expense it is seen to be" (Hutcheon 15). Rather than propose an analytical apparatus to mark *for* irony or a way to justify the discourse *as* irony, I have argued for irony as a more flexible mode of inquiry, disrupting the notion that it occurs only when certain elements reside or are seen as incompatible within a single frame or context (Kaufer, "Irony, Interpretive" 456), and that irony is only a conscious event (Kaufer, "Irony, Interpretive" 454).[3] As a critical paradigm for historical work, irony becomes more nascent and more humane. It inspires readings and conclusions beyond *isosthenia*—beyond the "balancing of opposites" that is imbibed in rhetorical theories of irony when they are based only in skepticism and disbelief (Olson and Olson 42).

BEING CRITICAL AGENTS AND TEACHING CRITICAL AGENCY

In addition to questioning what we value in historical practice, this project has also caused me to question agency as a historiographic imperative and to rethink our expectations of *agents* in feminist historical work. In her 1986 argument for gender as an analytic category, and later in her 1999 revision of this theory, Joan Wallach Scott encourages historians to "find ways (however imperfect) continually to subject our categories to criticism, our analyses to self-criticism" (*Gender* 41). For Scott at that time, *gender* could work as an analytic category because it was both constitutive of stated sexual differences and representative of blurred power relations (*Gender* 41–42). In the same way, *irony* works as an analytic category that reveals both actual and symbolic connections between subject and object and observer and observed, with greater potential for disruption than for coherence, inviting women to think of themselves as critical agents. By *critical agents*, I mean those who embody both individual and collective subjectivity and invent responses to critical problems by navigating both resources and restraints. More specifically, critical agents are those whose identifications are not determined solely within or beyond themselves, but are enriched in the interpretive actions of others.

In Elizabeth Flynn's revisionist feminist project, critical agents are those for whom meaning "does not reside in the text as it does for the New Critics . . . but in the transactional process that is the result of the merging of reader and text" (114). Indeed, this transactional claim echoes Carolyn Miller's assertion that agency "is not only the property of an event, it is the property of a relationship between rhetor and audience" (150), and it bears as much on present political discourse as it does on archived political performances, especially in performances whose nuances are often flattened or missed. For example, in the opening statement of Barbara Jordan's July 1974 impeachment address before the US House Judiciary Committee, a single instance of marked incongruity demonstrates how the whole of her speech could act as a euphemism for a more vital conflict of national identification, a more complex historicization, or both. After quoting extensively from James Madison at the 1788 Virginia Ratifying Convention, and interspersed with a forensic analysis of Watergate, Jordan ironically portrays Watergate as a potential material destruction of the Constitution that Madison helped ratify: "If the impeachment provision in the Constitution of the United States will not reach the offenses charged here, then perhaps that eighteenth-century Constitution should be abandoned to a twentieth-century paper shredder" ("Statement"). This statement resonated two years later in her keynote address at the Democratic National Convention and again twenty years later at the same convention, when Jordan alludes to her own historic participation as a black woman investigating Watergate in 1974 and addressing the DNC in 1976. Yet the historical and political capital of this address, and particularly of the paper shredder comment, still rests in certain expectations that Jordan's irony was constructed of contextualized tropes. More specifically, its historical and political capital resides in the single "rhetorical flourish" in a speech that was otherwise devoid of euphemisms (Morgan, "Barbara"). Rhetorically, Jordan's paper shredder comment has been historicized only within the logic of an ad hominem remark.

However, if we were to ask, *Of what is consciousness being raised in Jordan's address?* then irony works to reveal other logics—it both situates Jordan and reflects the forms and topoi in which she, her audiences, and her historians can and should be resituated. An analysis of irony in contemporary political discourse surrounding any singular event would need to account for more than merely the ironists' and audiences' attitudes toward the object, its subjects, and its targets. It would need to account for the extralinguistic positioning of the ironists and audiences as well as the topoi made possible in the various relationships constructed from these positionings. Otherwise, its agential properties cannot be effectively traced.

More recently, when Madeleine Albright delivered the keynote address at the annual Colloquium on Public and International Affairs at Princeton University in 2006, her positioning as former US secretary of state enabled her to outline her ninth point—that democracies should be inclusive—with unusual efficacy. In raising the subject of whether democracy could still be attained in the Middle East in spite of cultural intimidation tactics by dissident groups such as Hamas, Albright was able to deliver another message critiquing the wait-and-see tactics of developed nations, such as the United States, for their role in maintaining the status quo:

> Let us be fair—elections did not create Hamas. Hamas grew because prior Palestinian governments failed to deliver. Now, because of the elections, Hamas will be tested as it has never before been, and required to do what it has never before done. This will create pressures on the organization, including pressure from us, to refrain from violence and to moderate its policies toward Israel. Democracy did not create Hamas, but it may cause Hamas either to change—or to fail; either outcome would be an improvement over the status quo. ("Promoting")

In the context of the complete address, this passage illustrates a common discursive move for Albright and likely for other international heads of state: to return the power of governing a national conscience to the audience or to illustrate how the audience members had unwittingly relinquished that governance through their inattentiveness to Middle East policy.

However, its critical and historical efficacy are best seen not in this discursive interpretation, but in the interpretive spaces constructed among the address, its subjects, its timings, and its contexts—and in the possibilities for independently choosing between standpoints and positionings in our interpretation (Strauss 23). The relationships among Albright's status as a former US policymaker and an ongoing diplomat, her immediate audiences' self-awareness as students of diplomacy or teachers of policymaking, and her distant audiences' expectations as consumers of global media create many more spaces for observing how an ironic political agency is formed, circulated, historicized, and reused or recalled in contexts requiring diplomacy.

Critical, reciprocal agency is almost an imperative for historiographic work, for it empowers the historian to recognize when and where she can speak on behalf of historicized subjects—and speak to historical audiences—whose discursive subjectivities are not identical to her own or to each other (Carlacio 128). Without this enabling, for example, a number of white, middle-class feminist rhetoricians would likely "remain silent, wondering if it is we who are being addressed, spoken to, or invited to join in what ought to be perceived in many ways as a common struggle for our rightful place in a history that has elided our intellectual work and our rhetorical practices" (Carlacio 128). Kate Ronald and Joy Ritchie might call these agential relationships the kinds of "rhetorical strategies and stances" that make a difference in how we teach *rhetorica* ("Introduction" 3) or how we teach the attitudes that historians carry toward "doing" rhetorical history and toward "using" women's rhetorics productively (3). In order to serve (and advance) feminist historical research, dialectical studies like *Women's Irony* should make it more evident how *rhetorica* is teaching us (Ronald and Ritchie, "Introduction" 2). In the kind of study employed throughout this book, feminist agency is more than a "resource constructed in particular contexts and in particular ways" (Geisler 12); it is a knowledge-making practice that necessarily includes the agent's subjectivity through questioning and reflection. By understanding and practicing the interpretation of irony as agential—as something that makes dialectical constraints clearer as they emerge—readers can inhabit historicized discourse as a kind of usable past. As Inderpal Grewal writes in *Transnational America*, "The 'global' is not and never [is] quite global" (22). It is, rather, a "powerful imaginary produced through knowledges moving along specific transnational connectivities" that themselves are part of historicized trajectories (22).

NOT YOUR MOTHER'S IRONY: FROM RECOVERY TO EPISTEMOLOGY

More than likely, each of the women I study—from Anne Askew to Madeleine Albright—experienced occasions in which she could not speak, censored her own text in the early stages of her thinking, or felt its repercussions on her life, her family, and her vocational or political aspirations.

More than likely, the complexity of their experiences far exceeds the occasions in which they could reasonably write or speak. Under such rhetorical constraints, we might be tempted to argue that ironic discourse retroactively restores to these women a kind of inventive potential. I would rather argue that irony gives back to its own historicity, not by enabling transhistorical comparisons of women's political strategies when they are under duress or by revealing a stable taxonomy of their performances, but by enabling historiographers to be analysts, archivists, and activists at once, three roles that I have sought to conjoin throughout this project.

For example, at the end of chapter 1, I offered several ways that Anne Askew's ironic discourse invites critical readers to reexamine how the very limits of rhetorical understanding in Renaissance women's texts may be "moved and removed" (Ratcliffe 30). At the end of chapter 2, I argued for a disruption of Anne Hutchinson's traceability as a historically divisive figure by rereading the Antinomian controversy as something other than an ecclesiastical and rhetorical schism. In chapters 3 and 4, I reconceptualized Helen Gougar's suffrage archive as an epistemological placeholder based on the various *dynamis* relationships among all of the archive's agents. Each of these arguments reflects irony's potential to disambiguate as much as it ambiguates—to bring into deeper relief the various kinds of witnessing that are involved in a paradigmatic (re) construction of feminist political discourse. As a result, the case studies throughout this book have tried to reflect a panhistoriographic approach by offering a set of principles that guide how we can reasonably expect Renaissance, Colonial, and suffrage histories to demonstrate reciprocal agency, as well as a set of methodological questions to apply to more contemporary ironic performances. And as a result, I have found certain things to be "true" of irony's epistemic function in each performance.

Ideally, irony gives us a way in to histories and locations "other than our own" (Olson 79), helping us see history writing as complex, dialogical, and inventive. By focusing on what occurs (or *can* occur) in ironic discourse, historiographers can do more than simply "find things" in feminist texts that corroborate what history already tells them women have used irony to accomplish. While texts—even typologies—can serve as paradigms to direct or redirect thinking, it takes more than textual reconstruction to provide a paradigmatic understanding of irony for feminist studies in rhetoric and writing. Instead, it makes more sense to justify irony as a critical reading practice that brings together history and theory in such a way as to question our sense of normative categories when we do archival history on feminist subjects. Irony *as a whole discourse* draws historians' attention to the interstices of language, history, memory, and archive, embroiling while also liberating a present political problem in a past political narrative each time it is read. Whatever is liberatory about women's political irony is only fully realized in our interactions *with it* and *with them*. Thus I invite historians to take up the following "truths" as evidence of how using irony to think beyond recovery can facilitate the construction of new historical knowledge:

An irony paradigm encourages questioning of what can and should be the nature of contradictions in feminist discourse. Hui Wu articulates some of these contradictions that occur when theorists conflate postmodernism with feminist methods to arrive at a complete loss of the female subject (90). For Valerie Renegar and Stacey Sowards, irony raises the kind of critical consciousness that is necessary for feminist deliberation in the twenty-first century ("Liberal" 332). While they build on Richard Rorty's "liberal irony" as a unifying philosophical position,[4] I see it more simply as a phenomenon that—in my subjects' performances and in historiographers' interpretations of those performances—makes useful contradictions visible and thus invites new theorizations of *resource*. Rather than establish liberal irony as an overarching rhetorical theory, I articulate a paradigm that reveals the contradictions in my subjects' irony (and in our interpretations of it) as productive and agentive.

I am mainly interested in what historiographers in rhetorical studies can claim about discursive agency through a serious questioning of women's ironic political texts: What is the nature of the recovery work that irony makes possible, especially for moving feminist rhetorical methodologies beyond the study of *women's* texts, histories, and archives? What feminist identifications are reordered or transformed? What ideological assumptions are perpetuated or left? How are writers repositioned and readers disencumbered from the limits they create (Renegar and Sowards, "Liberal" 341)? How can writers and readers "engage in self-determination and self-definition through the disruption of traditional definitions, stereotypes, and identities" (Renegar and Sowards, "Contradiction" 8)? The dialectical potential in understanding liberal irony as a third-wave position is more fully realized when our examination of irony includes our role as interpreters of, or "second audiences" for, what women do.

In the case studies this book comprises, I associate ironic discourse with feminist contradiction by drawing on the same "three-pronged" definition that Renegar and Sowards provide. First and foremost, it is a

"temporally embedded process of social engagement" that is simultaneously informed by the past, oriented toward the present, and oriented
toward the future (Emirbayer and Mische 963, qtd. in Renegar and Sowards 4). Second, it is connected to language and rhetorical choice, and it
is articulated in terms of enactment, choice, and will (4) while also being
composed of extradiscursive acts, raising questions of voice, power, and
rights (Hauser, qtd. on 4). Finally, it is "communal, social, cooperative,
and participatory and, simultaneously, constituted and constrained by
the material and symbolic elements of context and culture" (Campbell,
qtd. on 4).

Renegar and Sowards draw positive elements from the notion of contradiction as "internally inconsistent or oppositional" (5), borrowing from
Michel Foucault, Mao Tse-tung, and Leslie Baxter to point to contradiction's usefulness in creating a "dilemma of identity construction" between
the "I" and the "we" of third-wave feminism (Baxter, qtd. on 5). I, in turn,
borrow from them to demonstrate that what becomes (dis)ambiguated
in historical examinations of irony are not only its various audiences but
also those audiences' positioning, as well as present and future readings
of their work. How can the various *dynamis* relationships between and
among an archive's agents make examinations of literacy, race, gender, and
class in rhetorical performances more rigorous for the feminist nexus?

What Royster and Kirsch have recently called "strategic contemplation"—a term of engagement they have developed to describe the simultaneously outward and inward journey of historical researchers as they
become conscious of how they interact with their histories and subjects
(85)—I call the *habitus* that describes not only the ways in which researchers and their subjects ironize together but also the temporal and spatial
interventions in which historians remember. Whether or not it applies
to discourse broadly construed as "ironic," this way of approaching the
archive posits archival remembering as a dynamic social practice that
reveals various acts of exclusion, omission, inclusion, and inscription.
Habitus is also reflected in the kind of patterning that taxonomies and
typologies reveal—that is, the various "ways in" to an archive that make
its extradisciplinary uses and functions more visible in its arrangement.

*An irony paradigm has a transformative effect on its own theory build-
ing and on building new theories of archive.* Richard Young has famously
presented epistemic similarity as a condition that "is more a symptom
of a widely shared paradigm than lack of imagination" (31). Although
he wrote these words partly to justify the role of composition texts in

making visible a current-traditional paradigm that was still prevalent in composition studies, Young makes a point that is of interest to revisionist historians even today: rather than articulate paradigms only in terms of their visible features or the ways in which they characterize entrenched discursive aims, we can consider how paradigms provide historians with a new way of imagining discourse, beyond simply "discovering" or "realizing" its tacit features.

To that end, I have not identified a set of tacit features in feminist ironic discourse, but rather tested Young's theories of invention on irony to determine whether it "provide[s] an adequate account of the psychological processes it purports to explain," "increase[s] our ability to carry out these processes more . . . effectively," and "provide[s] . . . a *more adequate* means for carrying them out than any of the alternatives" (40, original emphasis). For Young, a new paradigm "redraws the boundaries of the discipline" (45), adding to it while also leaving out, and comprising more the "*systems* composed of related beliefs, values, and methods," rather than the beliefs, values, or methods themselves (46, original emphasis). In my work, irony achieves epistemic status by highlighting its own movements between and within constraints, such as location, memory, and time.

An irony paradigm helps account for what Kirsch and Royster call "tectonic shifts" in the field (640), including new topographies, their underlying methodological challenges, belief systems about how knowledge is made, what counts as knowledge, how it is transferred, and the ways in which it can be used for good. Extracting theory from women's practices is important (Campbell, "Consciousness" 57), but it is not enough to fully justify the possibilities of irony in their political discourse across time and space. Feminist historiographers want not only to share in women's broad and diverse experiences but also to be cosharers in the experiences according to how they do (and can) interpret their texts. This may be the difference between *finding things* in their texts that conform to our expectations of what we always already can find and looking for residual interactions of something else. I am interested in the latter, not the former.

I am interested in imagining, rather than confirming or discounting, ways that ironic subjects (broadly construed) can be historicized, in much the same way as Joan Wallach Scott has imagined a theorization of sexual difference for more than feminist work. By merging feminist history with psychoanalysis, Scott considers sexual difference as a theoretically optimal site for interrogating how and why we classify subjects, groups, and behaviors in historical work and for considering how the "thinking of an historian [can be] an object of inquiry along with that of her subjects" (*Fantasy* 22). For Scott, the fact that *sexual difference* has eluded a terminal, stable definition and a singular motive points to

> the anxiety with which established boundaries are policed and the disciplinary power brought to bear on those seen to transgress established limits. . . . The elusiveness of sexual difference is both unrealizable and, for that very reason, historical. It is a quest that never ends. As such, it interrupts the certainty of established categories, thus creating openings to the future. (*Fantasy* 22)

For me, *irony* will have this status once it is realized as helping uncover the ways that historians are implicated in their own imaginative work and revealing the ways in which those practices we cherish and study diverge from those practices we teach.

While Jess Enoch and Jordynn Jack are not the first to attest to the importance of sites, spaces, and locations in creating new feminist methodologies for research, theirs is a powerful endorsement of how pedagogical projects *grow from* them, specifically by "construct[ing] new memories . . . that matter to them" (525), "understand[ing] forgetting as an action with various rhetorical nuances" (529), and realizing (or overcoming) a "recalcitrant 'presentness'" that often causes monuments to fall into or out of historians' immediate purview (533). Where ironic discourse is concerned, these same outcomes can be reached when rhetorical researchers consider the locatability of an archive's assemblage in order to identify the many ways that irony falls under the radar for serious historical consideration when it is studied apart from intentionality.

My decision to open up the various corpora of Albright's political memoirs, Meir's international media representations, and Jordan's public address for redefinition as *archives* reflects my own faith in their permeability, ironic antecedents, and interpretive value among my readers. That same decision reflects the permeability of genre expectations put on these texts that caused them to be so classified in the first place. Thus my examinations of Albright's, Meir's, and Jordan's archives—rather, my inclusion of all their texts into an arbitrarily considered archive—relies on both the robustness and the flexibility of that term, and my faith in that term to describe epistemologies, rather than containers.

An irony paradigm does not privilege one set of research methods over another, but inspires awareness of and attention to the (various) methods through which our research questions can emerge (Johanek 2).[5] Throughout this book, I have argued for irony's value in the teaching of historiography based on a kind of *facilitas* that occurs through its examination. I have also argued for irony's value as a historiographic tool based on how it inspires the development of analytic methods that disrupt old taxonomies and catalyze new ones. A paradigmatic understanding of irony can accommodate both tools and *facilitas*. What I call *ironic constructs* in the discourses that I study are actually intellectual constraints, rather than finite limits or boundaries on interpretive semantics. From these constraints emerges a set of investigative principles for defining a more transcendent practice. Ideally, this practice would expand the cultural memories of historiographers, cause us to rethink how we form cultural norms, and make us reconsider how to produce historical knowledge as simultaneously stable and unstable. Ideally, this practice would cause historians to question our assumptions about tradition, performativity, self, other, identification, and erasure that underscore how we think (ironic) discourse can and should be approached.

Ever since Cheryl Glenn's "Remapping Rhetorical Territory," feminist critics have collectively argued that perpetual terrain metaphors ultimately fail us in rhetorical studies, and we have turned to rearticulating (or reinvigorating) historiographical perspectives instead (Glenn and Enoch, "Invigorating" 13). Hui Wu has faulted our epistemological "confusions," or those dominant interpretive frameworks that conflate feminist history writing with postmodernism writ large, complicate the need for a feminist subjectivity, and prevent our work from impacting non-Euro-American traditions (82). Jacqueline Jones Royster has challenged the understanding that African women's rhetorical participation began in nineteenth-century America by being more inclusive of the terms of their generic and discursive "participation" ("Disciplinary" 151). Barb L'Eplattenier has reminded us that mapping and landscaping metaphors are simultaneously hobbled and "powerful tools" that "carry implications, possibilities, and limitations" for historical research and the biases we bring to it (133). Susan Miller, though not writing directly about ways to landscape the field, has appropriated the concept of "textual imaginary" to urge rhetoric and writing scholars to rethink how they write and rely on their own histories, so as not to exclude the multiple modes of and important "material intervention[s] in discourse production" (75). Although none of these historiographic projects has necessarily focused on irony, their critiques have helped establish the simultaneous fragility and dynamism of rhetorical recovery and encouraged us to find methods that historicize without essentializing. They have helped us understand that the success of one particular research method need not preclude all others.

Thus the most useful research paradigms for feminist rhetorical studies are those that *sustain complexity* (Royster and Kirsch 134), calling into question not only the ethics of our methodologies and our categories (e.g., "woman," "rhetor," "agent," "history") but also how researchers interpellate their subjects. Even multilateral historical interpretations need not lead to an enriched, objective conclusion—a single response, an analytic object, a thing. Instead, historical studies of ironic discourse can demonstrate the complex, often uneasy relationship between the individual and collective agency of women rhetors and their audiences, as a reminder of the dynamism of all historical practice. By extension, historians can reconsider what pedagogical assumptions this discourse should help them imagine in the first place (Enoch and Jack 519).

An irony paradigm represents rhetoric as a discipline that simultaneously focuses on its tasks, its knowledge makers, and its students as they evolve. Sowards and Renegar explicitly articulate a third-wave feminist consciousness raising as something "informed by predecessor feminisms as well as changing cultural conditions and expectations" (536–37), in turn capitalizing on Linda Heywood and Judith Drake's characterization of third-wave feminism as one that is concerned with "the development of modes of thinking that can come to terms with the multiple, constantly shifting bases of oppression in relation to . . . interpenetrating axes of identity" (3; qtd. in Sowards and Renegar 537). Such heightened consciousness raising has activist potential for shifting episteme because, as Sowards and Renegar note, "once something has been named and described, it can become the target of [further] social change" (546). Because it is both self- and other-directed, critical consciousness raising can occur in individual or small-group contexts; synthesizing irony in my subjects' texts reveals its capacity to make visible some different assumptions about equality and discrimination that circulate among and between various feminist rhetorical movements, whether we want to define those movements temporally or by some other set of working ideologies. It is dialectical and helps us "move beyond our own consciousness, embracing the interplay of the subjective and objective" (Johanek 113).

In Iris Marion Young's application of Sartre's *seriality* to feminist theory, the nature of the collective is but a temporary uniting factor. For

Young, one way to solve the dilemma between understanding "woman" as part of a social collective with its own feminist politics and accounting for the many individual women excluded from such a collective is to conceptualize social collectivity as a serial phenomenon (714, 723). Such a phenomenon binds figures together not by common attributes or a common identity politic, but by their engagement with pragmatic outcomes or a desire to attain them (717). This notion of defining a shared project according to its pragmatic outcomes and desires ultimately enables me to discuss the ironic discourse of past and present rhetors in the same theoretical space. Young's appropriation of seriality allows for that sharing to be accomplished individually or in groups and to be discontinued or otherwise made contingent. In other words, what joins together their projects is not a set of common traits observed in their discourse or a pattern of similarities observed in their ironic contexts, but their participation in a nascent field of activity that illuminates various motivations of, and possibilities for, all its agents.

The action of *joining a common project* or *being subjects in a common field of activity* does not necessarily lead to a lack of historical identification or to the constrained, practico-inert conditions that Sartre warns against (Young 726). In fact, it is not limited to traditional notions of subject or agent. The various *dynamis* relationships that occur among archival agents in figure 3.1 are intended to extend serial motivations toward those who historicize texts and construct archives. They further help bridge the rhetorician's agency with the agency of those whom she studies, and the rhetor's agency with those studying her, by offering new justifications for the construction of rhetorical histories and critical methodologies that span time and space. Finally, they are shaped by known as well as perceived norms of their discourse communities—temporal, cultural, and social (Hutcheon 143)—which means they ultimately invite historians to reimagine topos and *kairos* to account for more varied performances and more layered contexts. As of 2014, the International Women's Media Foundation reports that there are currently twenty-one female leaders of developed and developing countries. Not all of these women are popularized or historicized under the guise of irony (or "ironness," for that matter), but this fact does mark an occasion for our analytic methodologies to evolve along with their careers and for our motives underlying the *teaching* of historians of rhetoric to evolve as well. *Evolved* practices and motives allow not only for richer readings of their performances but also for more richly historicized contexts and disciplinary assumptions in which these performances are thought to abide and continue to abide.

An irony paradigm is interdisciplinary—occupying the spaces between disciplinary lenses for analysis and theorization—rather than multidisciplinary, which combines disciplinary lenses for analysis and theorization. In fact, it raises new ways of thinking about disciplinary inquiry. Rather than this work being thought of as rooted only in certain faculties (or fields of knowledge), and hence representing the methodologies that those faculties invite—or representing very limited movement among specific fields of knowledge—I want to reposition the work as epistemological in itself. In other words, while I have deployed disciplinary notions quite often throughout this study, I have deployed them as acts of *locating desires*, out of a conviction that *locations* are provocative, disruptive, transparent, and sometimes contradictory. Another central goal of this book has been to demonstrate irony as an original *techné* for reading Renaissance, Colonial, and suffrage texts, histories, and archives. Merely recognizing it as an expression of historical *ethos* presumes that Askew, Hutchinson, and Gougar employed ironic responses to overturn a system in which they were still participating. However, recognizing it as an original *techné* presumes that they—and we—can employ ironic responses for modeling or rewriting the historical processes in which we function.

In her own theory of historical agency, Karlyn Kohrs Campbell draws on Aristotelian *techné* to argue for agency's artfulness—its propensity for being learned and taught, inasmuch as agency invites recognition of "what means are available in a given situation" ("Agency" 6), and this includes learning how to read and valuate performances, even years or contexts beyond that given situation or moment. However, I differ somewhat from Campbell's appropriation of *techné* in justifying the learned, reasoned, and reproducible nature of irony as I observe it in Askew's, Hutchinson's, and Gougar's discourse. Campbell argues that "agency emerges out of performances or actions that, when repeated, fix meaning through sedimentation" ("Agency" 7). While patterns are important, I do not think sedimentation is a necessary condition for, or outcome of, understanding irony as agency. What I identify as panhistorical agency in figure 2.1 is hermeneutic but reciprocal; irony's paradigmatic potential is more aptly seen in the realizations it allows us about how we can read texts and notice ourselves as interpreters and interlocutors.

An irony paradigm enables a cross-cultural historical project. Achieving something like a global feminist rhetorical historiography requires a way for agents to "speak to each other across time and space" (Wang 29), to see the ways their texts and archives work toward global interdependence. It also requires a way for agents to realize locatability as something that is always evident but constantly fragile, and whose fragility can be embraced. Even so, panhistoriography is not necessarily boundless and free, operating apart from the confines of time, memory, and culture. On the contrary, what irony makes possible for historical work is precisely how it *illuminates these things*—time, memory, and culture—*as nuanced relations among archival agents.* Thus in chapter 2, I did not argue to overcome memory, but to overcome the notion that memory is necessarily in conflict with other critical aspects of historical work. Ironic interpretation not only should reflect what we believe enculturation looks like across and between rhetorical cultures, but it also should invent new tools and devise new challenges to the status quo (Wang 29). Ironic interpretation should also (or primarily) call into question historians' beliefs about enculturation and about who is authorized to narrate rhetorical history on whose behalf and in what terms (Carlacio 132).

By deemphasizing irony's interpretive outcomes and reemphasizing its interstitial gaps, the acts of reading, speaking, and addressing can serve a more authentically cross-cultural project. A truly cross-cultural rereading of Meir's 1969 statement, for example, could accomplish several things. It could destabilize theoretically limited notions of "identification" and "belonging" that permanently embroil it or reveal other troubled notions of diplomacy, citizenship, migration, and diaspora that occur in its discursive wake. Where Bo Wang argues for our disciplinary future in putting comparative rhetoric into dialogue with feminist rhetorical ethics, and where Christa Olson argues for our disciplinary future in putting our historical assumptions into dialogue with the ethical expectations of those being historicized, I argue for our disciplinary future in the realization of multistable associations between and among critical ironic agents.

Ultimately, I encourage feminist historians to question what it means to examine textual events, what it means to read histories of writing (and speaking) in political contexts as question building rather than problem solving, and how those acts of examining and reading can affect the formation of our discipline. Even more important than acknowledging these locations is striving for historical discourses in feminist rhetoric that do not follow the real, but rather signify it as something that resides not in the past, but in its own processes of recovery and discovery (Certeau 42).

NOTES

WORKS CITED

INDEX

INTRODUCTION: WHY AN IRONY PARADIGM FOR FEMINIST
HISTORIOGRAPHY, AND WHY NOW?

1. Resolution 181, known also as the "Plan of Partition with Economic
Union for Palestine," was presented to the UN General Assembly on 29
November 1947 and passed on the day of voting, but it was not popularly
received and ultimately not implementable as a strategy for "remapping"
such a conflicted empire (Benvenisti 14; UN General Assembly 3). Calling
for a planned evacuation of geographic Palestine by August 1948 and an
optional relocation of Arabs and Jews into population-majority states,
Res. 181 was intended to support the establishment of a future Palestinian
government in light of the fighting that ensued following Britain's 1937
proposal to partition the land. The UN Palestine Commission reported on
14 May 1948 that Res. 181 had failed for a myriad of reasons, including a
civil war that erupted almost immediately after its adoption, generational
distrust due to prior British support of Zionist oversettlement in Palestinian territories, and suspicion among both Arabs and Jews that such
a relocation would lead to a political and ideological separation, rather
than an equitable accommodation of two national peoples (Benvenisti
229–31).

2. Throughout this book, *feminist* is not used interchangeably with
feminine or *female*. Where it appears outside of a quoted context, feminist
refers to a particular approach or analytic lens, rather than to the qualities of texts written by or about women rhetors. Sometimes it describes
a particular historical or intellectual controversy—such as *la querelle des
femmes*, which dominated sixteenth- and seventeenth-century European
depictions of women rhetors—if I am theorizing that controversy according to today's variant understandings of the term.

3. I do not devalue these aims, but I deemphasize them when they
lead to tropes of engendering and victimhood.

4. Gearhart sought to separate academic practices in rhetoric from
persuasion and proposed rhetoric as communication, where the main goal

was not to change others but to "relate to each other, to other entities"
(198). For Gearhart, this kind of listening, receiving, collective attitude
reflected a "womanization of the discipline" (201). In their 1995 revision
of Gearhart's concept, Sonja Foss and Cindy Griffin further describe the
suasory nature of rhetoric as irresolvable, arguing that it goes against
basic feminist principles (4).

5. Sean Zwagerman's *Wit's End* opens with the premise that in the study
of women's twentieth-century literature, "humor" needs more nuanced
articulation as a term and concept but is best articulated according to
its various performative ends, rather than according to how it gets defined in limited speech acts. He in turn cites two other landmark studies:
Nancy Walker's *A Very Serious Thing*, which ultimately and usefully distinguishes between feminine and feminist humor but claims that humor
elides any clear definition for analytic usefulness in women's texts (xi,
qtd. in Zwagerman 2); and Linda Hutcheon's *Irony's Edge*, in which she
recommends studying irony as an interpretive scene, arguing that "the
dynamic and plural relations among the text or utterance (and its context),
the so-called ironist, the interpreter, and the circumstances" resist any
neat theorization (11). I wholeheartedly agree with these statements of difficulty, and I praise Zwagerman for beginning his project in the productive
quandary raised by studying humorous language as discursive attitudes,
rather than as discrete symbolic actions. I appreciate Zwagerman's work
because his redefinition of any *speech act* does not separate its linguistic
and rhetorical aspects. He calls it a "performative, explicit or implicit,
direct or indirect, . . . *act of communication, linguistic or otherwise, having a world-to-word—or world-to-symbol/gesture—direction of fit, toward
some perlocutionary effect*" (22, original emphasis). However, what may
result—what often results—is an implied conflation of women's irony
and humor, in spite of Candace Lang's and Hutcheon's own statements
to the contrary (*Irony's Edge* 4), and in spite of irony's recurrence as a
communicative mode in women's political discourse.

6. I use the word *performance* to emphasize simultaneously the textual, contextual, and extratextual dimensions of their rhetorical situations
as well as the deliberateness that informed how they wanted to be read
as women involved in discourses of struggle, recognizing that this is a
somewhat strained position for historiographers to take.

7. This undervaluing occurs in spite of key theoretical discussions of
irony's origins and uses, such as those offered by Wayne Booth, Hutcheon,
and C. Jan Swearingen, as I discuss in Chapter 1, and even more recent

case studies offered by Rachel Giora, Elizabeth Galewski, and Zwagerman, which I take up in later chapters.

8. Even while distinguishing ironies from one another, Lang's principal distinctions between irony and humor are based on the notion that irony "becomes serious only when it is negated, when signifier once again coincides with signified" (C. Lang 42), while humor is an entity that cannot be critically owned. What Lang calls "humor," "the acknowledged and assertion of the subject's fragmentation, a reaffirmation and exploration of the *inter*subjective nature of individual identity" (C. Lang 48), Gary Handwerk calls "ethical irony" and I also understand as irony. For Handwerk, "irony is a form of discourse that insists upon the provisional and fragmentary nature of the individual subject and thus forces us to recognize our dependence upon some mode of intersubjectivity that exceeds the furthest extension of any individual subject" (viii).

9. A 1904 *New York Times* article titled "The Tragedy of Anne Hutchinson" reported that Hutchinson's family tree included John Dryden, Sir Erasmus Dryden, and Jonathan Swift.

10. Allusions to Askew occur in documents surrounding Hutchinson's Antinomian controversy, while various *fin de siècle* reports of American Suffrage activities like Gougar's allude to the controversy itself.

11. The lack persists even though rhetoric scholars have acknowledged irony as alternatively "an effect, technique, or tone of linguistic, literary, or cognitive practice" (Kaufer, "Irony and Rhetorical" 90).

12. Throughout this book, *agentive* describes something that *has the semantic function of* an agent—in other words, the word's morphemes are agentive in some manner—whereas *agential* describes something that *is or acts as* an agent. This means that rhetors (e.g., Askew, Hutchinson, Gougar, and others), discourses, and interpretations are all referred to as *agential*, whereas particular texts, actions, and topical subjects are all referred to as *agentive*.

1. ON WOMEN AND AGENCY: IRONIZING TOGETHER

1. In his 1654 *Wonder-Working Providence of Sions Saviour in New England*, Edward Johnson portrays Hutchinson as a trophy in a spiritual war, describing her responses as a "Master-piece of Womens wit" through which the devil readily worked (134; qtd. in A. Lang, *Prophetic* 62).

2. Gougar spoke in almost every state, lecturing or appearing regularly in New York, Connecticut, Illinois, Indiana, Nebraska, Kansas, and Iowa. She wrote suffrage legislation for Kansas and Indiana and

corresponded for Chicago's *Daily Inter Ocean* for several years, earning notoriety from Hawaii (as seen in the *Honolulu Republic*) all the way to Washington, DC (*National Republican*). Between 1883 and 1907, these and other major newspapers mentioned or cited Gougar more than two hundred times.

3. After marrying against her wishes and bearing two children, Askew sought a divorce from Thomas Kyme of Lincolnshire and joined the Reformation movement in London, where she allegedly joined Queen Catherine Parr's inner circle. Before leaving Lincolnshire, Askew had come under suspicion by local clergy for "gospelling" (McQuade 2), and no public *record* indicates that a divorce was granted. However, it was not until she attracted the attention of ecclesiastical authorities in London that Askew was arraigned on the grounds of suspected heresy, jailed and interrogated, released without indictment, re-arrested three months later, interrogated by the King's Privy Council, imprisoned, illegally tortured, and finally—on 16 July 1546—burned at Smithfield, just outside the London Wall.

4. Even with this knowledge, it is not clear from historical records whether Askew was more influenced by classical rhetorical training or studies in formal logic. The former emphasized probable premises based on the laws of forensic discourse, while the latter emphasized certainty based on factual scientific premises (e.g., syllogisms).

5. The full title reads, "The first examinacyon of Anne Askewe, lately martyred in Smythfelde, by the wycked Synagoge of Antichrist, with the Elucydacyon of Johan Bale."

6. For a comprehensive look at how rhetorical silence has evolved in historical, theoretical, and pedagogical projects since *Rhetoric Retold*, see the introduction to Glenn and Ratcliffe's collection *Silence and Listening as Rhetorical Arts*.

7. Glenn specifically discusses Askew as one of these women who wrote and spoke "within the traditional constraints of women's deliberate and systematic marginalization from rhetorical activity" (*Rhetoric* 143), and she articulates several strategies through which Askew's performance can be understood as authentically feminist, effective *because of* rather than *in spite of* her identity as a woman (153).

8. The term "ironization" stems from Hutcheon's examination of how Michel Foucault's "semantic web of resemblance" *becomes ironized* in Umberto Eco's *Foucault's Pendulum* through active reading (129). Several of Eco's narrative elements help situate Foucault's understanding of Renaissance thinking as vast, logocentric, passive, esoteric, and waiting to be

discovered. Hutcheon calls this narrative strategy an *ironization* because it promotes commonsensical female characters who are closer to "the truth" than their male counterparts and who directly oppose Foucault's depiction of pre-seventeenth-century thought. It also defies some of the presuppositions that Hutcheon brought to her reading of Eco's novel (129).

9. In "Logic and Conversation," Grice stipulates that a speech act is "cooperative"—and speakers and hearers are in the same mode—when four conditions occur: the speaker relays exactly as much information as is necessary; the speaker says only what she or he believes to be true; the speaker says only what is relevant; and the speaker is direct and succinct. One or more of these conditions can be violated without jeopardizing cooperation, so long as the speaker signals the violation to the listener and the listener understands it (47).

10. The principle is something like Amadeu Viana's "asymmetry" in semantic script opposition, where one script takes prominence over another or, rather, where one set of cognitive structures or extralinguistic paradigms progresses and becomes dominant during the telling of a narrative or a joke (Viana 523; Raskin 81). What is implied by these theories is that any ironic text necessarily gives more information than is required for its comprehension, says more than what is believed to be true, and obfuscates relevance and succinctness. John Morreall has already argued that the requirements of non-bona-fide communication and script opposition need not apply to all instances of irony or even verbal humor, given the many ways that sophisticated and nonjoke humor often "violat[es] pragmatic rules" (398).

11. This notion of contextual inappropriateness makes it possible for ironical utterances to be technically relevant according to Grice's criteria, while also being semantically inappropriate in their context (Attardo, *Humorous* 116).

12. Attardo introduces the concept of multiple levels to account for the embeddedness caused by a narrative occurring within a narrative or when there is more than one narrative voice controlling a text (*Humorous* 81), an idea I extend here to justify Askew's second context.

13. Giora's and Attardo's definitions of irony may already accommodate interstitial awareness in examples such as this one, because they diverge from Gricean cooperation in distinguishing between *contextually relevant* and *situationally appropriate*. It becomes important, then, to trace how and where the incongruity occurs, whether it is resolved for both speaker(s) and audience(s), and how much of this (ir)resolution is

dependent on certain historical, literary, ideological, and critical contexts. However, I do not limit their tracing to linguistic analysis alone, because there are extralinguistic ways of determining incongruity.

14. The "kynges boke" refers to the circa 1543 publication *A Necessary Doctrine and Erudition for Any Christen Man*, issued by the king's authority and intended to restore essential Roman Catholic doctrine as the official national standard.

15. Cicero's "words antithetically used" and "ironic dissimulation" represented some theoretical development beyond Aristotelian functions of irony, making ironic statements "agreeable as well in grave as in humorous speeches" (*De Oratore* bk. 2, sec. 67). Irony's jocosity is discussed in these treatises as a property of the rhetor's self-representation and was not linked to epistemic processes until Wayne Booth's 1974 *A Rhetoric of Irony* or understood as a nonhumorous form until C. Jan Swearingen's history of irony as a paradigm for literate discourse (*Rhetoric and Irony*, 1991).

16. Booth's "rhetorical ironies" are designed by one human being deliberately to be shared with at least one other human being (234). From this, Booth devised an analytic classification of ironies as stable or unstable, covert or overt, and local or infinite, ultimately helping answer the questions "What does it mean—is it ironic?" and "How do I know?" (xi, 235). Ultimately, his rhetoric demonstrated how theories of irony that strive only to provide an infinite set of interpretations are more finite than they let on.

17. Swearingen indirectly addressed this limitation by demonstrating how the formation of ironic communication has worked alongside the various orality-to-literacy shifts that define Western rhetorical traditions. But in positing irony as a lens by which to view how rhetoric and literacy practices historically interrelate, Swearingen strengthened its ties to ethics and value. Her own framing of irony in the question "To what extent do beliefs about the nature of language shape how language is used?" and her discussion of how Augustine justified irony as an "edifying enigma" do come close to liberating irony from purely moral content, though not from notions of linguistic deceit. This follows Augustine's argument in *De Doctrina Christiana* that simply reporting or speaking ironic examples, if they were already present in scripture, is not deceitful without the intent to deceive (Swearingen 201). Words are signs; thus, when linked with scriptural hermeneutics, literary irony and rhetorical indirection become "edifying enigma" rather than "mendacity" or "indirection" (Swearingen 176, 180).

18. See, for example, the examinations and depositions of Dorcas Hell-yer and Hannah Claiborne in Fowles's *A Maggot*, subjugations of Henry Ayscough, whose sole purpose was to make a case for Ann Lee's mother as "devilish, wicked, a whore" (299) and whose principal technique involved appealing to the fantastical as a way of testing their belief in eighteenth-century realism (80–89, 157–65).

19. Ramus's *Training in Dialectic* was published and circulated pseud-onymously in the same year that Askew was burned. One can speculate as to how Askew's discursive strategies might have been affected by the circulation of this new text had she lived long enough to see these revisions to the classical system of *topoi* (Ong, *Ramus* 245).

20. For Prior, exposing the limitations of Bakhtinian situated utter-ances as too narrowly grounded in literary paradigms—rather than in linguistic, semiotic, psychological, or social paradigms that would allow written utterances to be situated historically (21)—reveals various "blind spots" in discourse theory that keep us from positing writing as action and activity (23). Prior's discussion of all utterances as multimodal—whether they are spoken or written (in fact, as "embodied, material, multisensory, multi-semiotic")—rather than fixed or concrete is meant to inform new methods of analytic practice for discourse studies writ large (27).

21. In her 1673 "Essay to Revive the Ancient Education of Gentle-women," Makin cites Askew as a "person famous for learning and piety" to argue that a gentlewoman's education is not only possible but also customary and beneficial (Beilin, *Examinations* xxxix).

22. Also known as the "Bloody Statute" or the "Bloody Whip with Six Strings," the Six Articles of 1539 (31 Henry VIII, c. 14) reaffirmed general tenets of Catholicism as parliamentary, including transubstantiation, clerical celibacy, chastity, and confession.

23. The "course of scoles," or "order of schools," refers to the rules of scholastic debate associated with Catholic scholarship at the time.

24. Karlyn Kohrs Campbell's best demonstration of this point is in her analysis of Frances Dana Gage's 1863 transcription of Sojourner Truth's "Arn't I a woman?" speech, delivered in 1851 in Akron, Ohio—a transcription that Campbell calls "fictive" for its assimilation of supposed with actual elements so as to represent Truth as the ideal African American woman speaker in her context.

25. The nuns' behaviors were called "possession" because that term could better account for the presence of two souls, two minds, and two voices struggling for agency in a single being; more specifically, the term

could better maintain the social homogeneity that was assumed to exist between those possessed and those who exorcised them. Were it labeled "altered" or "inhabited," the Ursuline nuns' discourse could be attributed to an authentic source, something that had been authored elsewhere and had since become lost or made inaccessible, fragmented by speech patterns that were determined ahead of time (Certeau 253). When it is labeled "possessed," the Ursuline women's discourse cannot wholly be attributed to an "other" beyond the priests' control, cannot itself be differently attributed, and cannot be identified beyond the locus prepared for the nuns on the demonological stage, because it is "established relative to the discourse that awaits [them] in *that* place" (Certeau 248).

26. In her study of Judith Sargent Murray's 1779 "On the Equality of the Sexes," Elizabeth Galewski identifies *ironic reversals*—movement between romantic irony and dialectical irony—as a narrative strategy for reconstituting the eighteenth-century female mind (Galewski 86).

2. ON LANGUAGE AND HISTORY: ELIDING DICHOTOMIES

1. Prophesying had not been against the law in England or new America. However, David Hall mentions that it made the authorities uneasy and that in New England, men derived a stricter hierarchical authority from their gender, which they could do by arguing that their learning was superior to women's (Hall xi). In the end, the ministers associated Hutchinson with the most radical separatists because of her tendency to value "the submersion of the self in the Holy Spirit" over anything in the material world (Hall xi), and the latter part of Hutchinson's trial before the Boston Church returned often to her claims of "authority by inspiration."

2. Although Antinomian histories do not often focus on William Hutchinson, it is important to note that his own magisterial aspirations took him to Portsmouth, Rhode Island, slightly ahead of Anne, where she joined him at the conclusion of her trial. They resided there until he died in 1642, prompting her to migrate to the New Netherlands (present-day New York).

3. Although scholars have taken up his claims with mixed criticism, Edmund Morgan's assertion that Hutchinson's activities went unproven still remains: "before her trial [she] had never publicly advanced her tenet of personal revelation. Neither had she openly professed any doctrines that could be sanely regarded as contrary to the Law of God. . . . [N]evertheless, . . . the synod of ministers had found eighty-two of them to condemn" (Morgan 644).

4. In Winship's definition, "Antinomian" refers to a justified believer who assumes exemption from divine moral law. Yet Hutchinson distinguished herself as believing differently than the Antinomians. Consequently, much of the trial was spent disputing "the nature of the grace that God freely bestowed on those whom He intended to save" (*Times* 3). Thus Winship cites nineteenth-century historians as the cause for labeling Hutchinson's trials the "Antinomian" controversy.

5. Lyle Koehler provides archival evidence that Winthrop was "harshly critical of female intellect" (58) and reminds us that John Cotton, during the 1638 trial, dissociated himself from Hutchinson far enough as to characterize Antinomianism as "a women's delusion" (Koehler 68).

6. They were not the first; Barker-Benfield argues that Hutchinson's responses were motivated by her desire to be included in the "priesthood of all believers" that Puritanism offered. He also maintains that Winthrop's reaction to Hutchinson's stance on needing no intermediary between herself and the deity was motivated by what he perceived as a sexual threat (Barker-Benfield 66) or by evidence of her being too "man-like" (Barker-Benfield 76).

7. This particular disagreement surfaced when Thomas Wilson questioned Hutchinson on what he thought to be a "contradiction" on the second, third, and fourth of sixteen alleged charges brought against her in the 1638 trial (Hall 351–52, 357): What becomes of the spirit when the body dies? and In immediate revelation, does the body die?

8. Westerkamp notes this as one of several discursive strategies employed by Puritan women: self-deprecatory language, passive voice, and the placement of God at the center of discourse ("Puritan" 586).

9. This could likely be an ironic reference to how the American church prohibited women from witnessing in the pulpit, yet tried them publicly for taking part in lay ministry.

10. While I do not disagree with popular historical opinion that Hutchinson posed contradictions at this point in the trial, it is worthwhile to note that Hutchinson's rhetorical deferral in the statement "I only believe as my minister has believed" is not unique.

11. Raymond contends that "a firm distinction between public and private is one we project backwards into the sixteenth and seventeenth centuries, a period which saw the formation of these categories as well as the construction of a division between the political and domestic spheres" (277).

12. Hutchinson's behavior did not go unnoticed by Robert Baillie, a minister writing from Glasgow at the time of the controversy, who is

highly critical of the Bay Colony church for what he perceives as a lack of attention to its wrongdoing (64). Baillie's criticism raises the possibility that Winthrop and the elders did not experience a crisis of negligence or obstinancy, but rather a crisis of definition regarding where ecclesiastical jurisdiction could be held—in the people or in the presbytery (181).

13. Backus's *Discourses* were indigenous to New England, calling for separation between church and state and lamenting that many preachers placed such extraordinary emphasis on their external appointments over their "internal call" that they were no different from the "rank Arminians" against whom John Cotton had argued (Backus 16).

14. Baillie argues that if "the people" enjoyed the power of ordination, it would not only "disable them in their Callings" but also introduce "Morellius Democracy and Anarchy" into the church (186–87), and he uses John Cotton's "Arminian Errours" and subsequent "obstinacy" as evidence of the church's waywardness (57, 65).

15. These gatherings eventually were attended by the governor himself and by deputies to the General Court (Williams 117; Buchanan, "Study" 246).

16. These images in turn echo the woman whom C. Jan Swearingen finds in Erasmus's *Praise of Folly*, posing as "a fool and a whore," able to expound on serious views only through an ironic pretense (228).

17. Winthrop, Welde, and others who departed from Hutchinson's views dramatically called up the fecund "monstrosities" suffered by Hutchinson's friend Mary Dyer, whose miscarriage created a small controversy of its own (Buchanan, "Study" 249).

3. ON LOCATION AND MEMORY: CHALLENGING *ETHOS*

1. The 1888 *Biographical Record and Portrait Album of Tippecanoe County* describes Gougar as "genuinely 'Western' by birth, education, and temperament" ("Biography" 638). However, Gougar was not limited in work, scope, or involvement to regional issues.

2. Gougar's lecture was titled "How Can the Civil and Political Rights of Indiana Women Be Enlarged without Constitutional Amendment?"

3. This remained a mainstay argument for Gougar throughout her career, juxtaposing foreign-born men given American privileges with native-born women denied these same privileges to reveal how current definitions of "citizenship" limited voting rights.

4. In January 1882, Gougar traveled to Washington, DC, to address the US Senate on behalf of Midwest suffrage, prompting this report in the *Inter Ocean*: "Mrs. H. M. Gougar of Indiana . . . is today a more able

statesman in power than two-thirds of those men who occupy those seats." Two years later, in 1884, the *Inter Ocean* reported favorably on Gougar's speech before the New York General Assembly ("Significant").

5. Gougar's "Bric-a-Brac" column encompasses a mixture of genres, but its contents exceed the sentimental and are not limited to "feminine" topics. In her columns, she lauds domestic efficiency, makes public service announcements, reprints personal letters, and protests US policies on immigration and foreign-born politicians, as well as religious hypocrisy. Gougar wrote more than a hundred installments between November 1878 and September 1880, filling anywhere from three to four and a half columns each time.

6. The 25 June 1896 *Chicago Tribune* reports that Gougar was running as Prohibition candidate for state attorney general (Kriebel, *Where the Saints* 162).

7. The front page of the 2 January 1897 *Milwaukee Sentinel* corroborates the story: "Mrs. Helen M. Gougar stepped down and out of the Nationalist party yesterday [31 December 1896]. . . . Ever since the election she has been criticized by some of the extreme members of the party for her part taken in speaking for the cause of bimetallism in the late campaign" ("Helen M. Gougar Ousted").

8. Ann D. Gordon's account does not explicitly consider that the Indiana State Suffrage Association may have moved in step with Gougar because alcoholism was a local phenomenon that undermined not only suffrage ideals but also emerging labor laws. It provided a regionally significant political platform.

9. Kriebel calls these later columns "long, laborious, highly opinionated, and at times obnoxiously egotistical," speculating that Gougar was probably reading less, "rewriting her own old themes," and becoming more absorbed with international travel and concerns (*Where the Saints* 198). I doubt she was reading less and "rewriting her old themes," since a number of references to her lecturing activity in the *Chicago Inter Ocean*, *Joplin (MO) Daily Globe*, and *Honolulu Independent* between 1896 and 1900 point to the involvement of both Helen Gougar and her husband, John, in bimetallism, foreign philanthropy, and US immigration law.

10. Gougar had been working on a history of global women's suffrage based on her extensive travels when she died from sudden heart failure at age sixty-four, leaving it unfinished. Thus Ida Harper's "Woman Suffrage throughout the World," published in 1907 by the *North American Review*, filled this role.

11. The 20 February 1897 *Chicago Daily Tribune* reports that Gougar "almost took away the breath of the learned jurists with a well-reasoned argument." She gave "a strong argument, free from female pyrotechnics and bristling with sound legal points that should cause some hesitation before the court decides against her" (Kriebel, *Where the Saints* 163).

12. Gougar's test case was reenacted in an interactive presentation on 10 November 2009 as part of the Indiana Courts in the Classroom Series called "My Place Is in the Voting Booth" (http://www.in.gov/judiciary/citc/lessons/gougar/).

13. As early as her 25 January 1879 "Bric-a-Brac" column, she writes:

> Our taxpayers are taxed for the support of the poor, for the administration of laws and justice, for the support of schools, reformatories and asylums; but over against all these they license, yes they actually throw the sanction of law around, the rum traffic which is the principal agent in making necessary all this heavy taxation for the support of the poorhouses, reformatories and asylums, as well as most of the expense in maintaining the courts of justice. (Kriebel, *Where the Saints* 52)

14. For a useful summation of Gougar's position against the gold standard and involvement with antitrust, see "Helen Gougar's Sunday Speech." Later, several city papers across the country dated 15–16 February 1900 note that Gougar was appointed to a nonpartisan committee with ten men to protest the currency bill.

15. Between 2004 and 2005, on behalf of the Tippecanoe County Historical Association (TCHA), I processed a reassembled collection of papers, documents, publications, memorabilia, and family history pertaining to the Jackson and Gougar families. A segment of the collection contained Robert Kriebel's research notes, acid-free copies of news clippings from Lafayette and Indianapolis that chronicled Gougar's activities, and meticulous genealogical work done by former archivist Sarah E. Cooke prior to 1983. Several new accessions in the late 1980s and early 1990s, updated research, and the integration of a new data management system made it necessary to process a new collection.

16. As a case in point, Gougar's portrayal as a public activist (and my processing of her collection in this way) also became the subject for other Gougar researchers, including Jennifer Adams, who has undertaken a thorough and systematic recovery of Gougar's performances, and Renee Stowitzky, who in 2006 researched a biographical chapter on Gougar

NOTES TO PAGE 116

for a course at Stanford Law School. Stowitzky's biographical chapter is itself public record, which illustrates how intricate the activity system for recovering women's political texts and suffrage performances is and how dynamic its revisions and recountings needs to be.

17. On 27 April 1983, Ann D. Gordon wrote a letter to Gougar's surviving grand-niece, Lura Sherry Hughel, querying about any surviving letters that Gougar might have exchanged with Stanton and Anthony during her service to the NWSA. Gordon was in the midst of preparing a documentary titled "Papers of Elizabeth Cady Stanton and Susan B. Anthony," now a series of volumes that is thoroughly and masterfully compiled, in which she argues that "Mrs. Gougar was an important co-worker of both Stanton and Anthony, and her correspondence with them, if it survived, would be an important source for scholars." Unfortunately for Gordon, Hughel, and the suffrage histories that have been constructed from Gordon's collection, little of Gougar's prolific correspondence had been retained or recovered. Hughel replied on 5 May 1983 with the unfruitful news that "Aunt Helen's" letters did not get passed on:

> At that time, the furnishings of the Gougar home were disposed of. . . . I was in grade school then and not on the scene, but my parents were involved and I am sure that my grandmother or my father or the housekeeper, Minnie [Wilhelmina Kalberer] would have separated such letters out for special disposition. All these memories lead me to believe that Uncle John must have made some disposition of Aunt Helen's correspondence sometime, not too long, after her death.

Excerpts from the letter, which resides with the accession papers of the Helen Gougar Colleton at TCHA, explain that Lura spent much time at Castle Cottage visiting her grandmother, Adelaide Eugenia Jackson Sherry, who moved there to direct housekeeping after Helen's death in 1907 and remained there after John's death in 1924.

18. A detailed list of contents is viewable at http://ecssba.rutgers.edu/pubs/publications.html. In volume 5, Gougar is mentioned on pages 64, 67, 119, 141–42, 166, 212–13, 221–23, 231–33, 308–09, and 583.

19. Francis Murphy was an American Temperance evangelist, associated for most of his profession with the Nazarene Church and active mainly from 1870 until his official "retirement" in April 1906 ("Francis Murphy"). Gougar's interview for the *Honolulu Independent* describes at length her own interactions with Murphy on three separate occasions

while attending his platform lectures, during which he tried to get audience members to sign the temperance pledge that he authored in 1876. Neither Gougar nor the people she was with, nor many in the audience she witnessed, could be persuaded to sign the pledge ("Gougar on Murphy"), although Murphy's obituary in the *New York Times* cites an estimate that approximately sixteen million people had signed the pledge worldwide ("Francis Murphy").

20. This is Coretta Pittman's argument in "Black Women Writers," where she articulates the dilemma faced by Harriet Jacobs, Billie Holiday, and Sister Souljah in trying to reconcile "an ethos of immorality to an ethos of respectability," yet in a rhetorical context where that reconciliation could not be accommodated. In other words, the slave narratives and autobiographies they used to document their life experiences and show their womanliness, to some degree, necessarily positioned them as promiscuous women according to how they fell short of dominant codes of womanhood (48), pious standards that even in the nineteenth and twentieth centuries *still* stemmed from Aristotle's *Nicomachean Ethics*. The paradox that Pittman notes is that "to acquire a positive and respectable ethos, [Jacobs] had to borrow and adapt a positive ethos from an Aristotelian model" (49); ideally, she instead would have liberated the black woman's ethos from extant racialized standards.

21. For example, Robert Kriebel lists several lawsuits in which Gougar participated where, rather than seek monetary damage, she demanded a "victory of principle" ("Suffragist"). At the end of the highly publicized and controversial Gougar-Mandler trial, Gougar won but chose not to pursue the $5,000 in monetary damages that the defendant, Henry Mandler, failed to pay ("War on the Wabash").

22. A common motif throughout Gougar's work is the idea that "there is no sex in good or evil. Male and female are equal before God" ("Bric-a-Brac," 20 Dec. 1879).

23. An 1885 article in the *Woman's Exponent* noted that Gougar was "like Anthony . . . a good organizer" ("Woman's Jubilee," qtd. in Stowitzky 38).

24. The trial ended on 11 April 1883, but Gougar had first filed suit on 5 December 1882. Henry Mandler was police chief at the time and circulated a rumor about Gougar's having an alleged affair with attorney W. Dewitt Wallace, the Republican candidate for Indiana state senator. Michael Goldberg recounts Gougar's exhausting three-year campaign from 1884 to 1887, during which she earned state suffrage in Indiana and

weathered the storm of another slander suit (Congressman Elijah Morse, from Massachusetts, and Mandler), experiences that "left her physically and emotionally battered; some said the experience had turned her hair white" (Goldberg 87; "War on the Wabash").

25. Unfortunately, Gougar would not get to speak at the event; she was called home from Washington, DC, to attend the funeral of her mother-in-law, Hannah Gougar Schlotman, on 17 March 1888.

26. According to Goldberg's history, Gougar's next three years were significant for the municipalities of Topeka and Leavenworth, as she earned Kansas municipal suffrage and encouraged the formation of a chapter of the NWSA there. She also continued her tours of Indiana and Utah on the same errands (Goldberg 88).

27. Anthony referred to Gougar's "Partisan and Patriot" address at the NWSA's convention, in which Gougar "arraigned the major parties for their lockstep hostility to the Prohibition party and their tendency to act only in partisan opposition to each other" (Gordon 222) and spoke so long and so critically that Anthony finally had to call her to order (Gordon 223).

28. In a letter dated 17 January 1890 from Anthony to Indiana suffragist May Wright Sewall, Anthony writes, "I trust [Helen] cannot entirely block Indiana's wheels!!" (Gordon 231). And in 1901, the *Honolulu Republican* satirically chastised her for being "narrow," "self-important," and like "the Pharisees" ("Example").

29. It is unfortunate that Kriebel's careful and extensive biography of Gougar—for which he admits having had to speculate as to how a number of events transpired—narrates her life as a coherent march forward in the spiritual realm. This portrayal causes us to overlook the historical complexities of such "forward" movement.

30. For example, in his employment of verbal devices reminiscent of Bush-era discourse, Stephen Colbert first invites viewers to differentiate between Democrats and Republicans before inviting them to transcend those divisions and see themselves as Americans. Colbert enacted a form of "presidential discourse" on Jon Stewart's *Daily Show* using tricolon and anaphora—discursive forms that he did not necessarily invent for this occasion, but that when put together in an expected cultural context, yielded the same kind of emotional result as when they were used by the president, "tap[ping] into (and then play[ing] with) the cultural power they yield" (Holcomb 74).

31. For Campbell, "feminine" is not limited to "having the qualities of a female" (*Man* 3) and "is not, today, a style exclusive to women" (*Man* 12).

Rather, "feminine" explains how suffragists invented their topics and debates, coped with masculinist denials of their ability to write or to speak (*Man* 11), and accommodated female audiences by performing the contradictions implied by their public and private lives. One major contribution of theorizing women's social discourse according to substance and style is its accommodation of interpersonal communication to enact social change ("'Rhetoric'" 141).

32. Gougar was cited in the *Atlantic Monthly* by would-be Colorado State Supreme Court justice John H. Denison, who chastised her "Almighty-centeredness" and claimed that her liberal views lost sight of the true natural "structure of things" ("Survival" 20).

33. In "Emancipated Women," Bierce refutes Gougar's argument for women's suffrage on purely "logical" grounds, and he takes issue with enlarged female participation in commercial, professional, and industrial outlets. Like many of his contemporaries, Bierce did not consider good government to be the ultimate end for anyone to strive for ("Opposing Sex" par. 3), and he believed political involvement was ruinous to a woman's superior moral character ("Opposing Sex" par. 4–5). The opening lines read, "It may please Helen Gougar and satisfy her sense of logical accuracy to say, as she does: 'We women must work in order to fill the places left vacant by liquor-drinking men.' But who filled these places before? . . . If my memory serves, there has been no time in the period that it covers when the supply of . . . abstemious male workers—was not in excess of the demand" ("Emancipated" par. 1).

34. This biography recounts the true story of Matthew Peters's immigration from Germany to New Orleans, covers his eventual involvement in the Underground Railroad and Civil War, and provides Gougar a platform to argue for temperance, suffrage, and philanthropy as necessarily interrelated causes.

35. In *Contingency, Irony, and Solidarity*, Rorty redefines "irony" as something that occurs in descriptions of the world and of phenomena in the world that can be evaluated as fluctuating or stable. On the one hand, for Rorty, it is descriptions themselves—not their representations or the phenomena they represent—that lead to the creation of new vocabularies to help humans explore and understand the world around them: "the world is out there, . . . descriptions of the world are not" (*Contingency* 5). On the other hand, the very contingent qualities of language allow it to do more than describe; that is, it can shape other human processes, such as memory, empathy, and understanding.

36. Additional text from this lecture includes the following:

> At the risk of being considered supremely materialist I shall lay down the proposition that the first concern of any human being should be to secure bodily comfort; next, intellectual growth and culture; next, spiritual supremacy over the earth. Every girl should receive such training, both in and out of school, as to consummate these desirable ends. . . . Many contend that the chief end for which a woman should receive training should be "for wife and mother." There is no more reason or justice for this than there would be in training every boy to be "a husband and father." ("Industrial")

37. The article's ironic title carries three meanings: it represents one of the most common objections to women's rights of her time; it symbolizes Gougar's own former apathy toward legislating women's rights; and it conveys Mary O'Toole's frustrated perception of the sheltered woman who saw no practical need to vote on her own behalf. In short, it demonstrates how Gougar's second strategic response often marks her reliance on cultural norms by drawing on "shared" feminine values to target problematic assumptions about domesticated women and justify their participation in public work.

4. FREEING THE *ARCHON*

1. Gougar's earliest confrontational essays were delivered in 1871 and 1876 for literary reunions of the Young Men's Christian Association (YMCA), attended by local writers, philanthropists, and faculty from the newly established Purdue University. In "Shirks," delivered on 15 December 1871, Gougar "attacked weak-spined people who shirked their duty to God, family, fellowman, and self, creating the need for social reforms and help agencies" (Kriebel, *Where the Saints* 33). Kriebel reports that the *Lafayette Daily Courier* wrote it up as "an admirable production" (16 Dec. 1871, qtd. on 33). In "Pimples," delivered on 24 March 1876, Gougar targeted the weak and inconsistent enforcement of "temperance laws, . . . liquor licensing, wobbling churchgoers, individual sloth, irresponsibility, atheism," calling them "impurities in the nation's life blood" (Kriebel, *Where the Saints* 40).

2. On 15 August 1882, the *Indianapolis Journal* printed an account of a satirical remark Gougar had made at the 1882 Democratic State Convention that was taken literally, then construed as a lie, causing the tenor of her whole remark to be understood as a vituperative endorsement

of the party and raising the ire of other suffrage organizers ("Gougar's Sarcasm").

3. The eight-page letter from Reverend Vaughan asks Gougar to send financial support for a third time, so he may continue his work at Christian socialist missions and attend to his ailing wife. It accompanied an ornate, hand-published, leather-bound book of Vaughan's poems and essays, only one of five such volumes that had been published by the time Gougar received hers. Gougar likely made Vaughan's acquaintance while he was street preaching in Boston and Providence during one of her lecturing trips to the Eastern Seaboard.

4. Having served as Indiana state senator, Harrison continued to view Indiana as a swing state of sorts.

5. It also was apparently well received. The printed transcript occupied more than seventeen sixteen-inch news columns and indicated three incidents of cheering, thirty-eight incidents of applause, ten incidents of great applause, a single incident of loud applause, two incidents of great laughter, and eight incidents of laughter.

6. This resonates with Gougar's criticism of the local Republican Party later in the address for employing moralistic rhetoric while actively seeking "whiskey votes." On 18 October 1882, Gougar replies to a letter from the Reverend B. Wilson Smith, in which he asked *Our Herald* to provide a platform for his campaign. Gougar advises him to stop being "cowardly on the Prohibition question" and seek instead to "sustain the change" by refusing to accept endorsements from the saloons ("Letter").

7. For example, Royster argues for challenging historical assumptions that African women's rhetorical participation began in nineteenth-century United States, when we can reasonably situate it thirty-five centuries earlier by being more inclusive with our examination of rhetorical practices across genre, space, and time—more inclusive of the terms of their "participation" ("Disciplinary" 151).

8. Examples include the Carlisle Indian School, the Laredo-based Spanish-language newspaper *La Crónica*, the historically black Wiley College, Texas Women's University, and East Texas Normal College.

5. TOWARD AN IRONY PARADIGM

1. In "Postnational Ethics, Postcolonial Politics," Jamil Khader considers how these difficulties of identification are compounded for Arabic women—even if they are not performing on a global stage—through journalist Raimonda Tawil's *My Home, My Prison*:

Ultimately, any womanist, or feminist, critique of Arab patriarchal structures and its nationalist master narrative had to be suspended until a collective subjectivity and a national sovereignty were affirmed. Especially in Palestine, since the convention of the Arab Women's Congress of Palestine in 1929, Palestinian women have been expected to commit themselves to the project of nationalist mobilization (*al-a'amal al-watani*) at the expense of their struggle for social rights and gender equity. (72)

2. For example, the Library of Congress's American Memory historical collections continue to grow, though supplied by a small number of repositories, while a good deal of other municipal and local feminist activity languishes unprocessed in underfunded historical associations. Because of what these collections condition us to value in suffrage histories and performances, historiographers might find it difficult to embrace more obscure types, genres, and traditions, or even to valuate them apart from their antecedents.

3. Today Kaufer might justify these claims by saying that in his 1983 article, he wished to articulate a concrete ironic *form*, rather than a more abstract theory of irony. However, the persistent linking of these traits with irony—especially in women's texts—has truncated the notion of what it means to interpret irony rhetorically, in spite of Kaufer's attempt to expand our uses of irony beyond simple application (via literary analysis) ("Irony, Interpretive" 456).

4. "Liberal irony" is a term that Rorty applies to the condition of hoping that "suffering will be diminished, [and] that the humiliation of human beings by other human beings may cease" (Rorty, *Contingency* xv).

5. In *Composing Research*, Cindy Johanek challenges methodological pluralism in composition research when it relies too much on untested ideologies or blocs of institutional power and privilege. She argues that past attempts at reconciling all of composition's research paradigms have fallen short of achieving cross-disciplinarity or actually "emerging from the need to know" (108), including Stephen North's 1987 "methodological egalitarianism" and Gesa E. Kirsch's 1992 "methodological pluralism." I extend her challenge to feminist rhetorical research more broadly.

WORKS CITED

Adams, Jennifer L. *Introducing Helen Gougar: A Midwestern Pioneer in the Women's Rights Movement, 1878–1907.* 2007. TS. Paper submitted to the American Society for the History of Rhetoric Division of the National Communication Association, Chicago.

"Aguinaldo a President Is Mrs. Gougar's Wish." *Washington Times* 27 Jan. 1903: 2. *Chronicling America.* Lib. of Cong. Web. 1 Apr. 2010. <http://chroniclingamerica.loc.gov/lccn/sn84026749/1903-01-27/ed-1/seq-2/>.

Albright, Madeleine Korbel. *The Mighty and the Almighty: Reflections on America, God, and World Affairs.* New York: Harper, 2006. Print.

———. "Promoting Democracy: 14 Points for the 21st Century." Princeton Colloquium on Public and International Affairs. Woodrow Wilson School of Public and International Affairs, Princeton University, Princeton, NJ. 29 Apr. 2006. Keynote Address. *PCPIA.* Web. <http://www.princeton.edu/pcpia/previous-colloquia/2006/keynote/transcript/>.

Alcoff, Linda. "Cultural Feminism versus Post-Structuralism: The Identity Crisis in Feminist Theory." *Signs: Journal of Women in Culture and Society* 13 (1988): 405–36. Print.

Allen, James. "Aristotle on the Disciplines of Argument: Rhetoric, Dialectic, Analytic." *Rhetorica* 23.1 (2007): 87–108. Print.

Anderson, Dana. *Identity's Strategy: Rhetorical Selves in Conversion.* Columbia: U of South Carolina P, 2007. Print.

Anonymous. "From *Dissoi Logoi.*" *The Rhetorical Tradition: Readings from Classical Times to the Present.* 2nd ed. Ed. Patricia Bizzell and Bruce Herzberg. Boston: Bedford/St. Martin's, 2001. 47–55. Print.

"Anti-Woman Suffrage: Don't Fail to Read This." Pamphlet. N.d. Western History Collection. *Women and Social Movements in the United States, 1600–2000.* Web. 22 Dec. 2005. <http://womhist.binghamton.edu/colosuff/doc19.htm>.

Aristotle. *Metaphysics.* Trans. Hugh Tredennick. 1933. Cambridge, MA: Harvard UP. 1989. Print.

———. *On Rhetoric.* Trans. George Kennedy. New York: Oxford UP, 1991. Print.

Attardo, Salvatore. "Humor, Irony, and Their Communication: From Mode Adoption to Failure of Detection." *Say Not to Say: New Perspectives on Miscommunication.* Ed. Luigi Anolli, Rita Ciceri, and Giuseppe Riva. Amsterdam: IOS, 2002. 159–79. Print.

———. *Humorous Texts: A Semantic and Pragmatic Analysis.* Berlin: Mouton de Gruyter, 2001. Print.

———. "Irony as Relevant Inappropriateness." *Journal of Pragmatics* 32 (2000): 793–826. Print.

———. "On the Pragmatic Nature of Irony and its Rhetorical Aspects." *Pragmatics in 2000.* Ed. Eniko Nemeth. Antwerp: International Pragmatics Association, 2001. 52–66. Print.

Attardo, Salvatore, and Victor Raskin. "Script Theory Revis(it)ed: Joke Similarity and Joke Representation Model." *Humor* 4.3–4 (1991): 293–347. Print.

Augustine. *The Enchiridion of Augustine, Addressed to Laurentius: Being a Treatise on Faith, Hope, and Love.* Ed. Rev. Marcus Dods. Trans. J. F. Shaw. Edinburgh: Clark, 1873. *Internet Archive.* Web. 1 Apr. 2011.

———. *On Christian Doctrine.* Trans. D. W. Robertson. New York: Prentice Hall, 1958. Print.

Backus, Isaac. "A Short Description of the Difference between the Bond-woman and the Free; as They Are the Two Covenants, with the Characters and Conditions of Each of Their Children: Considered in a Sermon, Delivered at Middleborough." *Discourses by Backus.* Boston: Green and Russell, 1756. TS. John Carter Brown Library, Providence, RI. 23 Apr. 2010.

Baillie, Robert. "A Dissuasive from the Errours of the Time." London, 1645. TS. John Hay Library, Providence, RI. 22 Apr. 2010.

Bakhtin, Mikhail M. "The Problem of Speech Genres." *Speech Genres and Other Late Essays.* Trans. Vern W. McGee. Austin: U of Texas P, 1986. 60–101. Print.

Barker-Benfield, Ben. "Anne Hutchinson and the Puritan Attitude toward Women." *Feminist Studies* 1.2 (Autumn 1972): 65–96. JSTOR. Web.

Barratt, Alexandra, ed. *Women's Writing in Middle English.* 2nd ed. Harlow, UK: Pearson, 2010. Print.

Barreca, Regina. *Last Laughs: Perspectives on Women and Comedy.* New York: Gordon, 1988. Print.

Baumlin, Tita French. "'A Good (Wo)man Skilled in Speaking': Ethos, Self-Fashioning, and Gender in Renaissance England." *Ethos: New Essays in Rhetorical and Critical Theory.* Ed. J. Baumlin and Tita French Baumlin. Dallas: Southern Methodist UP, 1994. 229–64. Print.

Beilin, Elaine V. "Anne Askew's Dialogue with Authority." *Contending Kingdoms: Historical, Psychological, and Feminist Approaches to the Literature of Sixteenth-Century England and France.* Ed. Marie-Rose Logan and Peter Rudnytsky. Detroit: Wayne State UP, 1991. 313–22. Print.

———, ed. *The Examinations of Anne Askew.* New York: Oxford UP, 1996. Print.

———. *Redeeming Eve: Women Writers of the English Renaissance.* Princeton, NJ: Princeton UP, 1987. Print.

Benhabib, Seyla. "From Identity Politics to Social Feminism: A Plea for the Nineties." Philosophy of Education Society, 1994. Keynote Address. Web. 1 Apr. 2011. <http://www.ed.uiuc.edu/eps/PES-Yearbook/94_docs/94contents.html>.

Benvenisti, Meron. *Sacred Landscape: The Buried History of the Holy Land since 1948.* Trans. Maxine Kaufman-Lacusta. Berkeley: U of California P, 2002. Print.

Bercovitch, Sacvan. *The Puritan Origins of the American Self.* New Haven, CT: Yale UP, 1975. Print.

Bierce, Ambrose. "Emancipated Woman." *The Shadow on the Dial and Other Essays.* San Francisco: Robertson, 1909. *Project Gutenberg.* Web. 16 Aug. 2008.

———. "The Opposing Sex." *The Shadow on the Dial and Other Essays.* San Francisco: Robertson, 1909. *Project Gutenberg.* Web. 16 Aug. 2008.

Biesecker, Barbara. "Coming to Terms with Recent Attempts to Write Women into the History of Rhetoric." Poulakos 153–72.

———. "Of Historicity, Rhetoric: The Archive as Scene of Invention." *Rhetoric and Public Affairs* 9.1 (2006): 124–31. JSTOR. Web.

Bilger, Audrey. "Laughing All the Way to the Polls: Do Female Politicians Need a New Punch Line?" *Bitch* 30 (Fall 2005): 48–53. Print.

———. *Laughing Feminism: Subversive Comedy in Frances Burney, Maria Edgeworth, and Jane Austen.* Detroit: Wayne State UP, 2002.

"Biography of Helen M. Gougar." *Biographical Record and Portrait Album of Tippecanoe County, Indiana.* Chicago: Lewis P, 1888. 637–43. Rootsweb.com. Web. 16 Feb. 2004.

Bizzell, Patricia, and Susan Jarratt. "Rhetorical Traditions, Pluralized Canons, Relevant History, and Other Disputed Terms: Report from the ARS." *Rhetoric Society Quarterly* 34.3 (2004): 19–26. Print.

Black, Edwin. "The Second Persona." *Quarterly Journal of Speech* 56.2 (1970): 109–19. Print.

Blair, Carol. "Contested Histories of Rhetoric: The Politics of Preservation, Progress, and Change." *Quarterly Journal of Speech* 78.4 (1992): 403–28. JSTOR. Web.

"A Bloody Record." *Evening Bulletin* 22 Apr. 1891: 3. *Chronicling America.* Lib. of Cong. Web. 1 Apr. 2010. <http://chroniclingamerica.loc.gov/lccn/sn87060190/1891-04-22/ed-1/seq-3/>.

Blouin, Francis. "Archivists, Mediation and Constructs of Social Memory." *Archival Issues* 24.2 (1999): 101–12. Print.

Booth, Wayne C. *A Rhetoric of Irony.* Chicago: U of Chicago P, 1975. Print.

Bourdieu, Pierre. *Outline of a Theory of Practice.* Cambridge, MA: Cambridge UP, 1977. Print.

Bremer, Francis, ed. *Anne Hutchinson: Troubler of the Puritan Zion.* Huntington, NY: Krieger, 1981. Print.

Brereton, John C., and Cinthia Gannett. "Learning from the Archives [Review Essay]." *College English* 73.6 (2011): 672–81. Print.

Brown, Robert L. "The Pragmatics of Verbal Irony." *Language Use and the Uses of Language.* Ed. Roger W. Shuy and Anna Shnukal. Washington, DC: Georgetown UP, 1980. 111–27. Print.

Buchanan, Lindal. *Regendering Delivery: The Fifth Canon and Antebellum Women Rhetors.* Carbondale: Southern Illinois UP, 2005. Print.

———. "A Study of Maternal Rhetoric: Anne Hutchinson, Monsters, and the Antinomian Controversy." *Rhetoric Review* 23.3 (2006): 239–59. Print.

Burke, Kenneth. *A Grammar of Motives.* Berkeley: U of California P, 1969. Print.

———. *Language as Symbolic Action: Essays on Life, Literature, and Method.* Berkeley: U of California P, 1966. Print.

———. *The Rhetoric of Religion: Studies in Logology.* Boston: Beacon, 1961. Print.

Caldwell, Patricia. "The Antinomian Language Controversy." *Harvard Theological Review* 69.3/4 (1976): 345–67. Print.

"Campaign of 1888: Mrs. Helen M. Gougar Replies to Anna Dickinson."
  Lafayette Daily Courier 6 Nov. 1888. Helen Gougar Collection,
  Scrapbook item 73.17.8. Tippecanoe County Historical Association
  (hereafter TCHA), Lafayette, IN.

Campbell, Karlyn Kohrs. "Agency: Promiscuous and Protean." *Communication and Critical/Cultural Studies* 1.1 (2005): 1–19. JSTOR.
  Web.

———. "Biesecker Cannot Speak for Her Either." *Philosophy and Rhetoric*
  26 (1993): 153–59. Print.

———. "Consciousness-Raising: Linking Theory, Criticism, and Practice."
  Rhetoric Society Quarterly 31.1 (2002): 45–64. JSTOR. Web.

———. *Man Cannot Speak for Her*, Vol. I: *A Critical Study of Early Feminist
  Rhetoric*. Westport, CT: Greenwood, 1989. Print.

———. "Gender and Genre: Loci of Invention and Contradiction in the
  Earliest Speeches by U.S. Women." *Quarterly Journal of Speech*
  81 (1995): 479–95. JSTOR. Web.

———. "'The Rhetoric of Women's Liberation: An Oxymoron' Revisited."
  Communication Studies 50.2 (1999): 138–43. JSTOR. Web.

———. "Theory Emergent from Practice: The Rhetorical Theory of Frances
  Wright." Miller and Bridwell-Bowles 125–41.

———, ed. *Women Public Speakers in the United States, 1800–1925: A
  Bio-Critical Sourcebook*. Westport, CT: Greenwood, 1993. Print.

Campbell, Karlyn Kohrs, and Kathleen Hall Jamieson. "Form and Genre
  in Rhetorical Criticism: An Introduction." *Form and Genre: Shaping Rhetorical Action*. Ed. Karlyn Kohrs Campbell and Kathleen
  Hall Jamieson. Falls Church, VA: Speech Communication Assoc.,
  1978. 9–32. Print.

Carlacio, Jami L. "Speaking With and To Me: Discursive Positioning and
  the Unstable Categories of Race, Class, and Gender." Royster and
  Simpkins 121–32.

Carlson, A. Cheree. "Limitations on the Comic Frame: Some Witty American Women of the Nineteenth Century." *Quarterly Journal of
  Speech* 74 (1988): 310–22. JSTOR. Web.

Carr, Jean Ferguson, Stephen L. Carr, and Lucille M. Schultz. *Archives
  of Instruction: Nineteenth-Century Rhetorics, Readers, and Composition Books in the United States*. Carbondale: Southern Illinois
  UP, 2005. Print.

Certeau, Michel de. *The Writing of History*. Trans. Tom Conley. New York:
  Columbia UP, 1988. Print.

Cicero, Marcus Tullius. *De Oratore. Cicero: On Oratory and Orators.* Trans. and ed. J. S. Watson. Carbondale: Southern Illinois UP, 1970. Print.

Clarke, Danielle. *The Politics of Early Modern Women's Writing.* Harlow, Eng.: Pearson, 2001. Print.

Cleaves, AnDrea. "You May Take My Body, but Not My Soul: The Analysis of Letitia Wigington's Confession." Fifth Annual Feminisms and Rhetorics Conference. Michigan Tech University, Houghton. 7 Oct. 2005. Address.

Colby, Clara Bewick. "Helen Gougar." *Woman's Tribune* 29 June 1907. Helen Gougar Collection, Newspaper item 73.17.26. TCHA, Lafayette, IN.

Coles, Robert. *Irony in the Mind's Life: Essays on Novels by James Agee, Elizabeth Bown, and George Eliot.* Charlottesville: UP of Virginia, 1974. Print.

Colston, Herbert L., and Albert N. Katz, eds. *Figurative Language Comprehension: Social and Cultural Factors.* Mahwah, NJ: Erlbaum, 2005. Print.

Connors, Robert J. "Women's Reclamation of Rhetoric in Nineteenth-Century America." *Feminine Principles and Women's Experience in American Composition and Rhetoric.* Ed. Louise Wetherbee Phelps and Janet Emig. Pittsburgh: U of Pittsburgh P, 1995. 67–90. Print.

Cooper, Marilyn M. "Rhetorical Agency as Emergent and Enacted." *College Composition and Communication* 62.3 (2011): 420–49. Print.

Cotton, John. "The Way of Congregational Churches Cleared" (1648). Hall 396–438. Print.

Davis, Natalie Zemon. *Fiction in the Archives: Pardon Tales and Their Tellers in Sixteenth-Century France.* Palo Alto, CA: Stanford UP, 1987. Print.

Deakins, Roger. "The Tudor Prose Dialogue: Genre and Anti-Genre." *Studies in English Literature, 1500–1900* 20.1 (1980): 5–23. *JSTOR.* Web.

Deleuze, Gilles, and Félix Guattari. *A Thousand Plateaus: Capitalism and Schizophrenia.* Trans. Brian Massumi. Minneapolis: U of Minnesota P, 1987. Print.

Denison, John H. "The Survival of the American Type." *Atlantic Monthly* Jan. 1895: 17–22. *The Making of America.* Cornell University. Web. 22 Dec. 2005. <http://cdl.library.cornell.edu>.

Derrida, Jacques. *Archive Fever: A Freudian Impression*. Trans. Eric Pre-
nowitz. Chicago: U of Chicago P, 1996. Print.

———. "Différance." *Margins of Philosophy*. Trans. Alan Bass. Chicago:
U of Chicago P, 1982. 1–28. Print.

———. "Structure, Sign, and Play in the Discourse of the Human Sciences."
A Postmodern Reader. Ed. Joseph Natoli and Linda Hutcheon. Albany: State U of New York P, 1993. 223–43. Print.

Dillon, Elizabeth Maddock. "New England and Its Others: Women, As-
semblage, and the Archive." 3rd Annual Women in the Archives
Colloquium. Brown University, Providence, RI. 24 Apr. 2010.
Address.

Ditmore, Michael G. "A Prophetess in Her Own Country: An Exegesis of
Anne Hutchinson's 'Immediate Revelation.'" *William and Mary
Quarterly* 57.2 (2000): 349–92. Print.

Donawerth, Jane. "The Politics of Renaissance Rhetorical Theory by
Women." *Political Rhetoric, Power, and Renaissance Women*. Ed.
Carole Levin and Patricia A. Sullivan. New York: State U of New
York P, 1995. 257–74. Print.

———, ed. *Rhetorical Theory by Women before 1900: An Anthology*. Lanham, MD: Rowman, 2002. Print.

"Editorial." *Indianapolis Daily Sentinel*. 15 Feb. 1881. Print.

"Editorial." *Indianapolis Journal*. 15 Feb. 1881. Print.

"Editorial." *Lafayette Morning Journal*. 7 June 1907. Helen Gougar Collection, Scrapbook item 73.17.8. TCHA, Lafayette, IN.

Edwards, Rebecca. *Angels in the Machinery: Gender in American Party
Politics from the Civil War to the Progressive Era*. New York: Oxford UP, 1997. Print.

Eliot, George. *Impressions of Theophrastus Such*. New York: Harper, 1894.
Project Gutenberg. Web. 1 Apr. 2010.

Emirbayer, Mustafa, and Ann Mische. "What Is Agency?" *American Journal of Sociology* 103.4 (1998): 962–1023. Print.

Engbers, Susanna Kelly. "With Great Sympathy: Elizabeth Cady Stanton's
Innovative Appeals to Emotion." *Rhetoric Society Quarterly* 37.3
(2007): 307–32. Print.

Engeström, Yrjo, R. Engeström, and T. Vähäaho. "When the Center Does
Not Hold: The Importance of Knotworking." *Activity Theory and
Social Practice: Cultural-Historical Approaches*. Ed. S. Chaiklin,
M. Hedegaard, and U. J. Jensen. Aarhus, Den.: Aarhus UP, 1999.
345–74. Print.

Enoch, Jessica. *Refiguring Rhetorical Education: Women Teaching African American, Native American, and Chicano/a Students, 1865–1911.* Carbondale: Southern Illinois UP, 2008. Print.

Enoch, Jessica, and Jordynn Jack. "Remembering Sappho: New Perspectives on Teaching (and Writing) Women's Rhetorical History." *College English* 73.5 (2011): 518–37. Print.

Enos, Richard Leo. "The Archaeology of Women in Rhetoric: Rhetorical Sequencing as a Research Method for Historical Scholarship." *Rhetoric Society Quarterly* 31.1 (2002): 65–79. Print.

Enos, Richard Leo, Karlyn Kohrs Campbell, Andrew King, Celeste M. Condit, Richard J. Jensen, Sonja K. Foss, Martin J. Medhurst, and David Zarefksy. "Symposium: Interdisciplinary Perspectives on Rhetorical Criticism." *Rhetoric Review* 23.4 (2006): 357–84. Print.

"The Examination of Mrs. Anne Hutchinson at the Court at Newtown." Hall 311–48. Print.

"An Example of Broad-Mindedness." *Honolulu Republican* 3 Feb. 1901: 4. *Chronicling America.* Lib. of Cong. Web. 1 Apr. 2010. <http://chroniclingamerica.loc.gov/lccn/sn85047165/1901-02-03/ed-1/seq-4/>.

Ferreira-Buckley, Linda. "Rescuing the Archives from Foucault." *College English* 61.5 (1999): 577–83. Print.

"Fighting for Women." *Indianapolis Sentinel* 20 Feb. 1897: 3. Print.

Finkelman, Paul, ed. *The Encyclopedia of American Civil Liberties.* Vol. 1. New York: Routledge, 2006. Print.

Flower, B. O. "Noble Type of Twentieth-Century American Womanhood." *Arena* (Apr. 1906): 384–85. Helen Gougar Collection, Pamphlet item 81.193.12. TCHA, Lafayette, IN.

Flynn, Elizabeth. *Feminism beyond Modernism.* Carbondale: Southern Illinois UP, 2002. Print.

Foss, Sonja K., and Cindy L. Griffin. "Beyond Persuasion: A Proposal for an Invitational Rhetoric." *Communication Monographs* 62 (1995): 1–17. Print.

Foss, Sonja K., and Karen A. Foss. "Our Journey to Repowered Feminism: Expanding the Feminist Toolbox." *Women's Studies in Communication* 31.1 (Spring 2009): 36–62. Print.

Foucault, Michel. *Language, Counter-Memory, Practice.* Trans. D. F. Bouchard and Sherry Simon. Ithaca, NY: Cornell UP, 1977. Print.

Fowles, John. *A Maggot.* London: Fowles, 1985. Print.

"Francis Murphy Dead: Famous Temperance Advocate Induced Millions to Sign Pledge." *New York Times* 1 July 1907: 7. *NYT* archives. Web. 1 Apr. 2010.

Galewski, Elizabeth. "The Strange Case for Women's Capacity to Reason: Judith Sargent Murray's Use of Irony in 'On the Equality of the Sexes' (1790)." *Quarterly Journal of Speech* 93.1 (2007): 84–108. JSTOR. Web.

Gans, Eric. "On Irony." *Signs of Paradox: Irony, Resentment, and Other Mimetic Structures.* Stanford, CA: Stanford UP, 1997. 64–74. Print.

Gearhart, Sally Miller. "The Womanization of Rhetoric." *Women's Studies International Quarterly* 2 (1979): 195–201. Print.

Geisler, Cheryl. "How Ought We to Understand the Concept of Rhetorical Agency? Report from the ARS." *Rhetoric Society Quarterly* 34.3 (2004): 9–17. Print.

George, Ann, M. Elizabeth Weiser, and Janet Zepernick, eds. *Women and Rhetoric between the Wars.* Carbonale: Southern Illinois UP, 2013.

Gibbs, Raymond W., and Christin D. Izzett. "Irony as Persuasive Communication." Colston and Katz 131–51.

Giora, Rachel. "On Irony and Negation." *Discourse Processes* 19 (1995): 239–64. Print.

———. *On Our Mind: Salience, Context, and Figurative Language.* Oxford: Oxford UP, 2003. Print.

Giora, Rachel, and Ofer Fein. "Irony Comprehension: The Graded Salience Hypothesis." *Humor* 12.4 (1999): 425–36. Print.

Glenn, Cheryl. "Remapping Rhetorical Territory." *Rhetoric Review* 13.2 (Spring 1995): 287–303. Print.

———. *Rhetoric Retold.* Carbondale: Southern Illinois UP, 1997. Print.

Glenn, Cheryl, and Jessica Enoch. "Drama in the Archives: Rereading Methods, Rewriting History." *College Composition and Communication* 61.2 (2009): 321–42. Print.

———. "Invigorating Historiographic Practices in Rhetoric and Composition Studies." Ramsey et al. 11–27.

Glenn, Cheryl, and Krista Ratcliffe, eds. *Silence and Listening as Rhetorical Arts.* Carbondale: Southern Illinois UP, 2011. Print.

Gold, David. *Rhetoric at the Margins: Revising the History of Writing Instruction in American Colleges, 1873–1947.* Carbondale: Southern Illinois UP, 2008. Print.

"Golda Meir Scorns Soviets." *Washington Post* 16 Jun. 1969. *LexisNexis*. Florida State University Library. Web. 20 Feb. 2015. <http://www. lexisnexis.com>.

Goldberg, Michael Lewis. *An Army of Women: Gender and Politics in Gilded Age Kansas*. Baltimore: Johns Hopkins UP, 1997. Print.

"Good Government League." *New York Tribune* 30 Nov. 1900. *Chronicling America*. Lib. of Cong. Web. 1 Apr. 2010. <http://chroniclingamerica.loc.gov/lccn/sn83030214/1900-11-30/ed-1/seq-6/>.

Gordon, Ann D., ed. *The Selected Papers of Elizabeth Cady Stanton and Susan B. Anthony*. 6 vols. New Brunswick, NJ: Rutgers UP, 2009. Print.

Gougar, Helen. "Address by Helen Gougar at the Indiana State Assembly on February 15, 1881." *Brevier Legislative Reports* 19: 193. Print.

———. "America in the Philippines: A Conversation with Helen M. Gougar." *Arena* Apr. 1906: 386–90. Helen Gougar Collection, Pamphlet item 81.193.12. TCHA, Lafayette, IN.

———. "Bric-a-Brac." *Lafayette Daily Courier* 25 Jan. 1879. Helen Gougar Collection, Scrapbook item 73.17.29. TCHA, Lafayette, IN.

———. "Bric-a-Brac." *Lafayette Daily Courier* 9 Feb. 1879. Helen Gougar Collection, Scrapbook item 73.17.29. TCHA, Lafayette, IN.

———. "Bric-a-Brac." *Lafayette Daily Courier* 11 Oct. 1879. Helen Gougar Collection, Scrapbook item 73.17.29. TCHA, Lafayette, IN.

———. "Bric-a-Brac." *Lafayette Daily Courier* 23 Nov. 1879. Helen Gougar Collection, Scrapbook item 73.17.29. TCHA, Lafayette, IN.

———. "Bric-a-Brac." *Lafayette Daily Courier* 20 Dec. 1879. Helen Gougar Collection, Scrapbook item 73.17.29. TCHA, Lafayette, IN.

———. "Bric-a-Brac." *Lafayette Daily Courier* 13 Dec. 1880. Helen Gougar Collection, Scrapbook item 73.17.29. TCHA, Lafayette, IN.

———. *The Constitutional Rights of the Women of Indiana*. Lafayette, IN: Journal Printing, 1895. Helen Gougar Collection, Purdue University Libraries, Karnes Archives and Special Collections, West Lafayette, IN. Web. <http://earchives.lib.purdue.edu/cdm/ref/collection/gougar/id/121>.

———. "Criticism vs. Gallantry." *Lafayette Daily Courier* 6 Dec. 1879. Helen Gougar Collection, Scrapbook item 73.17.29. TCHA, Lafayette, IN.

———. "Differing Views: Mrs. Gougar Says Prohibit or Repeal." *Voice* 23 May 1895: 3. Ohio State University Depository Film 14–96. Microfilm.

———. "Female Politicians: A Conversation with James G. Blaine." *Lafayette Daily Courier* Nov. 1888. Helen Gougar Collection, Scrapbook item 73.17.8. TCHA, Lafayette, IN.

———. "I Have All the Rights I Want: A True Story." *History of Women Series*. N.d. Reel 950, no. 9205. Indiana University. Microfilm.

———. "Industrial Training for Women." *Lafayette Evening Call* 3 Feb. 1900. Helen Gougar Collection, Newspaper item 73.17.3. TCHA, Lafayette, IN.

———. Introduction. *Women Wealth-Winners; or, How Women Can Earn Money*. 2nd ed. By Edna C. Jackson Houk. Cincinnati: E. C. Jackson Houk, 1894. 9–16. Helen Gougar Collection, Book item 86.63.1. TCHA, Lafayette, IN.

———. "Letter to Reverend B. Wilson Smith." 18 Oct. 1882. Helen Gougar Collection, Correspondence item 65.77. TS. TCHA, Lafayette, IN.

———. "Man's Rights." *Lafayette Daily Courier* 20 Dec. 1879. Helen Gougar Collection, Scrapbook item 75.17.29. TCHA, Lafayette, IN.

———. "The Man Who Blows." *Lafayette Daily Courier* 22 Nov. 1879. Helen Gougar Collection, Scrapbook item 73.17.29. TCHA, Lafayette, IN.

———. *Matthew Peters: A Foreign Immigrant*. Lafayette: Browne, 1898. Print.

———. "On Behalf of the National Republican Ticket." *Our Herald* 15 Nov. 1884: 7. Helen Gougar Collection, Newspaper item 82.195.11. TCHA, Lafayette, IN.

———. "Pictures from Cuban Life." *Lafayette Morning Journal*. 22 February 1898.

———. "A Plea for Woman Suffrage." N.d. Helen Gougar Collection, Newspaper item 73.17.13. TCHA, Lafayette, IN.

———. "Shall Educated Chinamen Be Welcomed to Our Shores?" *Arena* (Nov. 1906): 506–08. Helen Gougar Collection, Pamphlet item 81.193.12. TCHA, Lafayette, IN.

———. "Thinks Men Will Go to Heaven." *Lafayette Morning Journal* 29 July 1901. Helen Gougar Collection, Scrapbook item 73.17.29. TCHA, Lafayette, IN.

———. "Unrestricted Ballot." *Joliet News* 4 Nov. 1887. Helen Gougar Collection, Newspaper item 81.193.4. TCHA, Lafayette, IN.

"The Gougarine Is Stirring Things Up in Far Manila." *Hawaiian Gazette* 23 Jan. 1903: 2. *Chronicling America*. Lib. of Cong. Web. 1 Apr. 2010. <http://chroniclingamerica.loc.gov/lccn/sn83025121/1903-01-23/ed-1/seq-2/>.

"Gougar on Murphy." *Honolulu Independent* 2 Feb. 1901: 1. *Chronicling America*. Lib. of Cong. Web. 1 Apr. 2010. <http://chroniclingamerica.loc.gov/lccn/sn85047097/1901-02-02/ed-1/seq-1>.

"Gougar's Sarcasm: Explanations of the Nature of Her Address to the Democratic Convention." *Indianapolis Journal*. 15 August 1882. Helen Gougar Collection, Newspaper item 81.193.4. TCHA, Lafayette, IN.

Graban, Tarez Samra. "Emergent Taxonomies: Using 'Tension' and 'Forum' to Organize Primary Texts." Ramsey et al. 206–19.

———. "Toward a 'Second-Generation' Suffragism: Language Politics in the Ironic Discourse of an American Suffragist." *Gender and Language* 3.1 (2011): 31–60. Print.

Graff, Richard, and Michael Leff. "Revisionist Historiography and Rhetorical Tradition(s)." *The Viability of the Rhetorical Tradition*. Ed. Richard Graff, Arthur E. Walzer, and Janet M. Atwill. Albany: State U of New York P, 2005. 11–30. Print.

Gray, Ralph D. *Indiana History: A Book of Readings*. Bloomington: Indiana UP, 1995. Print.

"A Great Compliment." *Lafayette Morning Journal* 21 May 1887. Helen Gougar Collection, Newspaper item 81.193.4. TCHA, Lafayette, IN.

Grewal, Inderpal. *Transnational America: Feminisms, Diasporas, Neoliberalisms*. Durham, NC: Duke UP, 2005. Print.

Grice, H. Paul. "Logic and Conversation." *Syntax and Semantics*, Vol. 3: *Speech Acts*. Ed. Peter Cole and Jerry L. Morgan. New York: Academic, 1975. 41–58. Print.

Gross, Alan G. "Paradigm Shift." *The Encyclopedia of Rhetoric and Composition*. Ed. Theresa Enos. 1996. 491–92. Print.

Hall, David, ed. *The Antinomian Controversy, 1636–1638*. 2nd ed. Durham, NC: Duke UP, 1990. Print.

Handwerk, Gary J. *Irony and Ethics in Narrative: From Schlegel to Lacan*. New Haven, CT: Yale UP, 1985. Print.

Haraway, Donna. "A Manifesto for Cyborgs: Science, Technology, and Socialist Feminism in the 1980s." *Feminism/Postmodernism*. Ed. Linda Nicholson. New York: Routledge, 1990. 190–233. Print.

Harper, Ida Husted. *Life and Work of Susan B. Anthony, Volume 2*. Indianapolis: Bowen-Merrill, 1898. Print.

Haskins, Ekaterina V. "Between Archive and Participation: Public Memory in a Digital Age." *Rhetoric Society Quarterly* 37.4 (2007): 401–22. Print.

———. "A Woman's Inventive Response to the Seventeenth-Century *Que-relle des Femmes.*" Wertheimer 288–304.

Hauser, Gerard A. "Editor's Introduction." *Philosophy and Rhetoric* 37.3 (2004): 181–87. Print.

Hawhee, Debra, and Christa J. Olson. "Pan-historiography: The Challenges of Writing History across Time and Space." *Theorizing Histories of Rhetoric.* Ed. Michelle Ballif. Carbondale: Southern Illinois UP, 2013. 90–105. Print.

Hawthorne, Nathaniel. "Mrs. Hutchinson." 1830. *Writings of Nathaniel Hawthorne.* Ed. Eric Eldred. Derry, NH: Eldritch, 1999. Web. 13 May 2010.

"Helen Blazes Away Again." *Kansas City Journal* 16 Feb. 1899: 4. *Chronicling America.* Lib. of Cong. Web. 1 Apr. 2010. <http://chroniclingamerica.loc.gov/lccn/sn86063615/1899-02-16/ed-1/seq-4/>.

"Helen Gougar: Foot Soldier for Suffrage." *A Moment of Indiana History.* Indiana Public Media. WFIU Radio. 5 Mar. 2012. Web. 13 Sept. 2013. <http://indianapublicmedia.org/momentofindianahistory/helen-gougar-foot-soldier-suffrage/>.

"Helen Gougar's Sunday Speech: Answers Gold Arguments Advanced by Chicago Preachers." *San Francisco Call* 12 Oct. 1896: 2. *Chronicling America.* Lib. of Cong. Web. 1 Apr. 2010. <http://chroniclingamerica.loc.gov/lccn/sn85066387/1896-10-12/ed-1/seq-2/>.

"Helen M. Gougar." *Columbus Press-Post* July 1907. Helen Gougar Collection, Unnumbered newspaper item. TCHA, Lafayette, IN.

"Helen M. Gougar Expires Suddenly: Noted Advocate of Woman's Rights Drops Dead at Her Home in This City." *Lafayette Courier* 6 June 1907. Helen Gougar Collection, Unnumbered newspaper item. TCHA, Lafayette, IN.

"Helen M. Gougar Ousted." *Milwaukee Sentinel* 2 Jan. 1897. Print.

Heywood, Linda, and Judith Drake, eds. *Third Wave Agenda: Being Feminist, Doing Feminism.* Minneapolis: U of Minnesota P, 1997. Print.

Hoganson, Kristin. "'As Badly Off as the Filipinos': U.S. Women's Suffragists and the Imperial Issue at the Turn of the Twentieth Century." *Journal of Women's History* 13.2 (2001): 9–33. Print.

Holcomb, Chris. "'Anyone Can Be President': Figures of Speech, Cultural Forms, and Performance." *Rhetoric Society Quarterly* 37.1 (2007): 71–96. Print.

Howell, Wilbur Samuel. *Eighteenth Century British Logic and Rhetoric.* Princeton, NJ: Princeton UP, 1971.

——. *Logic and Rhetoric in England, 1500–1700.* New York: Russell, 1961. Print.

Hutcheon, Linda. *Irony's Edge: The Theory and Politics of Irony.* New York: Routledge, 1995. Print.

Jamieson, Kathleen Hall, and Karlyn Kohrs Campbell. "Rhetorical Hybrids: Fusions of Generic Elements." *Quarterly Journal of Speech* 68 (1982): 146–57. Print.

Janack, Marianne, and John Adams. "Feminist Epistemologies, Rhetorical Traditions and the *Ad Hominem.*" *The Changing Tradition: Women in the History of Rhetoric.* Ed. Christine Mason Sutherland and Rebecca Sutcliffe. Calgary, AB: U of Calgary P, 1999. 213–24. Print.

Jarratt, Susan. "Speaking to the Past: Feminist Historiography in Rhetoric." *PRE/TEXT: A Journal of Rhetorical Theory* 11.3–4 (1990): 190–209. Print.

Jerry, E. Claire. "Helen Jackson Gougar." *Women Public Speakers in the United States, 1800–1925: A Bio-Critical Sourcebook.* Ed. Karlyn Kohrs Campbell. Westport, CT: Greenwood, 1993. 267–78. Print.

Johanek, Cindy. *Composing Research: A Contextualist Paradigm for Rhetoric and Composition.* Logan: Utah State UP, 2000. Print.

Johnson, Nan. *Gender and Rhetorical Space in American Life, 1866–1910.* Carbondale: Southern Illinois UP, 2002. Print.

Jordan, Barbara Charline. "Democratic National Convention Keynote." 12 July 1976. New York. Address. *American Rhetoric.* Web. 1 Apr. 2010.

——. "Democratic National Convention Keynote." 13 July 1992. New York. Address. *American Rhetoric.* Web. 1 Apr. 2010.

——. "Statement on the Articles of Impeachment." 25 July 1974. House Judiciary Committee. Address. *American Rhetoric.* Web. 1 Apr. 2010.

Journet, Debra. "Writing Within (and Between) Disciplinary Genres: The 'Adaptive Landscape' as a Case Study in Interdisciplinary Rhetoric." *Post-Process Theory: Beyond the Writing-Process Paradigm.* Ed. Thomas Kent. Carbondale: Southern Illinois UP, 1999. 96–115. Print.

Kaufer, David. "Irony and Rhetorical Strategy." *Philosophy and Rhetoric* 10.2 (1977): 90–110. Print.

——. "Irony, Interpretive Form, and the Theory of Meaning." *Poetics Today* 4.3 (1983): 451–64. Print.

——. "Understanding Ironic Communication." *Journal of Pragmatics* 5 (1981): 495–510. Print.

Keith, George. "The Woman-Preacher of Samaria; a Better Preacher, and More Sufficiently Qualified to Preach Than Any of the Men-Preachers of the Man-Made-Ministry in These Three Nations (1674)." MS. John Carter Brown Library, Providence, RI. 23 Apr. 2010.

"Keith, George (1638?–1716)." *Oxford Dictionary of National Biography*, 2011. *Oxford DNB*. Web. 15 Oct. 2011.

Kerber, Linda K. "Separate Spheres, Female Worlds, Woman's Place: The Rhetoric of Women's History." *Journal of American History* 73.1 (Jun 1988): 9–39. Print.

Khader, Jamil. "Postnational Ethics, Postcolonial Politics: Raimonda Tawil's *My Home, My Prison*." *Arab Women's Lives Retold: Exploring Identity through Writing*. Ed. Nawar Al-Hassan Golley. Syracuse, NY: Syracuse UP, 2007. 71–89. Print.

Khalidi, Rashid. *Palestinian Identity: The Construction of Modern National Consciousness*. New York: Columbia UP, 1997. Print.

Kirsch, Gesa E. *Ethical Dilemmas in Feminist Research: The Politics of Location, Interpretation, and Publication*. Albany: State U of New York P, 1999. Print.

Kirsch, Gesa E., and Jacqueline J. Royster. "Feminist Rhetorical Practices: In Search of Excellence." *College Composition and Communication* 61.4 (Jun 2010): 640–72. Print.

Koehler, Lyle. "The Case of the American Jezebels: Anne Hutchinson and Female Agitation during the Years of Antinomian Turmoil, 1636–1640." *William and Mary Quarterly* 31.1 (1974): 55–78. Print.

Kolodny, Annette. "Inventing a Feminist Discourse: Rhetoric and Resistance in Margaret Fuller's *Woman in the Nineteenth Century*." *Reclaiming Rhetorica: Women in the Rhetorical Tradition*. Ed. Andrea Lunsford. Pittsburgh: U of Pittsburgh P, 1995. 137–66. Print.

Kriebel, Robert C. "Gougar Touted Abstinence from All Debt." *Lafayette Journal and Courier*. 25 June 1982: D1+. Helen Mar Jackson Gougar Clipping File, Reference Room Collection, Indiana Historical Society, Indianapolis.

———. "Mining Boom Turns to Bust for Gougars." *Lafayette Journal and Courier*. 11 June 1982: D1+. Helen Mar Jackson Gougar Clipping File, Reference Room Collection, Indiana Historical Society, Indianapolis.

———. "Suffragist Chooses New Direction." *Lafayette Journal and Courier*. 4 June 1982: D1+. Helen Mar Jackson Gougar Clipping File, Reference Room Collection, Indiana Historical Society, Indianapolis.

———. *Where the Saints Have Trod: The Life of Helen Gougar.* West Lafayette, IN: Purdue UP, 1985. Print.

———. "Writings Reflect Wit and Logic." *Lafayette Journal and Courier.* 18 June 1982: D1+. Helen Mar Jackson Gougar Clipping File, Reference Room Collection, Indiana Historical Society, Indianapolis.

Kristeva, Julia. "From *Women's Time* (1979)." *Feminist Literary Theory and Criticism: A Norton Reader.* Ed. Sandra M. Gilbert and Susan Gubar. New York: Norton, 2007. 460–73. Print.

Kuhn, Thomas S. *The Structure of Scientific Revolutions.* Revised ed. Chicago: U of Chicago P, 1970. Print.

La Flamme, Janice M. "The Strategy of Feminine Protest: A Rhetorical Study of the Campaign for Woman's Rights in Indiana, 1881." MA thesis. Indiana University, 1968. Print.

Lang, Amy Schrager. *Prophetic Woman: Anne Hutchinson and the Problem of Dissent in the Literature of New England.* Berkeley: U of California P, 1987. Print.

———. *The Syntax of Class: Writing Inequality in Nineteenth-Century America.* Princeton, NJ: Princeton UP, 2006. Print.

Lang, Candace. *Irony/Humor: Critical Paradigms.* Baltimore: Johns Hopkins UP, 1988. Print.

"Last Article Written." *Lafayette Sunday Morning Leader* 16 June 1907. Helen Gougar Collection, Scrapbook item 73.17.8. TCHA, Lafayette, IN.

Lauer, Janice. *Invention in Rhetoric and Composition.* West Lafayette, IN: Parlor, 2004. Print.

"The Law and the Ladies." *Indianapolis Journal* Feb. 1880. Helen Gougar Collection, Scrapbook item 73.17.8. TCHA, Lafayette, IN.

Lee, Julia Sun-Joo. "The Return of the 'Unnative': The Transnational Politics of Elizabeth Gaskell's *North and South.*" *Nineteenth Century Literature* 61.4 (2007): 449–78. JSTOR. Web.

Leff, Michael. "Tradition and Agency in Humanistic Rhetoric." *Philosophy and Rhetoric* 36.2 (2003): 135–47. Print.

L'Eplattenier, Barbara. "Questioning Our Methodological Metaphors." Royster and Simpkins 133–46.

Locke, John. *Essay Concerning Human Understanding* (1690). *Project Gutenberg.* Web. 5 Dec. 2010.

Logan, Shirley Wilson. *"We Are Coming": The Persuasive Discourse of Nineteenth-Century Black Women.* Carbondale: Southern Illinois UP, 1999. Print.

Lomicky, Carol S. "Frontier Feminism and the *Woman's Tribune*: The Journalism of Clara Bewick Colby." *Journalism History* 28.3 (2002): 102–11. Print.

Lunsford, Andrea, ed. *Reclaiming Rhetorica: Women in the Rhetorical Tradition*. Pittsburgh: U of Pittsburgh P, 1995. Print.

Mackinnon, Catherine A. "Feminism, Marxism, Method, and the State: An Agenda for Theory." *Signs: Journal of Women in Culture and Society* 7.3 (1982): 515–44. Print.

Makin, Bathsua. "An Essay to Revive the Ancient Education of Gentlewomen." *Bathsua Makin, Woman of Learning*. Ed. Francis Teague. Lewisburg, PA: Bucknell UP, 1998. 109–50. Print.

Martin, Randall, ed. *Women Writers in Renaissance England*. New York: Longman, 1997. Print.

Mattingly, Carol. "Telling Evidence: Rethinking What Counts in Rhetoric." *Rhetoric Society Quarterly* 31.1 (2002): 99–108. Print.

———. *Well-Tempered Women: Nineteenth-Century Temperance Rhetoric*. Carbondale: Southern Illinois UP, 1998. Print.

Mayhead, Molly, and Brenda DeVore Marshall. *Women's Political Discourse: A 21st Century Perspective*. Lanham, MD: Rowman, 2005. Print.

Mazzola, Elizabeth. "Expert Witnesses and Secret Subjects: Anne Askew's *Examination* and Renaissance Self-Incrimination." *Politics, Women's Voices, and the Renaissance*. Ed. Carole Levin and Patricia A. Sullivan. Albany: State U of New York P, 1995. 157–71. Print.

McQuade, Paula. "'Except That They Had Offended the Lawe': Gender and Jurisprudence in *The Examinations of Anne Askew*." *Literature & History* 3rd ser. 3 (1994): 1–14. Print.

Merrill, Yvonne D. "The Role of Language in the Construction of Mary Wortley Montagu's Rhetorical Identity." Miller and Bridwell-Bowles 44–62.

———. *The Social Construction of Western Women's Rhetoric Before 1750*. Lewiston, NY: Mellen, 1996. Print.

Meyer, Michaela D. E. "Women Speak(ing): Forty Years of Feminist Contributions to Rhetoric and an Agenda for Feminist Rhetorical Studies." *Communication Quarterly* 53.1 (2007): 1–17. Print.

Miller, Carolyn R. "What Can Automation Tell Us about Agency?" *Rhetoric Society Quarterly* 37.2 (2007): 137–57. Print.

Miller, Hildy, and Lillian Bridwell-Bowles, eds. *Rhetorical Women: Roles and Representations*. Tuscaloosa: U of Alabama P, 2005. Print.

Miller, Nancy Weitz. "Ethos, Authority, and Virtue for Seventeenth-Century Women Writers: The Case of Bathsua Makin's *An Essay to Revive the Antient Education of Gentlewomen* (1673)." Wertheimer 272–87.

Miller, Susan. *Trust in Texts: A Different History of Rhetoric.* Carbondale: Southern Illinois UP, 2008. Print.

Morgan, Edmund S. "The Case against Anne Hutchinson." *New England Quarterly* 10 (1937): 675–97. Print.

Morgan, Nick. "Barbara Jordan Gives a History Lesson on the Constitution." *Harvard Business Publishing Newsletter* 15 June 2011. *Harvard Business Review.* Web. 1 Feb. 2012.

Morreall, John. "Verbal Humor without Switching Scripts and without Non–*Bona Fide* Communication." *Humor: International Journal of Humor Research* 17.4 (2004): 393–400. Print.

Morris, Sammie L., and Shirley K Rose. "Invisible Hands: Recognizing Archivists' Work to Make Records Accessible." Ramsey et al. 51–78.

"Mrs. Gougar Lectures: She Will Grapple with the Question of a 'Way Out for the Unemployed.'" *San Francisco Call* 12 Mar. 1896: 7. *Chronicling America.* Lib. of Cong. Web. 1 Apr. 2010. <http://chroniclingamerica.loc.gov/lccn/sn85066387/1896-03-12/ed-1/seq-7/>.

"Mrs. Gougar Memorialized." *Lafayette Morning Journal* 5 May 1887. Helen Gougar Collection, Scrapbook item 73.17.8. TCHA, Lafayette, IN.

"Mrs. Gougar's Contest: Indiana's Most Celebrated Case." *Daily Bee* 10 Apr. 1883. *Chronicling America.* Lib. of Cong. Web. 1 Apr. 2010. <http://chroniclingamerica.loc.gov/lccn/sn99021999/1883-04-10/ed-1/seq-2/>.

"Mrs. Gougar's Test Vote." *Lafayette Morning Journal.* 7 November 1894.

"Mrs. Helen M. Gougar and Robert Schilling Meet in Debate." *Daily Inter Ocean* 19 Feb. 1896: 7. Helen Gougar Collection, Newspaper item 81.193.6. TCHA, Lafayette, IN.

"Mrs. Helen M. Gougar in Kansas." *Lafayette Morning Journal* 1 Feb. 1887. Helen Gougar Collection, Scrapbook item 73.17.8. TCHA, Lafayette, IN.

Munslow, Alan. *Deconstructing History.* New York: Routledge, 1997. Print.

"National Federal Suffrage Association." *A True Republic* 3.2 (1895). Helen Gougar Collection, Newspaper item 81.193.6. TCHA, Lafayette, IN. Print.

Natoli, Joseph, and Linda Hutcheon, eds. *A Postmodern Reader.* Albany:
  State U of New York P, 1993. Print.

Nora, Pierre. "Between Memory and History: *Les Lieux de Memoire.*"
  Representations 26 (1989): 7–25. Print.

"Noted Suffrage Advocate Dies." *Los Angeles Herald* 7 June 1907: 1. *Chronicling America.* Lib. of Cong. Web. 1 Apr. 2010. <http://chroniclin-
  gamerica.loc.gov/lccn/sn85042462/1907-06-07/ed-1/seq-1/>.

Octalog. "Octalog II: The (Continuing) Politics of Historiography." *Rhetoric Review* 13.1 (1997): 22–44. Print.

———. "The Politics of Historiography." *Rhetoric Review* 7.1 (1988): 5–49.
  Print.

Olson, Christa J. "Places to Stand: The Practices and Politics of Writing
  Histories." *Advances in the History of Rhetoric* 15.1 (2012): 77–100.
  JSTOR. Web.

Olson, Kathryn M., and Clark D. Olson. "Beyond Strategy: A Reader-
  Centered Analysis of Irony's Dual Persuasive Uses." *Quarterly
  Journal of Speech* 91.1 (2004): 24–52. JSTOR. Web.

Ong, Walter J. *Ramus, Method, and the Decay of Dialogue: From the Art
  of Discourse to the Art of Reason.* New York: Octagon, 1979. Print.

———. *Rhetoric, Romance, and Technology: Studies in the Interaction of
  Expression and Culture.* Ithaca, NY: Cornell UP, 1971. Print.

Oravec, Christine, and Michael Salvador. "The Duality of Rhetoric: Theory
  as Discursive Practice." Poulakos 173–92.

Perelman, Chaim, and Lucie Olbrechts-Tyteca. *The New Rhetoric: A Treatise on Argumentation.* South Bend, IN: U of Notre Dame P, 1969.
  Print.

Pexman, Penny M. "Social Factors in the Interpretation of Verbal Irony:
  The Roles of Speaker and Listener Characteristics." Colston and
  Katz 209–32.

Pittman, Coretta. "Black Women Writers and the Trouble with *Ethos*:
  Harriet Jacobs, Billie Holiday, and Sister Souljah. *Rhetoric Society
  Quarterly* 37.1 (2006): 43–70.

Polanyi, Michael. *Personal Knowledge: Towards a Post-Critical Philosophy.*
  Chicago: U of Chicago P, 1974. Print.

"Post Office Muddle." *Lafayette Morning Journal* 3 Jan. 1890. Helen Gougar Collection, Newspaper item 81.193.6. TCHA, Lafayette, IN.

Poulakos, Takis. "Human Agency in the History of Rhetoric: Gorgias' *En-
  comium of Helen.*" *Writing Histories of Rhetoric.* Ed. Victor Vitanza.
  49–80. Carbondale: Southern Illinois UP, 1994. Print.

———, ed. *Rethinking the History of Rhetoric: Multidisciplinary Essays on the Rhetorical Tradition*. Boulder, CO: Westview, 1993. Print.

Prior, Paul. "From Speech Genres to Mediated Multimodal Genre Systems: Bakhtin, Voloshinov, and the Question of Writing." *Genre in a Changing World*. Ed. Charles Bazerman, Adair Bonini, and Débora Figueiredo. 17–34. Fort Collins: WAC Clearinghouse and Colorado State. Web. 16 Nov. 2009.

Quintilian. *Institutio Oratoria*. Trans. H. E. Butler. Vols. 1–12. Cambridge, MA: Loeb-Harvard UP, 1922. Print.

———. *Institutio Oratoria*. Trans. Charles E. Little. Vol. 6. Nashville: George Peabody College for Teachers, 1951. Print.

———. *Institutio Oratoria*. Trans. Donald A. Russell. Vols. 1–2. Cambridge, MA: Loeb-Harvard UP, 2001. Print.

Ramsey, Alexis, Wendy Sharer, Barb L'Eplattenier, and Lisa Mastrangelo, eds. *Working in the Archives: Practical Research Methods for Rhetoric and Composition*. Carbondale: Southern Illinois UP, 2009. Print.

Raskin, Victor. *Semantic Mechanisms of Humor*. Dordrecht, NLD: Reidel, 1985. Print.

Ratcliffe, Krista. *Rhetorical Listening: Identification, Gender, Whiteness*. Carbondale: Southern Illinois UP, 2005. Print.

Raymond, Joad. *Pamphlets and Pamphleteering in Early Modern Britain*. Cambridge: Cambridge UP, 2003. Print.

Rayner, Alice. "The Audience: Subjectivity, Community, and the Ethics of Listening." *Journal of Dramatic Theory and Criticism* 7 (1993): 3–24. Print.

Renegar, Valerie R., and Stacey K. Sowards. "Contradiction as Agency: Self-Determination, Transcendence, and Counter-Imagination in Third Wave Feminism." *Hypatia* 24.2 (2009): 1–29. JSTOR. Web.

———. "Liberal Irony, Rhetoric, and Feminist Thought: A Unifying Third Wave Feminist Theory." *Philosophy and Rhetoric* 36.4 (2003): 330–52. JSTOR. Web.

"A Report of the Trial of Mrs. Anne Hutchinson before the Church in Boston." Hall 349–88. Print.

Reynolds, Nedra. *Geographies of Writing: Inhabiting Places and Encountering Difference*. Carbondale: Southern Illinois UP, 2004. Print.

Rhodes, Jane. "Mary Ann Shadd Cary and the Legacy of African-American Women Journalists." *Women Making Meaning: New Feminist*

Directions in Communication. Ed. Lana F. Rakow. New York: Routledge, 1992. 210–24. Print.

———. *Mary Ann Shadd Cary: The Black Press and Protests in the 19th
Century.* Bloomington: Indiana UP, 1998. Print.

Rickert, Thomas. *Acts of Enjoyment: Rhetoric, Zizek, and the Return of
the Subject.* Pittsburgh: U of Pittsburgh P, 2007. Print.

Riegel, Robert E. "The Split of the Feminist Movement in 1869." *Mississippi
Valley Historical Review* 49.3 (1962): 485–96. Print.

Ritchie, David. "Frame Shifting in Humor and Irony." *Metaphor and Sym-
bol* 20.4 (2005): 275–94. Print.

Ritzer, George. *Sociology: A Multi-paradigm Science.* Boston: Allyn and
Bacon, 1975. Print.

Rodríguez, Cristina M. "Clearing the Smoke-Filled Room: Women Jurors and the Disruption of an Old-Boys' Network in Nineteenth-
Century America." *Yale Law Journal* 108.7 (1999): 1805–44. Print.

Romano, Susan. "The Historical Catalina Hernández: Inhabiting the
Topoi of Feminist Historiography." *Rhetoric Society Quarterly* 37.4
(2007): 453–80. Print.

Ronald, Kate, and Joy Ritchie. *Available Means: An Anthology of Women's
Rhetorics.* Pittsburgh: U of Pittsburgh P, 2001. Print.

———. "Introduction: Asking 'So What?' Expansive Pedagogies." *Teaching Rhetorica: Theory, Pedagogy, Practice.* Ed. Kate Ronald and
Joy Ritchie. Portsmouth, NH: Boynton/Cook, 2006. 1–12. Print.

Rorty, Richard. *Contingency, Irony, and Solidarity.* New York: Cambridge
UP, 1989. Print.

———. "The Contingency of Language." *Rhetoric in an Anti-Foundational
World: Language, Culture, and Pedagogy.* Ed. Michael F. Bernard-
Donals and Richard R. Glejzer. New Haven, CT: Yale UP, 1998.
65–85. Print.

———. "Feminism and Pragmatism." Tanner Lectures on Human Values.
University of Michigan, Ann Arbor. 7 Dec. 1990. Address.

Rowbotham, Sheila. *Woman's Consciousness, Man's World.* Baltimore:
Penguin, 1973. Print.

Royster, Jacqueline Jones. "Disciplinary Landscaping, or Contemporary
Challenges in the History of Rhetoric." *Philosophy and Rhetoric*
36.2 (2003): 148–67. Print.

———. "Sarah's Story: Making a Place for Historical Ethnography in Rhetorical
Studies." *Rhetoric, the Polis, and the Global Village.* Ed. C. Jan Swearingen and David Pruett. Mahwah, NJ: Erlbaum, 1999. 39–51. Print.

———. *Traces of a Stream: Literacy and Social Change among African American Women*. Pittsburgh: U of Pittsburgh P, 2000. Print.

Royster, Jacqueline Jones, and Gesa E. Kirsch. *Feminist Rhetorical Practices: New Horizons for Rhetoric, Composition, and Literacy Studies*. Carbondale: Southern Illinois UP, 2012.

Royster, Jacqueline Jones, and Ann Marie Mann Simpkins, eds. *Calling Cards: Theory and Practice in the Study of Race, Gender, and Culture*. New York: State U of New York P, 2005. Print.

Royster, Jacqueline Jones, and Jean C. Williams. "History in the Spaces Left: African American Presence and Narratives of Composition Studies." *College Composition and Communication* 50.4 (1999): 563–84. Print.

Salter, Liora, and David Wolfe. *Managing Technology: A Social Science Perspective*. Toronto: Garamond, 1990. Print.

Sartre, Jean Paul. *Critique of Dialectical Reason*. Trans. Alan Sheridan Smith. Vol. 1. Brooklyn: Verso, 2004. Print.

Schilb, John. "Differences, Displacements, and Disruptions: Toward Revisionary Histories of Rhetoric." *PRE/TEXT: A Journal of Rhetorical Theory* 8.1–2 (1987): 29–44. Print.

———. *Rhetorical Refusals: Defying Audiences' Expectations*. Carbondale: Southern Illinois UP, 2007. Print.

Scott, Joan Wallach. *The Fantasy of Feminist History*. Durham, NC: Duke UP, 2011. Print.

———. *Gender and the Politics of History*. Rev. ed. New York: Columbia UP, 1999. Print.

———. "Gender: A Useful Category of Historical Analysis." *American Historical Review* 91.5 (1986): 1053–75. Print.

Sharer, Wendy. "Disintegrating Bodies of Knowledge: Historical Material and Revisionary Histories of Rhetoric." *Rhetorical Bodies*. Ed. Jack Selzer and Sharon Crowley. Madison: U of Wisconsin P, 1999. 120–42. Print.

Sheard, Cynthia Miecznikowski. "The Public Value of Epideictic Rhetoric." *College English* 58 (1996): 765–94. Print.

Sheffield, William P. "Persecuted by Puritans; Ann Hutchinson and Mary Dyer..." New Haven, CT, 1888. TS. John Hay Library, Providence, RI. 22 Apr. 2010.

"A Significant Scene: Mrs. Helen Gougar at Albany." *Inter Ocean* 26 Apr. 1884. Helen Gougar Collection, Newspaper item 81.193.6. TCHA, Lafayette, IN.

Simpkins, Ann Marie Mann. *The Professional Writing Practices and Dialogic Rhetoric of Two Black Women Publishers: Discourse as Social Action in the Nineteenth-Century*. Diss. Purdue University, 1999. Ann Arbor: UMI, 2001. Print.

————. "Rhetorical Tradition(s) and the Reform Writing of Mary Ann Shadd Cary." Royster and Simpkins 229–41.

Smith, Charles D. *Palestine and the Arab-Israeli Conflict: A History with Documents*. 7th ed. Boston: Bedford/St. Martin's, 2010.

Smith, Tania Sona. "*The Lady's Rhetorick* (1707): The Tip of the Iceberg of Women's Rhetorical Education in Enlightenment France and Britain." *Rhetorica* 22.4 (2004): 349–73. Print.

Southard, Belinda A. Stillion. "A Rhetoric of Inclusion and the Expansion of Movement Constituencies: Harriot Stanton Blatch and the Classed Politics of Woman Suffrage." *Rhetoric Society Quarterly* 44.2 (2014): 129–47. Print.

Sowards, Stacey K., and Valerie R. Renegar. "The Rhetorical Functions of Consciousness-Raising in Third Wave Feminism." *Communication Studies* 53.4 (2004): 535–52. Print.

"Speech of Helen M. Gougar to the Senate Committee on Woman Suffrage, March 7, 1884." *History of Woman Suffrage*. Ed. Elizabeth Cady Stanton et al. Vol. 4. New York: Arno and *New York Times*, 1902. 38. Print.

Stanton, Elizabeth Cady, Susan B. Anthony, Ida H. Harper, and Matilda Joslyn Gage, eds. *History of Woman Suffrage*. 6 vols. New York: Arno and *New York Times*, 1881–1922. Print.

Steedman, Carolyn. *Dust: The Archive and Cultural History*. New Brunswick, NJ: Rutgers UP, 2002. Print.

Stowitzky, Renee. "Gougar Biographical Essay." 2006. *Women's Legal History*. Stanford Law School. Web. 15 Aug. 2009. <http://wlh-static .law.stanford.edu/papers06/GougarH-Stowitzky06.pdf>.

Strauss, Leo. *Persecution and the Art of Writing*. Chicago: U of Chicago P, 1988. Print.

"Suffrage Worker Here: Mrs. Helen M. Gougar Visiting in Los Angeles." *Los Angeles Herald* 15 Apr. 1905: 10. *Chronicling America*. Lib. of Cong. Web. 1 Apr. 2010. <http://chroniclingamerica.loc.gov/lccn /sn85042462/1905-04-15/ed-1/seq-10/>.

"Susan B. Anthony Is Assailed." *Chicago Daily Tribune*. Helen Gougar Collection, Newspaper item 81.193.6. TCHA, Lafayette, IN.

Swearingen, C. Jan. *Rhetoric and Irony: Western Literacy and Western Lies.* New York: Oxford, 1991. Print.

Tebeaux, Elizabeth, and Mary M. Lay. "The Emergence of the Feminine Voice, 1526–1640: The Earliest Published Books by English Renaissance Women." *JAC: A Journal of Composition Theory* 13.1 (1995): 53–81. Print.

"The Temperance Question." *Honolulu Independent* 2 Feb. 1901. *Chronicling America.* Lib. of Cong. Web. 1 Apr. 2010. <http://chroniclingamerica.loc.gov/lccn/sn85047097/1901-02-02/ed-1/seq-2/>.

Tobin, Lad. "A Radically Different Voice: Gender and Language in the Trials of Anne Hutchinson." *Early American Literature* 23.3 (1990): 253–70. JSTOR. Web.

"The Tragedy of Anne Hutchinson: Disciple of Roger Williams, and a Born Leader, She Was Centuries Ahead of Her Time." *New York Times* 17 July 1904. *NYT* archives. Web. 1 Apr. 2010.

Turnbull, Nick. "Rhetorical Agency as a Property of Questioning." *Philosophy and Rhetoric* 37.3 (2004): 207–22. JSTOR. Web.

"Two Opinions of a Woman." *Kansas Commoner* 7 June 1907. Helen Gougar Collection, Newspaper item 73.17.26. TCHA, Lafayette, IN.

Ulman, H. Lewis. *Things, Thoughts, Words, and Actions: The Problem of Language in Late Eighteenth-Century British Rhetorical Theory.* Carbondale: Southern Illinois UP, 1994. Print.

UN General Assembly. *The Question of Palestine and the United Nations.* Brochure DPI/2517/Rev.1, chap. 2 (2 Dec. 1986): 1–8. Web. 15 Mar. 2014. <http://www.un.org/Depts/dpi/palestine/ch2.pdf>.

Verhoeven, Betsy. "'Caliope,' 'Mary Lovetruth,' and 'A Female American': Women Editorialists during the American Revolutionary Era." *Rhetoric Society Quarterly* 39.1 (2009): 25–45. Print.

Viana, Amadeu. "Asymmetry in Script Opposition." *Humor: International Journal of Humor Research* 23.4 (2010): 505–26. Print.

Volpe, Michael. "The Persuasive Force of Humor: Cicero's Defense of Caelius." *Quarterly Journal of Speech Communication* 63 (Oct. 1977): 311–23. JSTOR. Web.

Walker, Nancy. *A Very Serious Thing: Women's Humor and American Culture.* Minneapolis: U of Minnesota P, 1988. Print.

Wang, Bo. "Rethinking Feminist Rhetoric and Historiography in a Global Context: A Cross-Cultural Perspective." *Advances in the History of Rhetoric* 15.1 (2012): 28–52. JSTOR. Web.

"War on the Wabash: Editor Williams Routed by Lecturer Gougar—Mrs. Gougar a Victim of Malicious Persecution." *Washington Chronicle* 18 June 1888. Helen Gougar Collection, Scrapbook item 73.17.8. TCHA, Lafayette, IN.

Wertheimer, Molly. *Leading Ladies of the White House: Communication Strategies of Notable Twentieth-Century First Ladies*. Lanham, MD: Rowman, 2004. Print.

———, ed. *Listening to Their Voices: The Rhetorical Activities of Historical Women*. Columbia: U of South Carolina P, 1997. Print.

Westerkamp, Marilyn J. "Anne Hutchinson, Sectarian Mysticism, and the Puritan Order." *Church History* 59.4 (1990): 482–96. Print.

———. "Puritan Patriarchy and the Problem of Revelation." *Journal of Interdisciplinary History* 23.3 (1993): 571–95. JSTOR. Web.

Wheelwright, John. "Memoir of the Rev. John Wheelwright." *John Wheelwright: His Writings*. Ed. Charles Bell. Freeport, NY: Books for Libraries, 1970. 1–78. Print.

The Whole Duty of Woman Comprised in the Following Sections, viz. . . . By a Lady. Written at the Desire of a Noble Lord. 14th ed. 1793. MS. John Carter Brown Library, Providence, RI, 23 Apr. 2010.

Willard, Frances E., and Mary A. Livermore, eds. *American Women: A Comprehensive Encyclopedia of the Lives and Achievements of American Women during the Nineteenth Century*. Vol. 1. New York: Mast, 1897. Print.

Williams, Selma. *Divine Rebel: The Life of Anne Marbury Hutchinson*. New York: Holt, 1981. Print.

Winchester, Elhanan. "The Seed of the Woman Bruising the Serpent's Head: A Discourse Delivered at the Baptist Meeting House in Philadelphia, Sunday April 22, 1781." TS. John Carter Brown Library, Providence, RI. 23 Apr. 2010.

Winship, Michael P. *The Times & Trials of Anne Hutchinson: Puritans Divided*. Lawrence: UP of Kansas, 2005. Print.

Winthrop, John. *Antinomians and Familists Condemned by the Synod of Elders in New-England: With the Proceedings of the Magistrates Against Them, and Their Apology for the Same*. London, 1644. TS. John Hay Library, Providence, RI. 22 Apr. 2010.

———. "A Short Story of the Rise, Reign, and Ruine of the Antinomians, Familists & Libertines" (1644). Hall 199–310. Print.

Withington, Ann Fairfax, and Jack Schwartz. "The Political Trial of Anne Hutchinson." *New England Quarterly* 51.2 (1978): 226–40. Print.

"The Woman Suffrage Convention." *Washington Post* 20 Dec. 1884: 1. Print.

"Woman Suffrage in New York." *Voice* 31 (31 May 1894): 5. Print.

"Woman Suffrage Not on Trial." *Lafayette Daily Courier* 24 Feb. 1883. Helen Gougar Collection, Newspaper item 81.193.4. TCHA, Lafayette, IN. "Women at War: The Gougar-Sewall Imbroglio at the Woman's Congress." *Lafayette Journal* 24 May 1893. Helen Gougar Collection, Newspaper item 81.193.4. TCHA, Lafayette, IN.

"Women in Politics: Octave Thanet Writes about the Women Politicians of the West." *St. Paul Globe* 20 Sept. 1896: 17. *Chronicling America*. Lib. of Cong. Web. 1 Apr. 2010. <http://chroniclingamerica.loc.gov/lccn/sn90059523/1896-09-20/ed-1/seq-18/>.

Wu, Hui. "Historical Studies of Rhetorical Women Here and There: Methodological Challenges to Dominant Interpretive Frameworks." *Rhetoric Society Quarterly* 31.1 (2002): 81–98. Print.

Yarbrough, Stephen. *After Rhetoric: Studies in Discourse Beyond Language and Culture.* Carbondale: Southern Illinois UP, 1999. Print.

Yearwood, Lagusta. "Synopsis of the Letters in the Anthony-Avery Papers." 2000. *University of Rochester Department of Rare Books, Special Collections, and Preservation.* Web. 16 Feb. 2004. <http://www.lib.rochester.edu/>.

Young, Iris Marion. "Gender as Seriality: Thinking about Women as a Social Collective." *Signs: Journal of Women in Culture and Society* 19 (1994): 713–38. JSTOR. Web.

Young, Richard. "Paradigms and Problems: Needed Research in Rhetorical Invention." *Research on Composing: Points of Departure.* Ed. Charles R. Cooper and Lee Odell. Urbana, IL: NCTE, 1978. 29–47. Print.

Zahl, Paul F. M. *Five Women of the English Reformation.* Grand Rapids: Eerdmans, 2001.

Zwagerman, Sean. *Wit's End: Women's Humor as Rhetorical and Performative Strategy.* Pittsburgh: U of Pittsburgh P, 2010. Print.

INDEX

Page numbers in italics indicate illustrations.

Tarez Samra Graban is an assistant professor of English at Florida State University and a coauthor of *GenAdmin: Theorizing WPA Identities in the Twenty-First Century*. Her work in rhetorical historiography and archival theory has appeared in *Rhetorica, Gender and Language, College English,* and *Peitho,* as well as *Working in the Archives* and *Rhetoric and the Digital Humanities.*

Studies in Rhetorics and Feminisms

Studies in Rhetorics and Feminisms seeks to address the interdisciplinarity that rhetorics and feminisms represent. Rhetorical and feminist scholars want to connect rhetorical inquiry with contemporary academic and social concerns, exploring rhetoric's relevance to current issues of opportunity and diversity. This interdisciplinarity has already begun to transform the rhetorical tradition as we have known it (upper-class, agonistic, public, and male) into regendered, inclusionary rhetorics (democratic, dialogic, collaborative, cultural, and private). Our intellectual advancements depend on such ongoing transformation.

Rhetoric, whether ancient, contemporary, or futuristic, always inscribes the relation of language and power at a particular moment, indicating who may speak, who may listen, and what can be said. The only way we can displace the traditional rhetoric of masculine-only, public performance is to replace it with rhetorics that are recognized as being better suited to our present needs. We must understand more fully the rhetorics of the non-Western tradition, of women, of a variety of cultural and ethnic groups. Therefore, Studies in Rhetorics and Feminisms espouses a theoretical position of openness and expansion, a place for rhetorics to grow and thrive in a symbiotic relationship with all that feminisms have to offer, particularly when these two fields intersect with philosophical, sociological, religious, psychological, pedagogical, and literary issues.

The series seeks scholarly works that both examine and extend rhetoric, works that span the sexes, disciplines, cultures, ethnicities, and sociocultural practices as they intersect with the rhetorical tradition. After all, the recent resurgence of rhetorical studies has been not so much a discovery of new rhetorics as a recognition of existing rhetorical activities and practices, of our newfound ability and willingness to listen to previously untold stories.

The series editors seek both high-quality traditional and cutting-edge scholarly work that extends the significant relationship between rhetoric and feminism within various genres, cultural contexts, historical periods, methodologies, theoretical positions, and methods of delivery (e.g., film and hypertext to elocution and preaching).

Queries and submissions:

Professor Cheryl Glenn, Editor
    E-mail: cjg6@psu.edu
Professor Shirley Wilson Logan, Editor
    E-mail: slogan@umd.edu

Studies in Rhetorics and Feminisms

Department of English
142 South Burrowes Bldg.
Penn State University
University Park, PA 16802-6200

Other Books in the Studies in Rhetorics and Feminisms Series